"A deep, fascinating dive into a uniquely American brand of religious zealotry that poses a grave threat to our national parks, wilderness areas, wildlife sanctuaries, and other public lands. *American Zion* provides essential background for anyone concerned about the future of open space in the western United States. It also happens to be a delight to read."

—JON KRAKAUER, author of *Under the Banner of Heaven*

"Brilliant and electrifying . . . Gaines Quammen's voice is bright, engaging, and smart. She listens. She is fair. But she is not seduced by cowboy mythology. Her vision calls for an ecological wisdom that can govern our communities, both human and wild, with reverence and respect."

—TERRY TEMPEST WILLIAMS, author of *Erosion*

"A fascinating primer on the twisted and nefarious legacy of theology, entitlement, conquest, and patriarchy in the American West."

—FLORENCE WILLIAMS, author of *The Nature Fix*

"Betsy Gaines Quammen has accomplished something I thought impossible: combining a rich historical account of the Mormon push west and the accompanying conception of 'Zion' with clear-eyed reporting on the Bundys. This book is like a skeleton key, unlocking so many complicated, and largely unquestioned, myths of the West."

—ANNE HELEN PETERSEN, BuzzFeed News

"A creative, deeply thoughtful work on the origins, dynamics, and consequences of the Bundy legacy."

—JEDEDIAH ROGERS, author of *Roads in the Wilderness*

"I find the author's sense of the tribal perspectives spot on and sensitive. I enjoyed *American Zion* immensely—Betsy is a great storyteller!"

—WALTER FLEMING, department head and professor of
Native American Studies, Montana State University

"What J. D. Vance did with *Hillbilly Elegy* to explain small-town Appalachian angst, Gaines Quammen has done with *American Zion* to help people understand the long and convoluted issues in the American West."

—THANE MAYNARD, co-author with Jane Goodall of
Hope for Animals and Their World

"Historian Betsy Gaines Quammen recounts the history of Mormons in America to help us understand how a painful abyss has formed between some of that religion's believers and management of national public lands. Such understanding is essential for those of us working to cross that divide."

—MARY O'BRIEN, author of
Making Better Environmental Decisions

"A thorough and thoughtful analysis of the challenges we face in managing our public lands and an argument for why these lands should remain in public hands."

—JAMES LYONS, former deputy assistant secretary,
US Department of the Interior

"An empathetic and clear-eyed account of the intersections of faith, conservation, and Native rights in the skirmishes over western public lands."

—ANDREA AVANTAGGIO, Maria's Bookshop

"Well-researched and compelling . . . Gaines Quammen is a natural storyteller."

—ARIANA PALIOBAGIS, Country Bookshelf

American Zion

American Zion

Cliven Bundy, God & Public Lands in the West

Betsy Gaines Quammen

TORREY HOUSE PRESS

SALT LAKE CITY • TORREY

First Torrey House Press Edition, March 2020
Copyright © 2019 by Betsy Gaines Quammen

Published by Torrey House Press
Salt Lake City, Utah
www.torreyhouse.org

International Standard Book Number: 978-1-948814-14-0
E-book ISBN: 978-1-948814-15-7
Library of Congress Control Number: 2019936116

Cover photo "Members of the Bundy family and their supporters near
    Bunkerville, NV, in April 2014" by Jason Bean, *Las Vegas Review-Journal*
Cover design by Kathleen Metcalf
Interior design by Rachel Davis
Distributed to the trade by Consortium Book Sales and Distribution

This book is dedicated to my two big Ds,
David and Dad

CONTENTS

Introduction

A map of the American West is a Rorschach test—people see what they want to see as reflections of who they are. There are those who see land solely for human utility. And those who see a realm for wild creatures. Some see the West as a place of colonialization and genocide, where the indomitable mettle of Indigenous peoples nevertheless endures. Some see a land of plunder, evidenced by slag heaps, old mining pits, and the abandoned equipment of long-ago endeavors. There are empty corners where a look in any direction reveals no obvious human marks, though the marks exist. This is a land heavily trod. Dying towns punctuate the old highways, their Main Streets marred by boarded-up windows, their schools emptied by dwindling enrollments. These towns are just miles from robust cities, ballooning with the influx of new residents and tech businesses. The West is a place of a thousand destinations—on rivers, on mountains, on prairies, and on rocks. It's where cars speed down lonely roads, flanked by grazing horses and cattle, fence lines and range, billboards and baled hay. It is a place of differing points of view, a place of intersections and of loggerheads. People see their own ink blots here, spread across a land colored by custom, ambition, opportunity, and cows—sacred and otherwise.

The Intermountain West, a region of such differing interpretations, is geographically delimited by the Rocky Mountains to the east, the Cascade and Sierra Nevada Ranges to the west, and encompasses the Columbia Plateau, the westward drainages of the Northern and Southern Rockies, the Great Basin and the Mojave Desert. On the map, it is a large jumble of boundaries and ownerships with checkerboard designations and varying jurisdictions, sometimes running across state lines. A cartographic color code and a series of demarcations make one thing crystal clear: most of the Intermountain West is federal public land. Which means that all Americans, as citizens and taxpayers, are proprietors of some of the most incredible real estate on this planet. The best part of the West is that we share it—in all its fraught majesty. And this affords opportunity for further insights into how this land is variously construed. Somewhere between 280 and 560 generations of Indigenous people have been young and grown old here on the western landscape. Today, 327 million Americans participate in its proprietorship.

Public lands are precious and beloved places to westerners and non-westerners alike. They are finite and fragile, and have very real thresholds of tolerance to ruination. And there's the rub. Some people are asking too much of these lands and, in doing so, are declaring war both on nature and on the millions of people who also share public lands. This is nothing new. The West has always been a place of competing cultures and priorities that began with cultural and resource conflicts among Indigenous nations. As Europeans arrived and homesteaded, their claims to these lands were devastating for Native peoples. Not long after settlement slowed and the "western frontier" was closed, a battle between preservationists, timber barons, and ranchers spurred the creation of national parks and monuments and set the match to land wars that still burn today. Mining companies, four-wheel-drive enthusiasts, and those in livestock production have wrestled for control over lands that wildlife need and conservationists fight to protect. It falls to the American public to decide how these lands should be understood and managed. Should these lands be a place for recreation or for industry? For carbon sequestration or for resource extraction? For short-term gain or long-term viability? For everyone or a few individuals? To repeat the obvious: these lands belong to all Americans, yet their use is being determined by a limited number of politicians and rogue players.

I want to pause here and confess that the idea that these lands belong to all Americans is a laden one. Public lands are originally and rightfully Native lands. It seems like there is a way to reach some reconciliation, acknowledge the violations of the past, and engage collaboratively on issues of land use, wildlife, water, and sacred sites, among others. Such a partnership happened with the 2016 establishment of Bears Ears, a national monument in Utah, where five tribal nations worked with conservationists and federal land managers to protect cultural and ecological attributes. Under the current administration, this conservation effort, along with so many others, has been undermined by those who aren't concerned with Native rights or public interest. In the meantime, the priorities of Native peoples and a majority of other Americans have taken a backseat to the pursuits of fossil fuel interests, political agendas, and rural old-boy networks.

Within these networks and agendas, an old archetype inextricably linked to these lands has emerged, undeservedly, as a sort of ideological hood ornament in the fight over public lands. This archetype, embodied by certain western men and women, carries powerful cachet, over a hundred years in the making. His avatars might don bolo ties, boots, and big belt buckles. He, or she, might ride horses or drive ATVs and pickup trucks. An iconic figure lies behind those choices and affectations, looming large in the American imagination and in the career aspirations of children the world over. He is *the cowboy*, and he exerts an inordinate amount of power in public land management. But take a second glance and the cowboy isn't what he seems to be.

The cowboy made his way westward several decades after Meriwether Lewis, William Clark, and their Corps of Discovery returned from their expedition to the Pacific coast and back. Others followed in their footsteps, looking for economic opportunities and a place to call home. Some of these pilgrims pursued farming, others chased gold, and some began cattle-ranching. That's when the cowboy inserted himself into the western landscape, joining fellow settlers, railroad-track laborers, and the armies that protected them in a united campaign to drive Native peoples from their homeland.

The white cowboy hero may be a dwindled icon in our own age—his embodiments are fewer and further between, though a wonderful renaissance of the African American cowboy is resurfacing with the Compton Cowboys in California—but his mythic resonance remains, so potently was it charged by the romantic imaginings that arose around him when he first burst onto the scene. Newspapers, novels, films, and cigarette commercials have glorified him as brave, resourceful, and the very epitome of a hero. But the very term, *cowboy*, needs some critical unpacking. The real cowboy, the original, was a hired hand, not a boss rancher. His proud label became a useful catchall, because so many livestock producers relate to cowboys and look like cowboys and represent themselves as cowboys. Folks living outside the West might not even know the difference, but, given their meager wages, cowboys both know and feel the difference between themselves and the head honcho. Still, be it beef-industry executive or a proletarian cowpoke, imagine this figure seated on his saddle, atop his horse, under the wide brim of his hat. An imagined master of his home on the range, moving herds of lowing bovines to graze acre after lonely acre, sharing western grass, sometimes begrudgingly, with roaming buffalo, deer, and antelope. You get the picture—you've seen or heard about it a million times.

The cowboy made his first big public impression in 1902, swaggering into American popular culture by way of Owen Wister's novel *The Virginian*. Wister's book, adapted from several short stories he had earlier published in magazines, traced the life of a self-made cowboy, an amalgamated man who combined eastern gentility with western gumption and grit. This hero is simply known as the Virginian; he's a man without a name, and his story is told by a pal, Tenderfoot. The Virginian is handsome, tall, and the very epitome of decency. Plus he's sexy. "He climbed down with the undulations of a tiger, smooth and easy, as if his muscles flowed beneath his skin," according to Tenderfoot, deeply impressed by their first meeting.

The Virginian begins as a cow puncher, moves on to be foreman, and later becomes part owner of a Wyoming ranch—the ultimate cowboy dream. Over the past hundred years, Wister's work has been adapted into six movies and a TV series, and served as a template for countless other western novels, movies, TV series, comic books, video games, and marketing campaigns around the world. This original mythic cowboy, the Virginian, also set an example of individualistic entitlement. Toward the end of the novel, he proclaims: "I'm going my own course. Can't you see what it must be for a man?" His entitlement becomes his destiny.

Apart from books and imaginations, the cowboy figure carries real baggage—more than enough for a pair of saddlebags. In the nineteenth century, real cowboys and their trail foremen arrived in the Intermountain West with millions of cows, moving them through the rugged landscape, facing brutal winters and deep snows as well as blazing summers, high rivers, drought, and quicksand. These bovine residents helped the cowboys co-opt grasslands for the rancher bosses, working through both legal and illicit channels to acquire more ground and access to federal grass left unclaimed by homesteaders. When this era of the unregulated rangeland free-for-all came to an end, Native peoples had been displaced and killed. Bison were nearly extinct, in part due to an effort to starve the Indigenous population, and western lands were left trashed.

As the twentieth century began, the US government—and the cowboys themselves—realized that things had to change. Legislation to regulate grazing and to protect the land became a priority. Massive western cattle drives, in which millions of cows were moved from arid to green, or from pasture to market, came to an end. Herd limits and designated allotments for livestock producers on the public domain were developed, with a grazing management system that remains in place today. Over the years, regulations have increased in the West, in places once left unchecked, causing some public land cowboys to chafe with each new rule. Many permittees rely on public lands as range, because their own private ranch property is inadequate to support viable herds. You need thousands of acres of land to raise cattle, because the West can be dry and stingy. Luckily for those operators who depend on it, renting federal land is cheap. Livestock producers pay on average thirteen times less to graze on public range than they would if they were leasing private lands. The cowboy of yesteryear was grazing open, unregulated public domain on stolen Native lands. Today he grazes that same land on public subsidies.

Presently, the government manages 5,863 active grazing leases on Forest Service lands (which are held within the Department of Agriculture) and the Department of the Interior manages another 18,000 permits granting grazing privileges. While many of these modern-day leaseholders have perfectly workable relationships with the government, some do not. In fact, certain livestock operators who run cows on public lands have come to deeply, and even violently, resent federal controls. The cowboy once grazed his animals with no oversight, and for some, that open-range era represents the epitome of freedom and independence. But the lack of regulation was neither sustainable nor benign. The early liberties afforded this low-maintenance livestock production have come into conflict with shifting American values. The public's interest in western lands has evolved, from the romantic distortions of Wild West movies and television shows to today's better understanding of the damage unregulated livestock grazing wreaks on the landscape, from devastating erosion to noxious weeds to wildlife extirpation. Over the years, elected officials, encouraged by a voting public keen on conservation, have drafted and enacted measures to protect shrinking western resources by regulating livestock. And with the enforcement of these laws, as well as market forces, costly droughts, and alternatives to wool and leather, some ranchers on the public range, where seldom was heard a discouraging word, got—well, discouraged. The cowboy, once kingly, got stripped of a near-royal prerogative—the unimpeded reign over American western lands.

And this brings us to our story. There's a rancher in Nevada who is determined to preserve his cowboy image and the mythology, the prerogatives, that come with it. For over twenty years, Cliven Bundy has let his cows graze illegally on a chunk of Nevada public land (in the Mojave Desert's fragile habitat) without permission from the United States government or the public. Bundy has paid no grazing fees since 1993 when he stopped in protest, later ignoring the 1998 cancellation of his lease agreement. Nonetheless, Cliven feels justified. He says that he knows his rights better than anyone else, and has no interest in other notions about land management. Nor has he time for Native historical claims, wildlife habitat, federal laws, or the rights of all other Americans who share ownership of this common ground. Like the Virginian, Cliven Bundy has decided to go his own way.

Over a course of decades, this man, in the process of flouting the law, has become a hero to some in the West. He has engaged thousands of followers, from other ranchers to anti-government militia to officials in the Trump administration, in a fight against the principles governing public lands. He has gathered support to abolish public land ownership altogether. He makes frequent reference to himself and his followers as "we the people," as though only Bundy and his followers did "ordain and establish" the US Constitution. In representing himself as the proxy spokesperson for all Americans, he refuses to grasp that his positions defy the interests and the will of his fellow Americans. Americans who know and love public lands, love them—as wildernesses, parks, forests, prairies, monuments—not as rangelands. But Bundy believes that he has the corner on land-rights issues, and that his point of view is better informed, more substantial, and more warranted than the viewpoints of the rest of us. Why? In part, it's because he fancies himself a cowboy whose home is on the range. But there's so much more to his campaign. Cliven Bundy has gathered other potent myths to substantiate his fight—ones that orbit his religion. He is a member of the Church of Jesus Christ of Latter-day Saints and has employed a unique syncretism that blends the legend of the cowboy with early Mormon beliefs. Bundy has convinced himself and others that God wants him to go to war over our public lands.

The West is full of stories. In fact, there are a million more tales than there are cowboys. But this one is, among other things, a cowboy story. It is not a celebration of the cowboy. Nor is it a condemnation of all those who call themselves cowboys. It's the story of the emergence of rancher Cliven Bundy, his family, and his followers, onto the western stage. It's a story of magic, history, prophecy, AR-15s, gods, and cultural convictions standing at odds to one another. It is also my plea to the American public to come to the aid of lands now under siege on multiple and unimaginable fronts. This story has a long prelude, beginning nearly two hundred years ago on the other side of this country when a new religion arose, and that religion was then carried to Nevada and Utah by the people who practiced it. Those pilgrims, when they came west, not only brought their new faith, but also carried animosities and certitudes which they pounded into the very lands where Cliven Bundy runs his cows today. These characters of the prelude, these Mormon pioneers, are Bundy's people. They are his ancestors. And once they settled in the West, they were determined never to leave—most especially not at the insistence of the United States government. To the Bundy family, the land where their cattle graze, these publicly held lands, is their property, their homeland, and the family has vowed to defend it or die trying.

PART 1:

The Cowboy and the Prophet

The Battle of Bunkerville

The fight for freedom is God's fight.

—Ezra Taft Benson

On April 12, 2014, hundreds of protesters, including members of various militia groups, gathered near Bunkerville, Nevada, in the southeastern corner of the state, making their stand in solidarity with Cliven Bundy. They had gathered to shut down the court-ordered removal of the Bundys' cattle from public lands. Many in the crowd carried guns and a few were positioned as snipers, their rifles aimed at federal agents and police. Agents aimed back. Men in cowboy hats rode on horseback with a crowd pushing along to face Las Vegas police and Bureau of Land Management (BLM) officers. Some of the protesters threatened and yelled obscenities. One guy in a Pittsburgh Steelers jersey asked a police officer if he was ready to die.

Cliven and Carol Bundy told me that even a backfire could have triggered another Waco. Of course, militia members and anti-government protesters say this all the time. Waco, Texas, is the town where, in 1993, federal agents, along with state law-enforcement officers and US military, led a siege of the compound in which a group, the Branch Davidians, had barricaded themselves. That siege ended in a final assault and a fire, resulting in the deaths of dozens of men, women, and children, an event that became a rallying cry in anti-government circles.

Some allude to Waco as a cautionary tale, others with a kind of yearning, eager to have it out with a government they so despise.

During the Bundy standoff, Interstate 15 was shut down while north- and southbound traffic idled. On that spring day in Nevada, rifles aimed and ready, some of the protesters awaited a sign that would determine the outcome. Would the feds attack first, giving the protesters their chance to defend the Bundys? To protect them from the same evil forces responsible for the fate of the poor Branch Davidians of Waco? Or would the itchy fingers of an armed protester set off a volley of bullets? Perhaps divine intervention might take place, indicating God's sympathy for this Mormon rancher and his family. In the minds of the protesters there that day, all scenarios were possible.

After a tense standoff, no bullets were exchanged. It was no Waco. In fact, the feds and the police relented and drove away. The retreat thrilled the protesters, but left the officers and agents shaken. Sergeant Tom Jenkins of the Las Vegas Metropolitan Police Department said, "We didn't show any fear that day, but I can tell you, we all thought in the back of our minds, we all thought it was going to be our last day on earth." Although the law officers weren't interested in sacrificing their lives for cattle, many Bundy supporters evidently were.

Cliven's son Ryan declared to the crowd, "The West has now been won." Cliven Bundy, his family, and his followers reveled in the agents' retreat. "If the standoff with the Bundys was wrong," Cliven said later, "would the Lord have been with us? . . . Could those people that stood without fear and went through that spiritual experience . . . have done that without the Lord being there? No, they couldn't." To the Bundys, the day validated their position and demonstrated that God was on their side.

The Bundys and their public land battles initially sounded like a fringe cause—an isolated family caught up in a quixotic battle with the government over a bunch of cows. But in fact, in their crusade, they have inspired hundreds of thousands of supporters in the years following the Nevada standoff. The Bundys, as western "everymen," have become the heroic face of anti-government agitators. Taking a passionate battle from Nevada to Oregon, where members of the family later led an armed occupation of a wildlife refuge, the Bundys staked their own claims on American public land and traditional Native land. They have gotten away with illegal grazing, takeovers, standoffs, and expensive property damage. To some, they have become champions. And as such, their amalgamation of Mormon beliefs, libertarianism, and a right-wing reading of the Constitution continues to inform and embolden anti-government activism.

Now members of this Mormon ranching family have launched a campaign, meeting with thousands of people, including reporters, supporters, and other ranchers, urging their followers to flout government regulations and join Cliven in his crusade to take back the West. In addition, Cliven's reach online is incalculable. So, what is his message to these rapt audiences? Essentially this: *We the people get to tell the federal government what they can and can't do. And the government cannot own public lands. Therefore, federal regulations on lands do not exist. In fact, public land is just the wrong name. Really, it's YOUR ranch. It's all spelled out for you in the Constitution. And if you don't trust me, just ask God. That's what He'll tell you.*

Hardly the first member of his faith to break a federal law in favor of God's higher authority, Cliven Bundy comes from a long line of Latter-day Saints, or Mormons, who talk to God and take His word over the law of the land. The line starts with Joseph Smith, the first Mormon prophet, seer, revelator, and founder of the Church of Jesus Christ of Latter-day Saints, who was arrested over forty times during his life of offenses that ranged from fraud and polygamy to conspiracy to commit murder. Smith's loyal bodyguard, Orrin Porter Rockwell—nicknamed "the Destroying Angel of Mormondom," because he brazenly went after enemies of the church, perceived or otherwise—

killed many men in his lifetime and very probably tried to assassinate the governor of Missouri. Brigham Young, who succeeded Smith in 1844, spent decades ignoring federal laws as he established Mormon homeland in the Great Basin, while encouraging violence, fraud, and multiple deceptions.

And 172 years after Smith's murder, and less than a year after the Battle of Bunkerville, the Heavenly Father would tell Cliven's sons Ryan and Ammon Bundy to take up arms against an oppressive United States government. On January 2, 2016, the boys arrived with a small army of supporters, locked and loaded, to occupy the Malheur National Wildlife Refuge in Oregon until their arrest six weeks later. When Bundy family members heard the heavenly call toward the righteous direction, it was game on. Thy will be done.

The Bundy family is a product of a region where the corners of southern Utah and northern Arizona abut the state of Nevada; a place where Mormon communities today are scattered among the parks, monuments, and recreational areas. In the nineteenth century, their ancestors built settlements and livelihoods across the West, within what became a mosaic of federal and private holdings. Today, these places are visited, or at the very least driven past, by millions of tourists every year. It is a multilayered landscape, considered homeland to Latter-day Saints and sacred ground to the Southern Paiute people. Hikers, mountain bikers, and climbers in the thrall of writings by Terry Tempest Williams and Edward Abbey, find in these places both sanctuary and adventure. Ranchers look out and see lifestyle and legacy. It's desert and it's canyon country, a home to retired snowbirds, Park Service personnel, lodge managers, and outfitters who each see their own various cosmologies and values reflected in these rocks. Some see majesty. Some see money. Some see birthright. And some see God.

The Seeker

Know ye not that ye are in the hands of God?

—Book of Mormon, Mormon 5:23

Cliven Bundy will tell you that his land war is part of being Mormon, though many Saints would counter his presumption. The church has publicly condemned the family's claim that their anti-government agitations are justified through Mormon scripture. And this is very important. The Bundy family's position does not reflect teachings upheld in modern mainstream Mormonism. Yet some of his supporters, including prominent Mormon politicians, do embrace the same convictions that the Bundys espouse. In order to grasp these rationales, we need to go back to the beginnings of the church, this incredibly successful American religion that has a lot to say about proprietorship, rights, and sticking it to the man. We also need to trace how a culture of European and Yankee farmers became irascible cowboys. Then we can better understand Cliven Bundy.

When Cliven's ancestors arrived in the Great Basin in the late 1840s, finally safe from religious oppression, they made their home in a land most other white settlers had overlooked. They helped build a homeland there, one promised to them by their prophet but which had eluded them before they found it on the flanks of the Wasatch Range. For the Bundy family, their birthrights to this land came with the arrival and the settlement of their forefathers. To make sense of Cliven Bundy and his insurgency is to understand the philosophies, assurances, and prophecies that came from early pioneers devoted to Joseph Smith.

The Bundy family story intrigued me. I'd spent the last decade working with religious leaders on conservation initiatives and I'd not yet had the opportunity to work with Mormons. The church had been slow to issue any formal statement on the environment, and the Bundy family seemed to be using their faith as an argument to deplete the land rather than steward it. I visited the family on March 5, 2015, and left their compound with my own signed Book of Mormon, courtesy of the family patriarch, vowing to Ryan and his father that I would read it. Because Cliven's convictions were so tied to his religion, I thought this volume would shed light on the underpinnings of the Bundy war. Perhaps as someone raised outside the church, I missed a profundity and poetry that I've come to associate with other religious texts, though the Book of Mormon is informative when following Bundy's motivations. But *The Nay Book*, a homemade manifesto filled with prophetic quotes by Mormon prophets and warnings about the precarious state of the US Constitution, is even more so. Ryan thumbed through his own copy, one bound in a vinyl binder, during the time I spent with the family. Named for the neighbor who compiled it, Keith Nay, it is often seen in the hands of Bundy's inner circle at events and gatherings.

Three men came into view the day of my visit, each foundational to the Bundy family position and approach. Nephi Johnson, Cliven's spiritual great-grandfather. Cleon Skousen, a Mormon right-wing agitator. And of course, Joseph Smith, who built a religion defined by promises of homeland and a personal relationship to God. The first Mormon prophet established a community of people with a history of despising the government, yet a belief in some duty to keep it in check, no matter what this entailed. The world is in its latter days, he warned, which meant time is almost up, coining a "truth" that created, and still creates, an urgency to action. If a stand must be taken, take it now, because there's no time to lose. With this comes another implication, maybe also contributory to the uprising at Bunkerville, and later at the Malheur National Wildlife Refuge: an expectation that a standoff might have a domino effect, leading to larger events that fulfill prophesies outlined in the Book of Revelation, of the story of earth's destruction and of Christ's Second Coming.

So let's begin with Joseph Smith, the first leader of the Latter-day Saints and first Mormon prophet. Many books have been written about Smith, and they range from fawning to condemning. Alex Beam, Fawn Brodie, Richard Lyman Bushman, and even Smith's own mother, Lucy Mack Smith, told the story of this amazing human, a man who held many in his thrall while outraging and repulsing others. He was incontrovertibly impressive in what he achieved—his church now has over sixteen million members, among whom are the Bundys. And one would be hard-pressed to find a historical figure as curious and as striking as the founder of this ever-flourishing, influential, and inescapably American religion.

Before Joseph was a prophet, as a young man, he was a scryer, a trade that used magical tools in the search for hidden treasure. For his work, he used a device called a seer stone, a dark brown rock he used to seek riches rumored to be buried near his home on the New York frontier. This was a hobby not unusual to his time and place—one based on hearsay and wishful thinking. Stories about buried treasure abounded in upstate New York, where Joseph Smith's family, for a time, made their home. Tales of pirate Captain Kidd's gold bullion led hundreds to dig deep trenches in vain. Rumored Spanish and Indian silver called to the farmers in their stony fields, promising riches and escape from the grindingly difficult life of the frontier settler. It certainly called to young Joseph Smith.

In his lifetime, he would meet with unimaginable fame and infamy, leaving behind a legacy that swelled ever greater after his death. But he began his career by digging. The process went more or less like this: First, he would place the stone in the bottom of his hat, then plunge his face into the gloom. In order for the spell to work, all light needed to be occluded so that his stone could "see" treasure, and thereby ascertain its coordinates. But this was only the first of many fiddly steps. Once he determined the location, preparation for excavation began. Perhaps he drew concentric circles around the loot, a ritual his mother would years later write about in her memoir. Pressing circles into the dirt was said to foil supernatural guardians, the ghosts of murdered men charged for eternity to protect these mythic fortunes. Those in the treasure trade warned that phantoms pulled the valuables back deep into the earth if they sensed any threat. Coarse language or the garrulous talk of careless seekers, it was said, could tip the guardians off and cause them to spirit the treasure away.

Smith's father, Joseph Smith Sr., also a scryer, emphasized the importance of night digs to his son. During the day, he explained, solar warmth coaxed hidden chests with piles of precious objects from the depths of the ground. Best to do most of the work after sunset, when the booty sat just below the earth's surface. Night digs were thrilling (and booze-soaked) diversions for those living in this time and place, full of ceremony, ritual, and the delicious anticipation of instant wealth. It is easy to imagine that many of the stories of ghosts said to watch over the treasure sites were actually the invention of jumpy drunks startling themselves in the murk of the forest. Strong drink could make the mind rather credulous and prone to exaggeration. Blaming a ghost offered a good excuse for those coming home hammered and empty-handed.

Joseph was born in Vermont in 1805 to parents well-versed in the magic and the supernatural. His father claimed celestial visions and his mother talked regularly to God. This was quite common among folks of this region in nineteenth-century America, a time of great uncertainty and adversity. Having a personal relationship with God and the supernatural provided reassurance in a place where poverty, disease, and desperation abounded. As a boy, Joseph and his family moved from place to place, due to failed crops and burgeoning mortgages. Through difficult though necessary moves, the Smith family, following several failures and subsequent relocations, landed in an environment well-suited to their numinous hobbies. New York State's "Burned-over District" marinated in a stew of wild revivalism, cults, and extremists preparing adherents for end-times. And it was there Joseph Smith spent his formative years.

In his youth, millennialism was rampant, as were utopian societies promoting everything from sexual libertinism (Oneidans) to abstinence (Shakers). Protestant branches proliferated, especially those offering rebellion against Calvinist notions of predeterminism. In other words, folks did not want to believe that they were fated to either heaven or hell even before they were born. If this were true, then why would one stay upright and honorable rather than spend the days drunk and feckless? If God had already made up His mind, then what was the point of being virtuous? Calvinism left many searching for a faith that would give them some agency, some skin in the game, and the opportunity to be judged for their actions, whether meritorious or sinful. Be it harps and halos or pitchforks and flames, they wanted to feel like they had some ability to determine where they spent their afterlife.

Growing up, Joseph picked through hot embers of the Second Great Awakening, pursuing both buried riches and new versions of Christianity. Although the tray of options was overflowing, he was not satisfied with what was offered. Untrained ministers, aspiring prophets, and self-proclaimed Second Comings roamed the countryside alongside the scryers, all searching to fill that emptiness found both in pockets and souls. Would they discover gold or God? Joseph came of age amid spiritual promiscuity, where, under the drape of a tent, silver-tongued preachers brought their audiences into flailing, juddering, and jerking fits, as if the hand of the Lord himself had reached out and shaken them. So eager were the people for religious novelty, the enthusiasms of upstate New York even brought believers into fits of glossolalia, speaking in tongues known only to God.

This birthplace for so many religious movements provided the incubator for Shakers, Seventh-day Adventists, and Oneidans—sects that encouraged perfectionism. And communalism. And various riffs on hanky-panky. A hundred years after the death of Joseph Smith Jr., writer Fawn Brodie, who grew up in a family with a deep regard for his teachings, described the Burned-over District of upstate New York as a cadre of "the Baptists split into Reformed Baptists, Hard Shell Baptists, Free Will Baptists, Seventh Day Baptists, Footwashers and other sects." She mentioned Anna Lee, the founder of the Shaker sect who regarded herself as the reincarnation of Christ. And "Isaac Bullard, wearing nothing but a bearskin girdle and his beard, who gathered a following of pilgrims in 1817 in Woodstock, Vermont." He was a "champion of free love and communism, he regarded washing as a sin and boasted he had not changed his clothes in seven years." So many wanted to know God. Or to be God. These emerging religious leaders filled a great need, arising in response to a culture yearning for celestial reassurance. Further, if there was ever a place that might inspire someone to imagine his own version of a religion or fancy herself a mystic, the Burned-over District was it, with plenty of muses from which to draw encouragement.

Before upstate New York became a spiritual hotbed, it was homeland to a very different culture. This was the territory of the Seneca nation, one of six nations of the Iroquois Confederacy. The five other nations were the Mohawks, Cayugas, Onondagas,

Oneidas, and Tuscaroras: descendants of people who had lived here for thousands of years before the British and French came to colonize and spread their own cultural ideas. It should come as no surprise that at this time of white settler revivalism, the Seneca had their own prophet, Handsome Lake, who, after a near-death experience in 1799, began to have religious visions and hold conversations with George Washington and Jesus. Handsome Lake warned his people about the brutal penalties that awaited them if they succumbed to the vices of the settlers. Imbibing whiskey and partaking in gambling, according to Handsome Lake, led to an eternity of drinking molten iron and gaming with scalding cards—consequences of participating in the vices of white people. Like so many other mystics, Handsome Lake spoke of the impending end of the world. Tragically, unlike the Christian preachers' foretelling of an apocalypse, for the Seneca, Handsome Lake's prophecies were coming true. As environmental historian Matthew Denis pointed out, the Senecan culture and way of life ended with colonialism, Christian missionizing, and settlement.

In fulfillment of Handsome Lake's prophecies, settlers continued to arrogate Native land and occasionally, though not surprisingly, those farmers dug up the evidence of the original inhabitants. A projectile point or a shard of pottery, again adding to rumors and expectations of further treasure in the ground. Did the arrowhead indicate a large trove of valuables? Perhaps the riches of a chieftain's grave or a lost tribe? Farmers pinned their hopes of escaping drudgery and hardship on whispered chitchats of riches cached by the very population that they themselves had impoverished and displaced.

And yet the call of Indian riches rang in the ears of Joseph. As did the dream of an undiscovered conquistador chest of gold. Something precious, buried but undiscovered, waiting for the warmth of the sun and the talents of a true diviner. Yet he found nary a doubloon. Even so, for whatever reason, Joseph enjoyed a good reputation as a scryer during these years—so much so that, in 1825, Josiah Stowell bet on Joseph's unproven skills and hired him to find a Spanish silver mine rumored to be on his property in Pennsylvania. But after searching and digging and divining and incanting, there was no silver in sight. Angry over this failure, and convinced of Joseph's chicanery, the farmer's nephew took Smith to court as a disorderly person and imposter, the first of a lifetime of criminal charges for the soon-to-be religious leader.

In spite of this legal tangle, the next chapter in Smith's life was beginning to come into view. During his time in Pennsylvania, though he didn't strike it rich, he met his first of many wives, Emma Hale. By then, he'd learned that people eagerly believed in myths, like buried treasure, and in a region of smoldering religious passions, he'd seen a culture's need for belief as much as their hunger for it. Joseph had met a young Orrin Porter Rockwell, eight years his junior, and their consequential friendship was just budding. Rockwell would help bring Joseph's religion, as well as a Mormon code of vengeance, into the West, where it remains today. And despite his nephew's accusation of flim-flam, Josiah Stowell remained friends with the young, failed scryer. In an 1834 letter written on behalf of the ailing Stowell to Smith, who was then living in Nauvoo, Illinois, the old farmer promised to "come up to Zion the next season." Both men were dead within a year after the letter was written. But we'll get to that. And we'll also get to Zion.

It wasn't too long after the Stowell job that Smith announced something truly extraordinary, his mighty unearthing. It was not pirate plunder. Nor the contents of a chieftain's grave. Rather, as he would tell thousands of men and women, he stumbled onto something infinitely more marvelous. A stack of golden plates engraved with mysterious script, which he dug from the side of a hill called Cumorah. With this claim, he created a new identity on this account—the discovery of platters, scribbled with stories, that he told his followers he'd translated and written within the pages of the Book of Mormon.

These plates had not come from scrying, Joseph declared, but rather from a visiting angel named Moroni. Years later, and well into his launch of a modern world religion, he recalled an angel floating in the air who wore a robe of "exquisite whiteness."

> It was a whiteness beyond anything earthly I had ever seen; nor do I believe that any earthly thing could be made to appear so exceedingly white and brilliant. His hands were naked, and his arms also, a little above the wrist; so, also, were his feet naked, as were his legs, a little above the ankles. His head and neck were also bare. I could discover that he had no other clothing on but this robe, as it was open, so that I could see into his bosom.

After several more visits, the angel encouraged Joseph to go dig up the plates.

Though the words etched upon the plates were initially inscrutable, Joseph said that luckily he'd found magic tools along with the plates, an Urim and a Thummim, necessary for decoding what he declared was a type of reformed Egyptian writing. Using their power, Joseph went back to a process he knew so well, plunging his face into the opening of his hat and staring into the darkness toward his own seer stone perched in its crown. Conjuring the engraved contents from the darkness, Joseph translated the words, revealing the plate's tales to his trusty scribes, Emma, Oliver Cowdery, and Martin Harris. The process was first carried out from Joseph's and Emma's home in Harmony, Pennsylvania, and later, he and Cowdery went to Fayette, New York, to finish the work.

The platters, Joseph claimed, contained a history of America written by a man named Mormon and later edited by his son Moroni. They told of a lost tribe of Israel, a family who traveled west in 600 BCE, and the descendants who spread throughout the Americas. For over a thousand years, two lineages, one descended from a man named Laman and the other from his brother Nephi, fought battles against each other as they struggled with various degrees of success to follow the word of God. Eventually, the Lamanites, those descended from Laman, killed off the Nephites, those descended from Nephi, but, over the centuries, the Lamanites forgot their origins. Joseph Smith believed the Lamanites were in fact American Indigenous people, whom God had punished and left with dark skin for their transgressions.

This racist notion was not unique to Smith, as many white Christians regarded skin color as "the curse of Ham"—this in reference to the passage in Genesis in which Noah punishes a son by that name. Ham had come across his father lying naked in a drunken stupor, and for this act, which Noah felt was one of disrespect, he hexed both his son and the entire land of Canaan. Although there is no mention of Noah's actual spell, it was somehow decided in the Middle Ages that the curse of Ham conferred dark skin. This became a justification for enslaving those who were not white. By using the curse of Ham as a device, people in servitude were seen as deserving of their fates. Prominently used in nineteenth-century America to justify slavery, the idea was embraced by the Mormons, who carried it westward and into their Indian missions. The church maintained that the jinx could be reversed through an act of Mormon conversion, fostering a long history of pressure on Indigenous peoples to embrace Mormon culture and leave their own behind. The curse of Ham also influenced church policy prohibiting African American men from joining the Mormon priesthood until 1978.

In 1830, the Book of Mormon was published and it became an essential element, even the key, to building Joseph Smith's church. He had something the various sects of upstate New York did not—his very own bible. Joseph was offering an

American gospel, an actual sacred story that had been unfolding on American soil. The book told of Jesus visiting the Americas after his resurrection. It offered a history of the chosen people, who were Americans, and it explained the presence of Native peoples and where they'd come from. With the Book of Mormon, America was a new and improved Jerusalem. To believers, it was a restored gospel, a contemporary and comprehensive explanation of Christian theology. It attracted followers who saw in his Book of Mormon new information giving fuller meaning to the Old and New Testaments. Like fitting together pieces of a puzzle, when these texts were interpreted together, an up-to-date vision of God became available to Joseph's flock. Joseph's sacred book gave proof that God continued to engage in an ongoing dialogue with humanity.

Many were attracted to Joseph Smith and his bible written from golden plates, but not everyone. Many called it forged or a bad biblical rip-off. Among them was Mark Twain, who combined all of these accusations in his own assessment, written years after its publication, calling the Book of Mormon a "pretentious affair, and yet so 'slow,' so sleepy; such an insipid mess of inspiration. It is chloroform in print. If Joseph Smith composed this book, the act was a miracle—keeping awake while he did it was, at any rate." He continued, writing that "the book seems to be merely a prosy detail of imaginary history; the Old Testament for the model; followed by a tedious plagiarism of the New Testament. The author labored to give his words and phrases the quaint, old-fashioned sound and structure of our King James translation of the scripture." The text, Twain added, is so jammed with biblical-sounding expressions such as "and it came to pass," that, had this particular idiom been discarded in the final product, "his Bible would have been only a pamphlet."

Although the book had detractors, within a few years after its publication, Smith had hundreds of devotees, earning him the reputation of a real live, flesh-and-blood prophet of God.

This man, seemingly capable of revealing God's truth in real time, was like a modern-day John the Baptist. It wasn't just the Book of Mormon. Throughout his life, Joseph Smith received messages from God that influenced the direction of his religion and his people. Throughout his life, prophecy and revelation came fast and furious; after his death, "God's truths" spread out across the Great Basin and Colorado Plateau.

But while Joseph was able to share his book, the holy plates were another story. Moroni, Joseph claimed, wanted them back. A handful of witnesses did testify to their existence; some saw them in visions and others claimed to have glimpsed or "hefted" them while they lay draped in cloth. But it doesn't really matter. The truth of their existence is not the point. What really matters are the people who joined the Mormon Church and their descendants, those who brought Joseph Smith's ideas into their unique identity. Publication of the Book of Mormon earned Smith the authority to launch his ideologies along a far-reaching trajectory. His book was but one text in a career that produced voluminous doctrines, sundry revelations, and complicated theologies. What Joseph Smith left behind has superseded his thirty-nine years. Plates or no plates, interpretations of his prophecies are as important today as they were when he walked the earth.

Early Days

Hell may pour forth its rage like the burning lava of Mount Vesuvius, or of Etna, or of the most terrible of the burning mountains; and yet shall "Mormonism" stand.

—Joseph Smith

So why is Joseph Smith so important in this cowboy story? Because he left behind systems and beliefs that continue to motivate a growing group of people, many of whom aren't even Mormon. When looking at the Bundys, and the many supporters who back them, we see specific and notable pieces that Smith put forth to provide basis for their row. Among these pieces: God talks to the faithful and gives them higher truths. The world is in its latter days—hence their appellation, the Latter-day Saints (LDS)—so time is of the essence. And the Saints are entitled to homeland, and as such must serve as soldiers in defending their land, beliefs, and God-given liberties.

The way these facets became embedded into early Mormon worldview is based on the experience of the Mormon Church as much as Smith's character. The ideas came about over years as he defended his people and his community from oppression, violence and repeated exiles. But in the beginning, with the Book of Mormon in hand and in ongoing dialogue with God, he set about building both a collection of followers and a culture to enwrap them. That culture would combine talismanic elements of Americana with supernatural dashes, together with a commitment to punishing those they perceived had wronged them.

When rumors spread about the plates and the Book of Mormon, Smith began to draw devotees. A handsome fellow of six feet, with bright blue eyes, long eyelashes, and a profile defined by a striking Roman nose, he set about securing his own authority and muffling other religious enthusiasms and assertions that might detract from his new status as prophet and the credibility of his divine messages. Very early in his career, he crafted some rules, issued a few disclaimers, and made an example of an errant follower in order to ensure his own power.

In 1830, the year the Book of Mormon was published, Hiram Page, a jowly man who was among those who swore to the existence of the golden plates, told friends that he had received his very own prophecy from God using his very own seer stone. This boast was alarming and carried with it a challenge to the prophet's preeminent position, so Smith confronted Page before the small group of men who made up a nascent body of governance, telling them Page's insight was bogus. Smith said that God had decreed, in the form of a revelation, "No one shall be appointed to receive commandments and revelations in this church excepting my servant Joseph Smith, for he receiveth them even as Moses." Smith asked that Page's prophecy be discounted and the offending stone destroyed. And so, it was done.

Still, Smith did encourage his first followers to experience God and urged a personal relationship with the Almighty, but he recognized that this type of egalitarianism came with some risk. He did not want God talking to those who might contradict him. Historian Richard Lyman Bushman points out in his exhaustive biography of the prophet, *Joseph Smith: Rough Stone Rolling*, that part of the appeal of Joseph Smith as prophet was "the promise of gifts and visions." Smith recognized the charismatic merits of having rapport with God, and he conceded that, indeed, direct communication from God to other church members could occur. But each such message, he insisted, would need his vetting before it could be believed. Members receiving divine dispatches had to, according to Bushman, "follow the Spirit of the truth, not the mindless ecstasies of visionaries," and visions must "edify" and bring forth the "bright light" of truth, rather than sidetrack, create confusion, or devolve into passionate paroxysms. Joseph Smith aspired to create a system, even "rules," as described in the church Articles and Covenants, that would separate wheat from chaff—good prophecy from bad. Within a modern context, to someone outside the church, divine communication and individual prophecy sounds arbitrary and slippery. The power of a personal revelation among the credulous can be used to manipulate and mislead. Still, today the Mormon Church cites the story of Hiram Page to illustrate the difference between "imitation" (Page's assertion) and "truth" (Joseph Smith's true revelation). Page's claims, they say, came from Satan's whispers rather than from the real "work of God." But what is truth and what is imitation? Who acts as spiritual arbitrator now that there is no Joseph to do the vetting? And if someone feels "inspired" with deep passions, what keeps him or her from claiming to know, then act upon, the true words of God? This is a sticky wicket.

After the incident with Hiram Page, though Joseph Smith's authority was confronted in various other ways during his tenure as prophet, dueling revelations with congregants did not seriously jeopardize his leadership role during his lifetime. It was after the prophet's death that some church adherents, and a handful of excommunicated members, turned to the idea of personal revelation to confront church policies and the laws of the land. Author Jon Krakauer, in his chilling and jaw-dropping book *Under the Banner of Heaven*, illuminates, among other things, the menaces of individual prophecy. "In the beginning Joseph Smith had emphasized the importance of personal revelation for everyone," writes Krakauer. He goes on to detail that this imagined aptitude has triggered murders and many cases of statutory rape in modern Mormon fundamentalist circles. Although Smith tried to control revelation in his lifetime, "the genie was already out of the bottle," Krakauer asserts, and the appeal of personal prophecy persisted. Just ask Cliven Bundy and his sons.

By the time Bundy's great-grandfather, Nephi Johnson, was born into the new faith in 1833, Joseph Smith had left the Burned-over District. Though upstate New York had been a perfect place to forge a prophet, it was not the platform upon which to build his congregation. Already jammed with competing faiths, it was a crowded playing field. Plus, Smith's neighbors had turned on him, calling his prophetic abilities and his golden plates a sham. It wasn't just old friends—even his own father-in-law, Isaac Hale, had it in for Smith. Joseph eloped with Hale's daughter Emma in 1827 and, due to subsequent family friction, the fledgling prophet felt he needed to start anew beyond the reach of his indignant in-laws. So, in 1831, he headed south to Kirtland, Ohio, where Nephi Johnson was born two years later, entering a life defined by the complicated dynamics of this prophet's new church.

A growing number of people were hearing news of Smith and his American bible. Among them was lay minister Sidney Rigdon, a severe-looking chap with narrow eyes and bushy brows, who joined the faith after reading the Book of Mormon and seeing in it a truth for which he'd been hankering. Rigdon encouraged his own congregation to follow Joseph into what would become known as the Church of Jesus Christ of Latter-day Saints. The group set up shop in this small town, Kirtland, along the east branch of the Chagrin River, sixty miles northeast of Cleveland. Nephi's mother and father, Joel and Annie Johnson, trailed the Smiths to Kirtland, where they threw themselves into church work and the responsibilities of parenthood. The Rockwells, some of Smith's loyal neighbors who had since been baptized in the new church, left New York as well, bringing with them their son Porter, who'd befriended Smith years before. Unlike the Johnsons, the Rockwell family did not dally in Ohio but moved west to Missouri, joining other Mormon settlers buying land there.

Kirtland, by the mid-1830s, began to fill with converts who had heard about Joseph's golden bible, or, as it had also become known, his restored gospel. But Ohio was only a way station. Missouri was where Joseph imagined his religious kingdom, one he planned to build atop the very place where the Garden of Eden had once offered apples and fig leaves. Yes, Eden, Smith assured, had always been in North America, not the Middle East. It was there the Saints would bring forth their shining city, a New Jerusalem, along the same fertile real estate where Adam and Eve were created and bestowed the fish of the sea and the birds of the air. Missouri, the prophet said, was Mormon homeland, a place they would call Zion.

While dreaming of Zion during his seven years in Kirtland, Joseph erected a grand temple, raised and lost money for his church, and organized successful mission trips that mushroomed his congregation. By the time Nephi Johnson came into the world, the Mormon population of Kirtland was maybe a hundred citizens. When Nephi turned five in 1838, the town had roughly two thousand people, those lured by the religious promises of Mormon missionaries who were bringing converts into an overcrowded chaos. By one account, "the City of the Saints appeared like one besieged. Every available house, shop, hut, or barn was filled to its utmost capacity. Even boxes were roughly extemporized and used for shelter . . ." The disorder in Kirtland was made worse by the fact that many new converts were arriving with no money, having given up property and family connections to come join this man who talked to God. They were promised that the church would take care of them, and many arrived expecting both spiritual and material support.

Sidney Rigdon, the lay minister, converted hundreds of Ohioans hungry for Smith's prophecy. The two shared a somewhat tumultuous relationship and Rigdon wasn't the first, and was certainly not the last, nagged by doubt about Joseph's prophetic accuracy and leadership abilities. In spite of Joseph's charm and his skills in persuasion, many, even church members, found his revelations, at times, dubious. And early on, there was the gossip about Smith's not-so-secret carnal proclivities.

In 1832, a mob dragged Joseph and Rigdon into the road and proceeded to strip, tar, and feather them. These thugs had also engaged the services of a Dr. Dennison to castrate Smith. At the last minute, the doctor lost his nerve, but tried (unsuccessfully) to empty a vial of poison into the self-proclaimed prophet's mouth. Smith walked away, alive and intact, with a chipped tooth that gave him a lifelong whistle when he spoke. According to biographer Fawn Brodie, the assault came in response to Joseph's suspected dalliance with sixteen-year-old Marinda Johnson. (Bushman's biography casts doubt on this suspected liaison.) All the same, Smith was "sealed," a Mormon marriage, to Marinda Johnson ten years later.

In addition to nearly getting killed perhaps due to reports of Smith's appetites, Rigdon was also concerned over another of the prophet's revelations that members should relinquish personal and financial properties to the church. He was asking for funds from both poor and wealthy members to pay for the expensive Kirtland Temple, among other church outlays. Rigdon had tried financial communalism in another church, with mixed results, and the idea bothered him. (Smith's call, known as the Law of Consecration, is partially practiced today through membership tithing.)

The idea of sharing wealth came to the prophet quite early, after asking one of his scribes, Martin Harris, to hand over three thousand dollars for the first printing of the Book of Mormon. When Harris balked, Smith snapped, and as though speaking in God's own words, threatened, "I command thee that thou shalt not covet thine own property, but impart it freely to the printing of the Book of Mormon, which contains the truth and the word of God. . . . And misery thou shalt receive if thou wilt slight these counsels, yea, even the destruction of thyself and property. . . . Pay the debt thou hast contracted with the printer. Release thyself from bondage." Eventually Harris did heed God's warning, or rather the threat that Joseph made in God's name. He mortgaged his farm to pay the publisher. Misfortune befell Martin Harris anyway; his wife, Lucy Harris, angry about the transaction—and her husband's relationship with the prophet— packed up and left him.

While Joseph ran affairs in Kirtland, he created church structure, appointed a council of leaders known as the Quorum of the Twelve Apostles, and wrestled with issues of liquidity and mortgages. The church bought quite a bit of land in the region and was burdened with outstanding loans, so he schemed to find further financing. He did this all while raising Zion in Jackson County, Missouri, sending families to the lush prairies of the American western frontier. Jackson County wasn't as jam-packed as Kirtland, and as the Mormons worked to acquire land, they bought farms alongside Gentiles (the term Mormons once used to describe those outside their faith). One early convert, Oliver Cowdery, a man distinguished by a large forehead, prominent widow's peak, and one tuft of black curls above each ear, was appointed to help organize the new arrivals to western Missouri and to assist them in buying property. After purchasing lands along the prairie, families, including the Rockwells, put up cabins, prepared hay for winter feed, and went about the business of settlers. The region's first Mormon wedding was celebrated in 1832 when Smith's old friend Porter Rockwell, then a young man of nineteen who lacked the ability to read or write, married eighteen-year-old Luana Beebe, his neighbor's pretty daughter. Hundreds attended, seizing a welcome excuse to rest the plow for a day.

As Smith had first revealed God's promise of Zion, he warned that the land would not be easily won when he prophesized that it was in "the hands of enemies." This was indeed correct. As a group, the Saints were hardly inconspicuous. They were a clannish, primarily Yankee presence in a slave state, and their beliefs were off-putting to the Missourians. Even more irksome was the Mormons' unwavering conviction that western Missouri was theirs, and theirs alone—a God-given homeland. They boasted that all the land would fall into hands of Latter-day Saints, as they awaited God's return to earth. But in their smug and staunch posturing, the Mormon people didn't understand how much danger they were creating for themselves. Missourians were a rough type of people, and while church members comforted themselves in their certainty that God would shortly send the Gentiles packing, the Gentiles soon began forming mobs.

While the Missourians did not appreciate the Mormons' haughtiness, the last straw was their abolitionist leanings. In the 1830s, nearly 20 percent of Missouri's population was enslaved, and the slaveholders feared that the Saints would fill political seats to agitate for abolition. *The Evening and Morning Star*, a Mormon newspaper established primarily to publish the messages of their prophet, carried a story in July of 1833, welcoming "free people of color" into Missouri and into the church. The Mormon Church was encouraging African Americans to come to their state, which Missourians feared could lead to slaves rising up. Missourians went into a rage over this. Soon after the article came out, as many as five hundred Missourians assembled at the Jackson County courthouse and issued an ultimatum: no more Mormon people in Jackson County. Members of the church currently living there had to leave. Mormon businesses were required to shut their doors, most especially *The Evening and Morning Star*. When the Saints tried to stall the process, begging for time to confer with church leaders in Ohio, the mob took measures into their own hands, dragging church leaders through the streets and plastering them with tar and feathers. Mobbers ripped the roof from the home of the publisher of the newspaper and destroyed the printing press. Fearing further backlash, Missouri Mormons agreed to leave Jackson County, and a short lull in violence gave Oliver Cowdery the opportunity to ride to Kirtland and discuss the dangerous and heartbreaking situation with the prophet. Some church members decided to appeal to Missouri's governor, Daniel Dunklin, asking for protection and recourse. But the governor responded by advising that the Mormon people seek legal counsel. When the Missourians heard that the Mormons were going to lawyer up, their fight against the religious sect became fierce. And sadistic.

On October 31, 1833, the mob members brutally beat Hiram Page and George Beebe, Porter Rockwell's brother-in-law. For days they unleashed their fury, razing homes, including Rockwell's own—something he would not soon forget. They looted LDS-owned stores and clubbed men bloody. Mormons fought back, killing two Missourians while losing four of their own. Still, they were outnumbered and out-gunned. In early November, days after the Saints successfully routed an attack near Independence, a Missouri official promised their safety in exchange for their weapons. But this was a ruse, depriving the Saints of protection against continued attacks as marauders torched Mormon farms and crops, leaving many of the now-defenseless people without homes or food as winter settled. The Latter-day Saints begged for mercy, but it wasn't to be found in their putative Garden of Eden.

Missouri Saints besieged Joseph to intercede on their behalf, but he hesitated, vacillating—first telling his Missouri disciples to trust in God, then rationalizing that the cold-blooded attacks were a deserved punishment for some lack of faithfulness among his flock—it wasn't just Rigdon who was questioning Joseph Smith's abilities and direction, others in Missouri were as well. In December of 1833, the prophet delivered a message to them that he said came straight from God. "Concerning your brethren who have been afflicted, and persecuted, and cast out from the land of their inheritance . . . ," God said to the prophet, "there were jarrings, and contentions, and envyings, and strifes, and lustful and covetous desires among them; therefore by these things they polluted their inheritances." This dispatch further offered that, although God was still upset about the sins of those not fully supporting Joseph Smith, "my bowels are filled with compassion towards them. I will not utterly cast them off." The decree promised that God would make available "all the land which can be purchased in Jackson County, and the counties round about, and leave the residue in mine hand." In other words, the Missouri Saints had it coming, but God would make it right. Yet, in spite of God's compassionate bowels, the situation in Missouri just kept getting worse.

As oppression mounted in Missouri, Joseph contemplated the best course of action, while counting on God's intervention. He sent a plea to President Andrew Jackson and was rebuffed, with Jackson deferring to the state of Missouri on grounds of states' rights. (It seems ironic today, with Mormon politicians in Utah comprising an exceptionally vocal contingent of this country's states' rights advocates.)

After Jackson's refusal to intercede, Smith struggled further to find some way to save Zion. Until now, Joseph Smith had preached and practiced pacifism. But mounting violence in Missouri tested this stance and pushed Smith to conceive a military campaign. Despite initial plans to engage an army of five hundred men to march to Zion and protect it from enemies, he managed to round up only two hundred volunteers; a thirty-four-year-old Brigham Young was among them. Smith led this campaign, named Zion's Camp, to Missouri, marking the beginning of a Mormon militancy with the goal of defending homeland. This ethos still echoes in Utah and Nevada today.

As it unfolded—that is, before Zion's Camp became a rewritten and sacred memory—the operation was fraught, its strategy unclear. Militia members squabbled and challenged their prophet's authority throughout the journey; supplies were thin and often unsuitable. A cured ham rotted and was chucked, instead of filling empty stomachs. The water supply became befouled. Army members fell ill, fourteen dying from cholera. Adding insult to injury, the expedition did not rescue the Missouri brethren, but rather turned around and marched back to Kirtland after Missourians threatened violence, again leaving the pioneers of Zion defenseless. These facts notwithstanding, historian Matthew C. Godfrey has noted that the Zion's Camp military drive is a much-ballyhooed chapter in church history, in which bad memories have been replaced with miraculous recollections. The church casts the endeavor as a God-given trial and an essential stepping stone in the development of the Mormon Church. But in reality, it was a total rout.

But before their retreat weeks later, while Zion's Camp marched toward the Mormon settlements in Missouri, the Missouri Saints were engaged in a last-ditch attempt to secure a peaceful agreement with the Gentile authorities. They wanted compensation for their property in exchange for their departure. But during negotiations, terms remained unacceptable, tipped to the advantage of non-Mormons. When news of Smith's oncoming army reached Missouri, discussions came to a halt, as this armed rescue mission rekindled the murderous spirits of the Missouri mobs. The fact that the prophet was trying to protect his people did not seem to impress the Missourians; instead, the Missouri gangs became even more organized, emboldened, and bloodthirsty.

After the long weeks spent marching across the grasslands of Middle America, sometimes covering forty miles in a day, the Saints arrived just north of Jackson County, setting up camp on the Fishing River. On June 19, 1834, two hundred Missourians requisitioned ferries to confront Zion's Camp. Later, the Saints would recollect that on this night, ominous weather rolled in, sending twisters screaming from the skies and a shower of huge hailstones that battered the ground. Though gunfire was exchanged during the long night, Mormons reported that the heavens stymied the Missourians; their dazzling and disorienting storm kept Zion's Camp safe.

Another Zion's Camp story, still a favorite in Mormon lore, tells of a Missouri tough named James Campbell, who boasted he would take down the Mormon prophet. If he failed, Campbell said, "eagles and turkey buzzards shall eat my flesh." Campbell commandeered a boat to the Saints' encampment, but it capsized, and he drowned. A few days later, his corpse was found ravaged by birds of prey, which Joseph Smith pronounced was a sure sign of God's favor.

Soon afterward, a Missouri sheriff approached the Mormon camp, warning that the Missouri militia was planning to attack. Smith capitulated and surrendered Jackson County. With the Ohio army's return to Kirtland, the Missouri Mormons were more vulnerable than ever. And with this failure to protect his people, Smith faced ever more upheaval. Some of his flock were beginning to worry they had placed their confidence in a poor leader. Or even worse, a false prophet.

A Militia Theology

It was then the rule that all enemies of the Prophet Joseph should be killed, and I knew of many a man who was quietly put out of the way by the orders of Joseph and his apostles while the church was there.

—John Doyle Lee

Jackson County was abandoned shortly after Zion's Camp returned to Ohio. Church members packed up what they could and fled into Clay County, Missouri, but after only two years, they again were told by locals to get out. Ohio adherents, on the other hand, seemed to be faring better. Nephi Johnson would later write that among his earliest memories was one of watching his father cut wood for the first Mormon temple, a big white cathedral with large gothic arched windows, dedicated on March 27, 1836. This was a new religion, awash in spiritual frenzy. Fresh converts fell into paroxysms, experiencing visions inspired by a contagious passion and shared yearning for God. Spectators at the 1836 Kirtland Temple's dedication recalled celestial winds blowing through the assembly room and angels hovering above church pews, phenomena suggested by their charismatic leader. Joseph Smith later wrote that he "beheld the Temple was filled with angels, which fact I declared to the congregation. The people of the neighborhood came running together (hearing an unusual sound within and seeing a bright light like a pillar of fire resting upon the Temple) and were astonished at what was taking place." It all sounds like a page torn from the wild revivals of the Burned-over District. The temple's opening ceremony, and the many stories that were told afterward about the heavenly visitations, gave the community bright reassurance, of both God's favor and their prophet's ability to court the supernatural.

But Joseph's allure came with a downside, and in some ways the church was the victim of his renown. Many new converts crowded into Kirtland, seeking religious direction as well as escape from a crushing poverty. According to Smith's Law of Consecration, the decree to share wealth, more-affluent church members were expected to support poorer ones. But there were just too many mouths to feed and families to house and the church was falling into debt. Joseph cast about looking for ways to relieve his situation. He even pursued another treasure hunt to Salem, Massachusetts, in an attempt to track down riches rumored to be hidden in the attic of a house; but just as was the case in his early days, he was left empty-handed.

During the 1830s, the banking industry was expanding nationally, in speculative and unsustainable directions. Church leaders, including Joseph, thought a bank could be just the thing they needed to take care of their congregation and continue to acquire property through loans. Though it lacked hard currency, the church did own real estate. A joint-stock enterprise, Kirtland Safety Society Anti-Banking Company, though never actually licensed by the Ohio legislature, opened in January of 1837. It was very short-lived. By November of that year, the bank, or rather anti-bank, had collapsed due to a national financial panic, mismanagement, and an anti-Mormon campaign that encouraged a run on the institution. Smith faced seventeen lawsuits from creditors for over one hundred thousand dollars of debt.

The bank wasn't the only thing that was short-lived. So was all that glowy confidence the Saints had in the prophet after the temple dedication. Many blamed Smith for the failure of the Kirtland Safety Society and their own financial straits. And the pitchforks came out. While Joseph was traveling on a missionizing expedition, two church leaders—one a member of the Quorum of the Twelve, the other involved in the Kirtland Society banking debacle—led an armed takeover of the temple. Though their efforts were thwarted, the church became badly fractured among those who maintained faith in Joseph's abilities and those who scorned him. The loyal were targeted by former church members who felt bamboozled and fleeced. Between 1837 and 1838, up to three hundred people, or 15 percent of church membership, abandoned Smith. In January 1838, Joseph Smith fled Kirtland after hearing of a plot to kill him, and rode to Missouri, trailed by Sidney Rigdon.

Church leaders had secured property on Shoal Creek in Caldwell County, in a place known as Far West, Missouri. By 1838, it was regarded as the Mormon headquarters. Defiance against the prophet was in full swing in Missouri as well, but once there, he dug in. His detractors were scattered throughout his own congregation as well as among the Gentiles, and the internal rebellion needed to be quelled in order to create a united front against a new wave of Missouri mobbism. So Smith and his inner circle devised a plan to shame and threaten those disloyal to the church to shore things up. This marks a big pivot—Mormon culture embraced a belligerence that would become a hallmark of the early church.

The first fusillade was verbal: Sidney Rigdon's warning in June of 1838, when he delivered what is known as the Salt Sermon. In the homily that warned disloyal Saints about what awaited them in their treachery, he quoted Matthew 5:13. "If the salt have lost his savor, wherewith shall it be salted? It is thenceforth good for nothing, but to be cast out, and to be trodden under foot of men." The salt, in this case, was the unfaithful Mormon. Rigdon was telling those insurgents that they would face retaliation if they continued. A boot to the head or worse.

Rigdon's threats were to be backed up with a newly formed gang of Mormon men, who came to be known as the Danites. Though their legend is far more formidable than their actual record, both lore and history are central to the Mormon story of theocratic militarism. This was no Zion's Camp—the Danites were taken seriously and they were feared. Although the Saints had until this point purportedly been pacifists, there was apparently a contingency plan. The year after the publication of the Book of Mormon, Smith issued a prophecy that not only allowed for force but encouraged vendettas. This decree held that any nations or people who went against the Mormons should at first be approached peacefully. But if that posture didn't work—a first, a second, or even a third time—then "I, the Lord, would fight their battles, and their children's battles, and their children's children's, until they had avenged themselves on all their enemies, to the third and fourth generation." Mormon historian D. Michael Quinn contends that Smith, during his tenure as prophet, built a theological justification for violence and "unlike other American religious denominations, 'the church militant' was a literal fact in Mormonism, not just a symbolic slogan." In Smith's reveals, if crossed, Mormons, and God for that matter, acted to take violent action against any perceived oppressor, generation after generation.

During this time of strife both within and outside of the church, Rigdon, John Doyle Lee, Sampson Avard, and Porter Rockwell became initiates of this secret gang, whose mission was to quell treachery, dish out retribution, and deal with the Gentile threat. First they called themselves the Brothers of Gideon. Then they played with the name Daughters of Zion, an appellation plucked from the biblical verse in Micah that reads, "Arise and thresh, O daughter of Zion: for I will make thine horn iron, and I will make thy hoofs brass: and thou shalt beat in pieces many people. . . ." Although the sentiment was clearly bellicose, apparently "daughters" didn't set the right tone. Finally they settled on a name from a passage in the Book of Daniel, recounting Babylonian King Nebuchadnezzar's dream about a stone "cut out without hands," which was the instrument sent from God to crush all false kingdoms. So from Daniel they became Danites, a Mormon gang pledged to serve as this tool, swung to smash the enemies of their prophet.

Porter Rockwell had grown up listening to Joseph Smith and loving him. He'd come with his family to Missouri because of their longstanding friendship and his lifelong devotion to the prophet. He'd watched the violence play out against Missouri Mormons, including the destruction of his own home. He'd seen Gentile hatred aimed at his brothers and sisters, which drew him into an increasingly devoted relationship to both his faith and Joseph. Over the years, Rockwell grew inclined to do whatever was asked of him, legal or illegal, to protect both the prophet and the church. And that made him a fine Danite.

Also well-suited was Danite ringleader Sampson Avard, a Mormon convert who moved from Kirtland to Far West, where he encouraged all sorts of retributions against their enemies, bidding his men in typical church parlance to "go scout on the border settlements to take yourselves spoils of the goods of the ungodly Gentiles." This idea of appropriating property from people outside the church found some footing in Mormon culture, well beyond the Danites. Stealing from Gentiles (which includes the government) became viewed, by some, as not only acceptable but merited. When Zion found its final home in the American West, Saints, inspired by the Danite code, continued to steal the possessions bundled on wagon trains belonging to non-Mormon families. During the early decades of the church, animosity calcified (again, among some but not all members) into a hard conviction: Mormon people were different from other Americans and beholden only to other Mormons. Transgressions against Gentiles did not count.

John Lee was among those, like Porter Rockwell, who later

brought aspects of the Danite ethos westward. He had come to embrace the church completely in a moment of deep sorrow when his second child, Elizabeth Adoline, succumbed to scarlet fever. In his grief, he stayed up all night reading the Book of Mormon and feeling the power of its truth. (Sidney Rigdon had a similar conversion experience when reading Joseph's bible.) Of his years handing out vigilante justice, Lee wrote in his memoir that the Danites carried out "the most sacred obligations," supporting one another and "the Church under any and all circumstances unto death," so that "to divulge the name of a Danite to an outsider or to make public any of the secrets of the Danites, was to be punished by death." The clandestine and sacred bond among Danites offered them the heady thrill of being holy thugs. Some members even became convinced of their own infallibility, which led to a dangerous and unsustainable bravado. In spite of their secret rituals and symbols, in time, they would find out that they were still just men.

On July 4, 1838, a month after Rigdon delivered the Salt Sermon, he went even further, warning Gentiles that the Mormon people were done with being denied their rights and "trampled on with impunity." Henceforth, Rigdon declared, "that mob that comes on us to disturb us" shall spark "between us and them a war of extermination; for we will follow them till the last drop of their blood is spilled, or else they will have to exterminate us: for we will carry the seat of war to their own houses, and their own families, and one party or the other shall be utterly destroyed." Though he claimed that the Mormon people "will never be the aggressors," his words launched a war.

On Election Day in August of 1838, in Gallatin, Missouri, John Lee got his first taste of vigilante justice. A group of bullies accosted an LDS man while he attempted to cast his vote. Suddenly the Danites in the crowd flashed one another their secret sign of attack—right hand to right temple, thumb to ear—and fell upon the Gentiles. Lee would later express exhilaration at meeting enemy flesh with the end of an oaken club, declaring, "Like Samson, when leaning into a pillar, I felt the power of God nerve my arm for the fray. It helps a man a great deal in a fight to know that God is on his side." Nine men left the brawl with broken skulls, Lee reported. But "all the Mormons voted."

By the fall of 1838, the region had fallen into open warfare between Mormons and Missourians. On October 25, during what is known as Missouri's Battle of Crooked River, the Saints saw their beloved leader David W. Patten wounded. Their reaction was one of shocking barbarity. Patten, nicknamed "Captain Fearnaught," had believed, like many other Mormon militants, that he was impervious to Gentile bullets. Sadly for him, this was not the case. Gut shot, Patten died a slow and agonizing death in front of the rattled Danites and other Mormon soldiers, who must have realized that they too were as penetrable to slugs as any mortal. In reaction to their friend's death, some retaliated by disfiguring an injured Missourian. According to one account, they mutilated "the unconscious [Samuel] Tarwater with their swords, striking him lengthwise in the mouth, cutting off his under teeth, and breaking his lower jaw; cutting off his cheeks . . . and leaving him [for] dead." It's not hard to understand why the Mormons were so incensed, after the brutal years spent trying to establish Zion in the face of venomous antipathy, thrashings, and property destruction. But the Danite ethos made a volatile atmosphere even worse.

Following the battle, rumors flew among Saints and Gentiles. Chaos and fury bred stories both exaggerated and inaccurate. *Dozens of Mormons butchered and left unburied! Fifty Missouri militia members slain! Savage Danites are thirsting for blood!* Two days after the fight at Crooked River, Missouri governor Lilburn Boggs signed Missouri Executive Order 44, ordering the Saints to leave the state or risk extermination. Because of "open and avowed defiance of the laws, and of having made war upon the people of this State," the order stated, "the Mormons must be treated as enemies and must be exterminated or driven from the State if necessary for the public peace—their outrages are beyond all description."

On October 30, a Missouri mob attacked several Mormon families in east Cardwell County. The small town where the incident occurred, Haun's Mill, was named after Jacob Haun, and home to about thirty Mormon families, a blacksmith shop, and the namesake mill. According to assistant church historian Andrew Jenson's 1888 account, survivors recalled that the massacre happened on a glorious, warm autumn day. In flowery prose, Jenson presents a scene in which children's laughter, the smell of corn ripening, and a recently signed peace treaty with one Missouri mob just two days before, had lulled the little village into a sense of false security. That afternoon, a group of men from another militia surrounded Haun's Mill and launched a savage attack. The assault lasted somewhere between thirty minutes and an hour as the mob set about killing seventeen people. One man was hacked up with a corn knife. Three boys, ages seven, nine, and ten, tried to take cover in a blacksmith shop but were found and executed at close range. Mobber William Reynolds placed a musket barrel to ten-year-old Sardius Smith's temple and blew the boy's brains out, explaining to his comrades, "Nits will make lice, and if he had [lived] he would have become a Mormon." When those who escaped the Haun's Mill attack returned to the site of the carnage, they placed their murdered loved ones at the bottom of an unfinished well, laying the boys' bodies next to the bullet-ridden corpses of their neighbors. Then they covered the dead with straw and left, on to the next Zion.

Nauvoo

The best way to obtain truth and wisdom is not to ask from books, but to go to God in prayer, and obtain divine teaching.

—Joseph Smith

In 1838, Joseph Smith had only six more years on earth before going to his glory. A review of events that unfolded during these final years suggests the prophet's runaway narcissism fueled acts of heedless and fatal bravado. But a member of the church might well consider these years the most productive period in Joseph's life. He was at the height of his prophetic force, the pinnacle of his authority, and the zenith of his productivity. By the time he was killed, a prodigious amount of theology had been left behind, some ideas that continue to excite those on the fringes of the Mormon religion. His most controversial revelations were on plural marriage and the idea that men could be gods, prophecies that led to his murder. But one of his most enduring prophecies, at least to our story, was that God divinely revealed the US Constitution. In fact, Cliven Bundy told me that it was Jesus who wrote it.

After the Battle of Crooked River, Joseph was arrested, chained, jailed, and awaiting trial. No Missourian involved in the Haun's Mill Massacre faced any such fate—a bitter pill for the Latter-day Saints. Smith narrowly avoided a firing squad, thanks to the sympathies of Missouri general Alexander William

Doniphan, who objected to an initial denial of due process. Charged with treason, murder, arson, burglary, robbery, larceny, and perjury, Smith spent a long and miserable winter in the fetid Liberty County jail awaiting trial. During his confinement, he corresponded with church leadership as well as with a property broker about acquiring roughly twenty thousand acres of land from one Dr. Isaac Galland, a con man known to be a genuine horse thief but not a genuine doctor. With this purchase and the acquisition of lands in Iowa and in Commerce, Illinois, Joseph once again envisioned Zion, this time straddling the wide Mississippi River on both the Iowa and Illinois shores.

After a six-month incarceration, Joseph and his men were allowed to escape. This in part may have been because many in Missouri were embarrassed over the whole Mormon affair and did not want further negative national attention that Smith's trial, and potential execution, would have brought. In any case, after bribing the guards with eight hundred dollars and a bottle of whiskey, Joseph saddled up a horse and made for the new homeland, a place he called Nauvoo, on the river's Illinois side. The name is an anglicized Hebrew word, *na'ah*, which means "comely" or "befitting."

Nauvoo was actually a pestiferous swampland. During their first year, many converts died of ague, typhoid, and cholera. Those lost included Joseph's father, his brother, and his youngest son, Don Carlos. His people were in rough shape when they arrived after their brutal experience in Missouri, and the boggy river land of this new home was not an easy place to alight. But as they settled, drained malarial swamps, built homes, gardens, and orchards, they shaped a place that held enormous promise.

Still, the Saints were poor. The state of Illinois was poor. And the country had yet to create any national legal tender. The financial panic of 1837 still rippled throughout, including, of course, among the Mormon community. In Nauvoo, residents relied on a system of barter and credit. Their detractors, however, spread gossip about their business practices, claiming that Latter-day Saints stole and counterfeited in their dealings with Gentiles as they set up business dealings in Nauvoo. Although this shady business may have happened, there is little evidence that it was as widespread as the regional rumors suggested. Still, just the allegations were enough to fan the flames of anti-Mormonism, which the Saints faced yet again.

In 1840, Smith secured the Nauvoo City charter and began to create municipal government. After years of finding no reliable advocate on either state or federal levels, Smith started to entertain his own political ambitions. He made himself mayor and filled the courts with Mormon judges, and with these appointments created more anti-Mormon sentiment among those who viewed his actions as theocratic and biased. But the prophet's intentions were understandable. The Mormon people had been run out of Missouri with no reparations. And although Joseph had pleaded for justice throughout the years, he'd repeatedly been disappointed by elected officials and the court system. With all the lessons learned, Smith was going to make Nauvoo a permanent safe haven for his people by packing offices with his own.

Another step toward defending his church was to build a militia. Danite ethos remained a deep cultural vestige, but in the 1840s, Smith wanted something grander than a gang of vigilantes. He gained authorization from the state of Illinois to raise an army, one he called the Nauvoo Legion. At its peak, his Mormon force topped five thousand members, making it the second-largest armed force in the country next to the US Army. Although he had no military experience, the prophet gave himself the title Lieutenant General, a rank that, at the time, had not been held by any military figure since George Washington. He rode in military parades, dressed in a splendid blue coat with epaulets and crisp white pantaloons. Around his waist he wore a gold sash, and atop his head a French-style military hat adorned with eight gold stars. This was a man who saw himself growing ever more mighty—one who spoke to God, shepherded an exploding number of supporters, and now had his own army.

Joseph's Nauvoo Legion engaged in grand acts of pageantry; both Latter-day Saints and Gentiles flocked to see the troops march and conduct military exercises. The festivities were meant to dazzle and entertain, but Smith's legion was foremost a calculated display of military might. It warranted that the Mormons were capable of challenging the authority of the state and the nation. Zion was coming into its glory. In 1839, construction began on the Nauvoo Temple, a large white limestone structure in a Greek revivalist style with star, moon, and sun adornments. Encased in scaffolding, this new sanctum, so full of promise, sat on a bluff above a horseshoe bend in the river. The Kirtland Temple, once filled with angels, was a thing of the past. God was now with Smith and his people in the state of Illinois. Mormon missionaries met with great success on their trips throughout Europe and converts were streaming into Nauvoo and into the faith. The *Nauvoo Neighbor* boasted that their city was "the great emporium of the West, the center of all centers," and had a "population of fifteen thousand souls congregated from the four quarters of the globe." It looked like the Mormons had found their home.

Nauvoo also had a great deal of security, with a police force that rivaled those of much bigger cities. The constabularies' primary charge was to provide the church leaders, primarily Joseph Smith and later Brigham Young, with personal protection. The prophet remained a wanted man in Missouri and he worried over bounty hunters and sheriffs who hoped, if they could lay hands on him, to trade their fugitive for a pile of cash. He was under guard at all times, night and day. Joseph continued to blame Lilburn Boggs for the horrors of Missouri. The former governor of Missouri, Boggs was the man who had issued Executive Order 44 after the Battle of Crooked River, calling for Mormons to be "exterminated or driven from the State." Smith and the brethren were still reeling emotionally and financially, and they wanted justice for those who were killed. And maybe something more.

Many believe that the prophet tapped his fiercest Danite, Porter Rockwell, to mete out justice upon this former governor. By then, the Danite leader Sampson Avard had long since left the church, after he testified in Missouri that it was Joseph Smith who had ordered Danite violence and raiding. Danite codes of vengeance had not disappeared, but the gang had disbanded after Far West. The injustices that the Mormon people had endured had hardened Rockwell and made him indubitably loyal to both the prophet and the church. In 1842, he traveled to Independence, Missouri, to work as groom for an expensive stallion stabled down the way from the Boggs family residence. May 6 was a drizzly spring day. That night, Lilburn Boggs, a stern and handsome man with a face framed by great white sideburns, sat in his study with two young daughters at his side. It was a scene of sweet domesticity, the retired governor reading a newspaper as his older girl rocked her younger sister in a cradle. But the tranquility was shattered as buckshot cracked the window behind them, and several balls pierced Boggs's neck, throat, and skull. The little girls were not injured, though they were badly shaken. Everyone thought this was the end of old Boggs, and news of his death drifted back to Nauvoo, a community that did not mourn over a rumor of his demise.

Yet Boggs survived, despite his grievous wounds. Rockwell was arrested for the attempted murder and held in the Independence jail for nine months. At his trial, he denied any role in the assassination attempt, rejecting the suggestion that his prophet had put him up to it. But Rockwell had been in the area, near the Boggs residence, and a storekeeper testified that he saw him handling the gun used to shoot Boggs. In fact, this weapon had been stolen soon after Rockwell inspected it in that store. But while many in Missouri (and elsewhere) believed the Mormon had tried to pluck the biggest and most painful thorn from the prophet's side, the evidence against him was too circumstantial and he was let free. All the same, the episode earned Rockwell a nickname—the Destroying Angel of Mormondom.

When Porter Rockwell returned to Nauvoo from Missouri and stood before his prophet, he was so caked in grime from hard overland travel that he was unrecognizable. As he later told friends, when the prophet finally identified him, he revealed God's utmost favor. Rockwell, Joseph declared, would not be felled by his enemies so long as he didn't cut his long and shaggy hair. And so, with locks long past his shoulders and a beard to match, Rockwell took the prophet at his word, did not visit a barber, and lived to the age of sixty-four. As Joseph predicted, neither "bullet or blade" could fell Rockwell. He died, instead, from a heart attack in Salt Lake City, shortly before his sixty-fifth birthday.

Although Rockwell lived a few more decades after the assassination attempt, his beloved prophet did not. His prophecies, and his appetites, affronting to both church members and Gentiles alike, became the death of him. In 1843, he revealed to his inner circle the doctrine of plural marriage. That same year, he wed fourteen women. He'd taken eleven new wives the year before and he married three others in 1841, though he may have been practicing polygamy as early as 1831. His confidence, or his audacity, was overflowing—even beyond taking multiple companions. In 1844, his final year, he decided to run for president of the United States. But that wasn't all. He urged his counselors to crown him King of the Earth (the minutes from this 1844 meeting are sealed and unavailable to the public), and he also pondered whether he and others were gods in the making.

During his tenure as the first Mormon prophet, Joseph offered many endowments to his brethren, bestowing the gifts of personal revelation, a God-given homeland, and his assurance that the Second Coming was imminent. To his male followers, he gave the doctrine of plural marriage and promised that, beyond this earthly veil, they could take their wives into the heavens (the most faithful would receive their own planets). He absolved his women followers of original sin, a very liberating gift for Christian women blamed in other denominations for the Fall and disparaged for centuries as shameful and devious. And the prophet gave his people agency—the ability to choose their own path and not be bound to the predestination of Calvinism.

But there was more that he would offer. Three months before Joseph died, he gave a eulogy for his friend King Follett. Follett was an early convert and with his wife, Louisa, he was baptized in Ohio in 1831. Both went on to Missouri and experienced its oppression. Follett and his family most likely had few possessions after Ohio and Missouri and must have struggled with the rest of the brethren as they settled in Nauvoo. Because of the malarial conditions, city officials encouraged residents to build deep wells to avoid disease; Follett was in the process of doing just that when a big bucket of rocks fell from fifteen feet overhead, crushing him. He lingered for eleven days after the accident, finally dying from his injuries.

The King Follett Discourse, a stirring funeral sermon dedicated to Smith's friend, was delivered on April 7, 1844. Smith began his talk during a storm, first asking the attendees—thousands, by some accounts—to pray for the weather to settle. It did. He talked about all of the beloved dead that families so missed, addressing Louisa Follett specifically, telling her that King had gone to his "celestial glory." And then he rolled out his most radical revelation. Heavenly Father was once only man. Additionally, there exists a multiplicity of gods and, as such, men can aspire to become gods themselves. (Sorry, ladies.) "Here, then, is eternal life—to know the only wise and true God; and you have got to learn how to be gods yourselves, and to be kings and priests to God, the same as all gods have done before you," he told his people.

This sermon, in addition to all of his other bold acts and declarations, pushed friends and followers into a rage. They felt that Smith's behavior was dangerously untoward, blasphemous, and self-aggrandizing. The *Nauvoo Expositor*, a slim, four-page journal, was published on June 7, 1844. It avowed Smith's original teachings, but it mercilessly attacked him for his recent revelations. The authors lambasted Joseph as a fallen prophet, mocking his role as a "Plebeian, Patrician, or self-constituted Monarch," in reference to his many ways of presenting himself, including "King of the Earth." The newspaper went on to detail the prophet's "open state of adultery" and called the King Follett Discourse a "false doctrine of many gods."

Upon seeing the *Expositor*'s exposé, the prophet retaliated. He met with the Nauvoo city council, who agreed with him that the paper was a public nuisance, and their printing press must be destroyed. Smith called upon a group of men, including Porter Rockwell, to loot the *Expositor* offices and smash and burn all of their printing tools. News of the destruction spread beyond Nauvoo's city limits and into surrounding Gentile communities. Law enforcement from Carthage and Warsaw, two townships near Nauvoo, attempted to arrest Joseph and the gang he dispatched. Given that Smith had filled the Nauvoo courts, it was unlikely any Mormon judge would hold their prophet or their brothers accountable for crimes against apostates. They didn't.

Mobs formed, including former Mormons, as crowds gathered in the streets of nearby townships and demanded that the Saints leave their state. In desperation, Smith wrote a letter to Illinois governor Thomas Ford on June 12, asking for protection against the mob's calls. He called the proprietors of the printing press all of the things Gentiles had accused Mormons of being: "a set of unprincipled, lawless, debauchees, counterfeiters, bogus makers, gamblers, peace disturbers." He wrote that "the grand object of said proprietors was to destroy our constitutional rights and chartered privileges; to overthrow all good and wholesome regulations in society; to strengthen themselves against the Municipalitiy; to fortify themselves against the church of which I am a member, and destroy all our religious rights and privileges, by libels, slanders, falsehoods, perjury." Governor Ford knew things were ready to boil over in his state and responded by asking that Joseph come to Carthage to face charges.

Did Joseph know that his own time was nigh? There is a mention in his journal, written in a strange moment of contemplation during the days leading up to his death. He started the entry, June 15, 1844, talking of recent visitors, reports of militia drills, and the arrival of several boxes of arms in the nearby Gentile town of Warsaw, Illinois. Then his entry goes from details of an impending conflict to mention of an image, Benjamin West's painting "Death on the Pale Horse." A beautiful and terrifying depiction of the Book of Revelation's Four Horsemen of the Apocalypse (famine, death, conquest, and war), West's painting was touring the United States at the time. It's not clear whether Smith was in possession of the actual masterpiece or a facsimile, but in his journal he wrote that a steamboat named the "Maid of Iowa come down the river about 2 or 3 o'clock While I was examining Benj Wests painting of Death on the Pale Horse which has been exhibiting in my reading room for 3 days." West's work is that of eschatological mayhem tied to a millenarianism that was in full bloom when it was painted in 1817—at the time, Joseph was twelve years old. The masterpiece depicts the story of Armageddon, Satan, agony, and hell, as foretold in Revelation. "And I looked, and behold a pale horse: and his name that sat on him was Death, and Hell followed with him. And Power was given unto them over the fourth part of the earth to kill with the sword, and with hunger, and with death, and with the beasts of the earth." This passage from the last book in the Bible tells of what will occur with the Second Coming of Christ, and for three days before his death, Joseph Smith gazed at its unfolding.

In his final years, Smith had explored various ways that he and his brethren could find power that he felt eluded them. Although he did not find a champion among politicians, he did believe in the virtue of the US Constitution. Joseph considered it divinely inspired—as God's will wrought by the founding fathers' ink and quill. He felt this document had the ability to defend his people, their freedom to practice religion as well as their entitlement to "life, liberty or property"—all of the supposed rights they'd been deprived of in Missouri. This founding document had been on his mind since his early days as prophet when in 1831, he revealed that, in the words of God, the "law of the land which is constitutional, supporting that principle of freedom in maintaining rights and privileges, belongs to all mankind, and is justifiable before me. Therefore, I, the Lord, justify you, and your brethren of my church, in befriending that law which is the constitutional law of the land." In understanding the Constitution, Joseph assured followers, lies true freedom.

Joseph's invitation to embrace the Constitution was later stretched by others, both prophets and apostates alike. There emerged an idea in the twentieth century that a Mormon might actually be better able to understand the true meaning of the Constitution than non-Mormons—this and the idea that the Latter-day Saints were responsible for its safekeeping. Smith's embrace of the founding document made it almost as sacred as those texts that resided in the Mormon canon, the Book of Mormon, the Doctrine and Covenants, the Bible, and the Pearl of Great Price. And because of this association, subsequent generations of Mormons have claimed the right to read the Constitution as divine, and at times to infuse it with subjective, and inaccurate, interpretations. Together, ideas of latter days, the sacred nature of the Constitution, and the essential role that Mormons have in its protection have embedded themselves, in Mormon circles of course but also within the American anti-government movement.

There is a revelation said to have been issued by the prophet in the year before his death, although it's not mentioned by church leaders until a decade later. It's likely apocryphal, but nonetheless influential, especially to the Bundys. This revelation is known as the White Horse Prophecy, in reference to the very scene (though not necessarily the actual painting) that Joseph pondered in his office for three days. The revelation states that "this Nation [America] will be on the very verge of crumbling to peices [*sic*] and tumbling to the ground and when the Constitution is upon the brink of ruin this people will be the Staff upon which the Nation shall lean and they shall bear the Constitution away from the very verge of destruction." If the 1831 prophecy to make friends with the Constitution was a whisper, this one was a shriek. The White Horse Prophecy foretells a time when the Mormon people will have to come to its rescue, when that document is at stake through the tyranny of the government at the time of Armageddon.

While regarding West's painting, so dark and unsettling, Smith's world was devolving and his control slipping. The people of Illinois were organizing, protesting, and calling for violence. Fearing attacks, Smith declared martial law in Nauvoo. He also ordered the Legion to engage in daily training exercises in preparation for war. Standing in front of his army, the prophet rallied his troops for battle. The speech, recorded in church records, called on "all ye lovers of liberty, break the oppressor's rod, loose the iron grasp of mobocracy, and bring to condign punishment all those who trample under foot [*sic*] the glorious Constitution and the people's rights." It wouldn't be hard to imagine this same rallying cry at the Battle of Bunkerville.

Joseph and his brother Hyrum tried to escape from what he was now sure was his own death. In a boat commandeered by Porter Rockwell, they crossed the Mississippi onto the Iowa shore, but turned back after Joseph read a letter from Emma pleading with him to return. On June 24, 1844, Joseph, Hyrum,

Porter Rockwell, and a few other church leaders rode to Carthage, where the prophet signed an order to disband the Nauvoo Legion. He also handed over hundreds of rifles and some cannons. The town was jammed with mobbers and militia members and as Smith and the others walked from their hotel to the court under heavy guard, people taunted the brothers, some shouting, "Kill the damn Mormons!" Joseph and Hyrum were found guilty of starting a riot in Nauvoo and were told they'd be held until their hearing on treason charges. Awaiting their fate in the heat of a Missouri summer, the men tried to calm themselves in the two-story Carthage jail with prayers and hymns, while mob members heckled throughout the long nights. On June 27, a gang of two hundred men, faces dirtied with wet gunpowder, rushed the jail, ran up the stairs, killed Hyrum, and as Joseph tried to escape out of a window, shot him. His last words were, "Oh Lord, my God!" as he fell down two stories before hitting the ground.

One of Joseph's wives, Eliza R. Snow, wrote a poem summing up the passions of the Mormon people in the wake of the fallen prophet.

> For never, since the Son of God was slain
> Had blood so noble, flow'd from human vein
> As that which now, on God for vengeance calls
> From "freedom's ground" from Carthage prison walls!
> Oh! Illinois! thy soil has drank the blood
> Of Prophets martyr'd for the truth of God.
> Once lov'd America! what can atone
> For the pure blood of innocence, thou'st sown?

The last legacy that Joseph Smith assured was the call to settle scores.

Brigham Young's Deseret

We ought to have the building up of Zion as our greatest object.

—Joseph Smith

In the wake of his death, confusion befell his grieving community, as Joseph Smith left behind no appointed or clear successor. So, while mourning the death of their prophet, the Latter-day Saints had to face the utter disarray and dissent within their community and a population of seething Gentiles, and do it without a leader. The beginnings of a church infrastructure were in place, including the Quorum of the Twelve Apostles, the group of church leaders among Joseph Smith's closest advisors, but there was no leader.

Nephi Johnson and his family were living in Carthage at the time of Joseph's assassination; his father, Joel, was employed in the construction of the town's jail, whose walls were left splattered in blood. Porter Rockwell had been in Nauvoo during the murders and John Lee on a mission in Kentucky. Though absent at the crucial moment, these men, over the next decades, came to avenge the blood of their prophet in various and brutal ways.

According to *History of the Church*, an official collection of Joseph Smith's edited writings and observations published twelve years after his death, he had prophesied that "the Saints would continue to suffer much affliction and would be driven to the Rocky Mountains." Those who made the journey would go on to "assist in making settlements and build cities and see the Saints become a mighty people in the midst of the Rocky Mountains." Like the White Horse Prophecy, this revelation is probably apocryphal, written after his death and slipped into church annals in order to bolster Smith's reputation as a prophet and provide the "proof" that indeed the Great Basin had been designated as Zion. It offered reassurance that the prophet had foreseen their troubles in Nauvoo and had known all along that a safe haven awaited them in the West.

When he heard about Joseph's death, Brigham Young made his way back to Nauvoo from the East Coast, where he'd been campaigning on behalf of the prophet's presidential bid. Smith's running mate Sidney Rigdon also returned to Nauvoo, from Pennsylvania, where he'd moved after agreeing to be the vice presidential candidate on Smith's ticket. These men, and a man named James Strang who claimed to hold a letter from Joseph granting him authority over the church, all vied for the role that Joseph had left vacant. In a sermon delivered on August 8, 1844, in the same grove where the King Follett Discourse had been given, Brigham Young made his case to assume leadership. He so moved the gathered crowd that many felt he channeled Joseph himself. With this passionate outpouring on why he felt called to steward the Mormon people, Young became a clear front-runner for doing just that. At the same event, Sidney Rigdon, known for his fiery Salt Sermon, also made his appeal to lead, but lost audience attention with rambling non sequiturs on end-times and Queen Victoria. After the men finished their elocutions, Young demanded that the crowd choose the next leader. "Do you want the church properly organized?" he asked. "Or do you want a spokesperson"—referring to Rigdon—"to be chief cook and bottle washer?" The crowd voted unanimously for Young to serve as president of the Quorum of the Twelve, apparently understanding their grave need for management over speechifying if the church was going to survive.

Young was convinced that Joseph Smith died due to Mormon disloyalty. He resolved that he would not abide disobedience or perfidiousness. He harbored grudges, did not admit to his own wrongdoings, and allowed no criticism of his directives. Redheaded, broader, and less sure of his prophetic skills than Smith, he secured Zion and under his authority the church grew from 26,000 members to 115,000, spread out through Utah and parts of Nevada, Idaho, and Arizona. He became church president in 1847 and served as prophet for thirty years, until his death in 1877. Young is the one to thank for the prosperity that his people would find in the West. He is the reason the church remains fixed to the Great Basin today. Honored with nicknames such as "Lion of the Lord" and "American Moses," Young believed utterly in the Mormon doctrine, and was resolute in his knowledge that he led God's chosen people. Cliven Bundy may be guided by the doctrine of Joseph Smith, but he wouldn't be battling over the land he is today without the resolve of Brigham Young.

Most thought Strang's letter from Joseph Smith had been forged, so he was excommunicated. He went on to build another Church of Jesus Christ of Latter-day Saints, a sect that grew to 12,000 members, called the Strangites. Among those who followed him to Beaver Island, Michigan, were Hiram Page, the man who had long ago proffered a rival seer stone that Joseph ordered destroyed, and Lucy Mack Smith, Joseph's mother. Though Strang initially opposed the practice of polygamy, he ended up married to five women. Like Joseph Smith, he also declared himself King of the Earth before he was murdered in 1856 by two disgruntled ex-Strangites.

After losing the coveted position to Brigham Young, Sidney Rigdon returned to Pennsylvania and also began his own sect, the Church of Christ. He continued to believe that the Book of Mormon was God's truth and that he was the rightful successor to the Mormon faith. Emma Smith and her children remained in

Nauvoo and, in 1860, her son Joseph Smith III became the leader of a third splinter sect, the Reorganized Church of Jesus Christ of Latter-day Saints, a branch of the Mormon Church that did not condone plural marriage, an idea Emma so despised. Freed from polygamy by widowhood, Emma went on to remarry. Still, throughout her life she never doubted that Joseph had dug up the sacred golden plates chronicling America's sacred early history and providing a restored gospel for modern America.

Immediately after Joseph Smith's death, the Gentile outrage seemed to abate, but only for a short time. By 1846, the Illinois House of Representatives unanimously passed a resolution demanding that Mormons leave the state. These religious adherents were no longer as defenseless as they had been in Missouri, nor were they without culpability in the violence perpetrated against them. They had weapons, martial capabilities, and a ferocious spiritual mandate for getting even. With acquittal of the five men charged in Joseph's murder (among them a commanding officer in the Illinois militia, a state senator, and the publisher of the anti-Mormon newspaper, the *Warsaw Signal*), the prophet's murder had infuriatingly gone unpunished. But as the Saints prepared to leave Illinois, some church members took retribution into their own hands.

Porter Rockwell shot and killed a reported leader of the militia effort called "the Carthage Greys," a young lieutenant named Frank Worrell. Rockwell was later acquitted of the murder because Worrell, fiercely anti-Mormon, had been threatening the life of a Mormon sympathizer, Sherriff Jacob Backenstos. To save his own hide, Backenstos ordered Porter to defend him from Worrell's advance. So Rockwell, the Destroying Angel, shot Worrell—to defend Backenstos and avenge the blood of the prophet.

For some time, the Latter-day Saints had felt very unlike other Americans, whom many regarded as both vicious and godless. This invidious distinction encouraged the Saints to believe they were governed by different laws, higher laws, both religious and jurisdictive, than the rules laid out by Gentiles. Joseph Smith had given his people the freedom to ask for private revelations directly from God, and left his followers with confidence that they possessed the raw materials and moral compasses of gods themselves. And if men were gods in the making, then all of their revelations, convictions, entitlements, and transgressions must also be infused with the divine. The Mormons were certain in the Lord's guidance—Gentiles and their laws were nothing compared to God's bidding.

By the time the Nauvoo Temple was dedicated in April of 1846, Brigham Young had already begun to prepare for the journey across the Oregon Trail. The doctrine of plural marriage continued during Young's reign, most steadfastly practiced by Young himself. Before walking west, he married twenty-one women in 1846 alone. He took fifty-five wives during the course of his lifetime. In the last months before leaving Nauvoo, the Saints kept the temple hopping with ceremony. It wasn't only marriages being performed. Families were sealed together for eternity and younger males were spiritually adopted by older men. Brigham Young embraced these bonds as well, adopting John Lee, among others. This was a time of endowments, washings, anointings, and sealings performed furiously before they departed Nauvoo—the rituals offered the idea of lasting spiritual bonds that would persist in spite of what might befall them on the journey ahead.

Before he departed west in 1846, Young wrote a letter to President Polk telling him of his plan for the Mormon people as well as sharing his sentiments. "We would esteem a territorial government of our own as one of the richest boons of earth, and while we appreciate the Constitution of the United States as the most precious among the nations, we feel that we had rather retreat to the deserts, islands or mountain caves than consent to be ruled by governors and judges whose hands are drenched in the blood of innocence and virtue, who delight in injustice and oppression." Young was not one to mince words.

On the first passage west during the winter of 1846–1847, Young bore the enormous burden of ushering 1,200 families—people who had laid their lives and their destinies at his feet—across a dangerous stretch of country on the 1,300-mile journey. The first families wintered along the trail 266 miles west of Nauvoo in what was called Winter Quarters, in Nebraska. There, hundreds died of illness, malnourishment, and exposure, their remains buried in a graveyard built for those lost.

In the only prophecy he ever made, shared with the first families to cross to Zion, Young spoke of a dream in which God likened the Saints' experience to that of the ancient Israelites. He told his followers, "I am he who led the children of Israel out of the land of Egypt; and my arm is stretched out in the last days, to save my people Israel." With that, their journey was given a religious justification, sacralizing their enormous efforts and trials in following this fledgling faith. They were walking in the footsteps of the children of Israel, across the lands of the Nephites and Lamanites, led by their own Moses.

Porter Rockwell served as scout and runner in the advance party as they made their way from Winter Quarters to the Great Salt Lake Valley. An excellent marksman, taunting death with his long and magical hair, he kept team members supplied with game and functioned as lookout to help thwart raids from justifiably outraged Native peoples in Nebraska, who were experiencing the crush of whites and the pains of Manifest Destiny. When his party reached Wyoming, a wet, cold spring left snow resistant to melt, creating a prime environment for ticks. Many in the first team suffered from what was called mountain fever or tick fever, including Brigham Young.

On the last leg of their journey, the forty-six-year-old Brigham Young convalesced, packed into a "sick" wagon as the team made its way down the western slope of the Wasatch

Range. His wagon bumped along the same steep gulches and rocky terrain crossed by the ill-fated Donner Party one year before. According to legend, when Brigham Young first spied the Great Salt Lake Valley, he announced, "This is the place!" A year later John Lee and the Johnson family, who brought with them the first domesticated sheep in the territory, joined Young and the others.

At first, they were on Mexican soil. But in 1848, millions of acres, including the fledgling Mormon settlement, were transferred from the Mexican government to the United States with the signing of the Treaty of Guadalupe Hidalgo, which marked the end of the Mexican-American War. This act covered lands that today lie within the states of Utah, California, Colorado, Wyoming, New Mexico, and Arizona. But signing the treaty put his people back in the United States, the place they'd been so desperate to escape, so Young made plans straightaway to isolate the Saints from further violence and tyranny and create their own religious realm on earth. He dreamed of a Mormon empire, a kingdom called *Deseret*, a word in the Book of Mormon, possibly derived from a Hebrew root, that in Mormon tradition means "honeybee." To build it, he planned settlements that stretched across the map, from the Sierra Nevada to the Southern Rockies, from Oregon to Mexico.

A couple of years after his arrival, Nephi's father, Joel, wrote a poem titled "Deseret." Joel, like his children and others, had seen the horrors of the Mormon experience firsthand. He'd lived in Kirtland and trailed the Saints through Missouri and Illinois. He'd helped build the blessed Kirtland Temple as well as the cursed Carthage jail. Joel Johnson's verses became a beloved Mormon hymn, "High on the Mountain," encouraging its listeners never to forget their history:

For God remembers still,
His promise made of old.

That He on Zion's hill,
Truth's standard would unfold!
Her light should there attract the gaze
Of all the world in latter days.
Then hail to Deseret! A refuge for the good,
And safety for the great, if they but understood.
That God with plagues will shake the world,
Till all its thrones shall down be hurled.

His song was sung in warning to Gentiles—if you mess with the Mormons, you mess with God, and that has serious consequences.

This homeland, finally found, felt providential and glorious. One church official wrote in 1849 that, after the Mormon people had "received nothing but one continued series of persecutions since the rise of the church," they had finally found their home in the Great Basin, free of Gentiles, those "inhuman, bloodthirsty savages who dwelt in the United States under the pious name of Christians." It was a wild and romantic country, this official noted, its landscape of mountains, saline lakes, desert, and extraordinary geological formations allowing for easy comparisons to the Holy Lands of the Middle East. Here they were, modern Israelites as Young's prophecy had foretold, making their home next to the Great Salt Lake Valley's most defining feature, the eponymous lake, which became the Mormon Dead Sea. The river emptying into this large saline body became the Jordan River. Mormon pioneers named their settlements accordingly—Eden, Moab, and Hebron. The tallest mountain in the Wasatch Range became Mount Nebo, after the one from which Moses first glimpsed the promised land. The Great Basin was not the verdant grassland of Missouri, and it was far from their swampy bend of the Mississippi River in Nauvoo. In this land, Yankee and European farmers continued to cultivate, yes, but they also began to run wide-ranging sheep and cattle in a vast and parched desert. This Zion made them ranchers.

But there was a reason the Great Basin was not occupied by other white settlers. It was not an easy place to plant stakes, in this country better suited to mobile communities that moved with the seasons, finding forage here and there, or following the prey depending on the time of year. People of such habits already lived here before the Saints arrived. This landscape may have been passed over by other Europeans before the arrival of the Mormons, but it was far from empty.

The Mormon people were colonizers who claimed Zion by homesteading. Before long, it became clear that the Salt Lake Valley was not big enough to sustain the tens of thousands of Mormons who arrived over the next two decades. Though Deseret never manifested in full (it was originally plotted for over one-sixth of the United States), a smaller version emerged in Young's plan to become economically independent from, and competitive with, other American states.

In 1849, Young sent teams to reconnoiter arable territory. One scout, Parley Pratt, who had been an early adherent of Joseph Smith, led his party down to what is now the site of Cedar City, Utah, and continued along the Virgin River. He later gave Young a detailed report of iron deposits and farmland, but also noted that "a wide expanse of chaotic material presented itself, huge hills, sandy deserts, cheerless grassless plains, perpendicular rocks, loose barren clay, dissolving beds of sandstone." Pratt's report was dreary, but it informed Young's scheme for settlement campaigns along lands that today make up some of the most celebrated scenic destinations in the world.

As Young considered how to establish Zion, he faced a people already living there. Though the Indigenous population presented a conundrum for the Saints, there was also opportunity. Bringing Native people into the church had been a priority from the beginning—one of Joseph Smith's aspirations had been a Native missionary campaign in Missouri: reversing the curse of Ham with the gift of a new faith that promised a renewed virtue and thereby took the world one step closer to the Second Coming. All the same, the Native people didn't act like God's chosen people. They didn't farm. Nor did they live in developed communities. And they did not like, as one could easily imagine, white people poaching their resources. At times they expressed this resentment by helping themselves, in their turn, to Mormon property.

There were early conflicts with the Timpanogos band of Utes, as Mormons settled along Utah Lake and the Provo River. Horse and cattle rustling became offered recourse against the pressures the Saints put on limited water and food. Jacob Hamblin was living near Tooele, Utah, south of the Salt Lake, when he watched Porter Rockwell shoot and kill five Utes who were wrongly accused of stealing horses. The last few years had made Rockwell a ruthless man, cynical and resolute, who would not question commands or overthink orders from church leadership. Brigham Young and others were exasperated with the Indian raiding, and for a time the new prophet adopted a position that justified killing any Native people found stealing from the Mormons. And when Young ordered the killing of horse thieves, that's what Rockwell did, whether they were culpable or only suspected.

A resourceful frontiersman, Jacob Hamblin was solemn-looking, his face defined by a heavy brow and elongated by a stiff, brushy beard. He had become a Latter-day Saint in 1842 and was serving as a lieutenant in the Nauvoo Legion when Joseph Smith was murdered. After the emergency decampment from Nauvoo, he had initially planned to join the Mormon wagon train, and even started heading west with his family. But in Council Bluffs, Iowa, just three hundred miles along, his wife, Lucinda, looked at the trail ahead with trepidation. After all that the congregants had been through, she just didn't have the heart to go forward into the unknown and refused to proceed. The already unhappy Hamblin marriage dissolved in 1849, leaving Jacob with their four children: Lyman, Martha Adaline, Duane, and Maryette Magdaline. And yet this lonely chapter for Hamblin was brief. The Lord Almighty evidently favored him, and soon another woman was in the picture. By the time he walked into the Great Salt Lake Valley a year later, he was accompanied by seven children—his own plus three stepchildren—and the new Mrs. Hamblin, Rachel.

Shortly after Rockwell killed the Ute men, a Goshute group, a Western Shoshone tribe, came under suspicion of taking cows. Hamblin gave chase and found himself face-to-face with one of the raiders. But when he aimed his gun at the Goshute man and fired, the shot went wild. Again, he took aim and this time his gun misfired. The man retaliated, shooting arrows that pierced the Mormon's hat and tore his coat, but not his flesh. Eventually both men fled the confrontation, in a close call that Hamblin came to believe was a result of divine intervention. After the encounter, Hamblin claimed that God had spoken, assuring him that if he never killed an Indian, neither would an Indian ever kill him.

To create Zion in the hills, deserts, and grassless plains of Utah Territory (designated in 1851) that Pratt's report described, relations with Native peoples became a priority. Recognizing the need for diplomacy and alliance in further settling homeland, Young arranged to send a crew who could earn the trust of the Indigenous peoples. Though he had spent a few years already as emissary to the southern tribes, in 1854, Jacob Hamblin moved his family, including his brother, William "Gunlock" Hamblin, to the lands along the Santa Clara River, a tributary of the Virgin. They built their homesteads among the yucca and sagebrush growing out of deep red soil. This was Southern Paiute territory, home to one of the region's most vulnerable cultures.

These bands possessed no horses and slept in simple brushwood shelters suited to their mobile culture. Slave traders from other tribes preyed on Paiute people, and their bands hoped an alliance with the Mormon people might offer them protection.

With a knack for languages, Hamblin became known as "the Indian Apostle," admired for his ability to understand Native people and broker relationships. But he showed little charity toward the Paiute people in his early encounters, writing in his journal, "there is not a day passes over my head, but that I consider it so great a privilege to have an hour to myself, where the Piutes [*sic*] cannot see me. . . . They are in a very low, degraded condition indeed; loathsome and filthy beyond description."

Mormons did establish relations, of varying degrees of closeness, with Native peoples. The church today includes many Indigenous members of the Southern Paiute and Navajo Tribes, converts to Mormonism—but this path was full of the heartbreak of assimilation, land grabs, white supremacy, and political maneuvering. Young mostly wanted partnerships with Native people so that together they could unite in case of attack on Mormon territory. He wasn't convinced, as Joseph Smith had been, that Native people would turn white with any religious conversion. And after a few years in the Great Basin, Young decided the tribal leaders would never be won over to Mormonism. Instead, he focused on children and intermarriage between his Saints and the Indigenous population. The biracial children born into such marriages could be brought up as Mormons—another piece of a cynical campaign.

The Virgin River watershed proved insufficient homeland for two such distinct cultures. Mormons were farmers and the Paiute people, for the most part, were not. Though Paiute communities did plant and harvest in lean years, they mainly lived off natural bounty. But in homesteading, the settlers took the choicest places, near springs and lands best suited for livestock forage. A region that had once amply supported the many bands of the Southern Paiute people disappeared as Mormons shaped the land for their own lifestyle.

The Southern Paiute people were left devastated in what they considered sacred homeland as well. These were a people who came as descendants of Tabuts, a wolf god. In one story, Tabuts carved people from sticks, in all shapes and sizes, placing them inside a sack, with a plan to "scatter them evenly around the earth so that everyone would have a good place to live." Tabuts had a younger brother, a trickster known as Shinangwav, the coyote. "Shinangwav cut open the sack," according to legend, "and people fell out in bunches all over the world." Somehow, according to their beliefs, the Southern Paiute people managed to stay in the sack. And as a result, "Tabuts blessed them and put them in the very best place." But with the arrival of the Mormons, the land became Zion: a place promised by Joseph Smith and conquered by Brigham Young.

After Mormon presence in the West was well established and the Native people had been run off or killed by disease and starvation, Young finally admitted his mistreatment of the Indigenous population and announced during a talk in 1866, in Springville, Utah, "This is the land that they and their fathers have walked over." It was "their home, and we have taken possession of it." After the Saints had been in the West for seventeen years, the prophet decreed that "it is our duty to feed these poor ignorant Indians; we are living on their possessions and at their homes." Young's condescension was shared by his followers, people who felt superior to the region's inhabitants and entitled to their lands—though the church continued its efforts to convert and control Native people well into the twentieth century.

Utah War

I have never willingly committed a crime. I have acted my religion, nothing more.

—John Doyle Lee

Brigham Young grew the boundaries of the Mormon empire, establishing farms, mines, and rangeland. Like the namesake of their kingdom, Deseret—the honeybee—the Mormon people assembled themselves into a hive, communally milling, milking, irrigating, harvesting, praying, and building Zion. Some of their settlements thrived; others succumbed. They fought drought, floods, and insect infestations. Travel was arduous and water was precious. It was a region that required grit to eke out enough to live on, making for a particularly trenchant and undaunted subculture of Mormonism in the desert. This is especially true of the Dixie and Iron Mission Mormons.

Beginning in 1854, Young ordered families to establish a network of small settlements and farms where the Mojave Desert abuts the Colorado Plateau and the Great Basin, today northern Nevada and Arizona and southern Utah. Several of the founding families were converts from the southern United States, earning by their efforts the "Dixie Mission" nickname. They planted cotton, though the land and soil would ultimately prove inadequate for sustainable production (the last mill closed in 1910). Instead the region became famous for tobacco, olive oil, almonds, and many varieties of fruit. McIntosh apples,

Winesap apples, banana apples, quinces, peaches, plums, melons, and even grapes all ripened under the Dixie sun.

But as the desert bloomed, relations with the rest of the country withered. While the Latter-day Saints had been in Utah Territory for a decade, they'd been largely left to their own devices. Brigham Young was appointed the Utah Territorial Governor in 1851 as well as Territorial Indian Superintendent, which gave him authority over both the Mormon population and tribal affairs. He, and his people, continued to harbor huge resentments against the United States and its citizenry. Gentile administrators serving in his territory—including judges, Indian agents, and other political appointees—were harassed when they tried to do their jobs. Not surprisingly, this unwillingness to cooperate with the federal officials drew Washington's gaze. Americans were already vexed over the issue of polygamy, which affronted a population who worried about the safety of the women and children living in such a remote corner of the country. Rumors about sexual depravities made newspaper headlines and supposed debaucheries became the fodder for bestselling novels. Metta Victor's 1856 *Mormon Wives*, an early anti-polygamy novel, offered the salacious tale of sister wives and a lecherous husband. Anti-Mormon tomes appeared for decades following Victor's work; the most famous were Arthur Conan Doyle's first Sherlock Homes adventure, the 1886 *A Study in Scarlet*, and Zane Grey's 1913 *Riders of the Purple Sage*. Both featured Mormon polygamist villains attempting to force women into unwanted marriages, with a backdrop of murder, thievery, kidnapping, and other savageries.

Both polygamy and slavery were deeply unpopular with much of the American populace. There was a worry, among national politicians, that if Utah Territory was to become a state, the practice of polygamy would be justified with the same rationale the Southern states used to justify slavery—state sovereignty. Congress pressured President James Buchanan to stand up to Governor Young, both for his refusal to work with non-Mormon agents and for the ritual of plural marriage. Tackling the Mormon problem was seen as less incendiary than addressing slavery, so when one advisor urged the president, in 1857, to "supersede the Negro Mania with the almost universal excitements of the Anti-Mormon crusade," Buchanan dispatched troops to march to Utah.

If the American public hated the Mormons, rest assured that the feeling was mutual. When rumors flew about the army heading to confront Mormondom, Young began to prepare for war with the United States. And he started with destabilizing Utah Territory by making travel hazardous for wagons crossing overland trails. At the time, Utah was a thoroughfare for migrants moving across the Rocky Mountains and the Great Basin. Before the friction, Young encouraged the Saints to do business with these settlers bound for the West Coast, helping them resupply on their long journeys. But as hostilities with Washington increased, Young ordered that any provisions not consumed by Mormon families were to be stored for wartime, not sold to desperate homesteaders who might be down to their last bags of beans. Those headed toward better lives in California found themselves caught between Young and the federal government. The prophet whipped up his adherents, telling them that "God has commenced to set up his kingdom on the earth, and all hell and devils are moving against it." Thousands of Mormons had already taken oaths in Nauvoo, vowing to avenge their prophet. If President Buchanan planned to challenge Young's authority or impede the building of Zion, he would get a fight.

In his riveting book, *Blood of the Prophets: Brigham Young and the Massacre at Mountain Meadows*, Will Bagley, a writer and historian, explores the climate in Mormon Zion just prior to the little-known Utah War, observing that in the mid-nineteenth century, for "all practical purposes, in Utah, there was no law but God's law." Prophecy, scripture, and revelation, not the law of the land, reigned supreme. The prosperity that the Mormon people would come to enjoy was still years in the future. Many of the Saints in Utah Territory were destitute after years of being forced to move and leave possessions behind. The Mormon community had intentionally tried to isolate itself, but their territory was on the way to the California gold fields, and the American quest for westward expansion pressed directly into them. Brigham Young understood the tactical situation, and as sabers rattled, he tried to shut down traffic across his territory. He also threatened that if Washington tried to invade Utah, Gentiles would be attacked by the Native peoples that he, as the Territorial Indian Superintendent, had thus far kept in check. He told Washington that all overland travel must cease because Gentiles could no longer move across the continent safely. "The deserts of Utah [will] become a battle for freedom. It is peace and rights—or the knife and tomahawk—let Uncle Sam choose." What he didn't say was that it was Young himself who started to intentionally provoke attacks.

In his official role, Young had been responsible for providing support to the tribal nations. With Buchanan barring down, he began to use his position to turn Native people against non-Mormons. Jacob Hamblin, in his dealings with the tribal nations, made abundantly clear the difference between himself—a Latter-day Saint—and Gentiles. The Southern Paiute people came to distinguish Mormons, "Mormoni," from other Americans, "Mericats." Mormoni were friends, Hamblin told the Native peoples, and the Mericats were not. Prophet Young instructed Hamblin to tell his Native network to join the Saints in the mounting conflict, or "the United States will kill us both."

The Utah War or, as it is also called, Buchanan's Blunder, was not very momentous. When the troops arrived in 1858, members of the Nauvoo Legion blocked routes into the Salt Lake Valley and wouldn't let them enter. They harassed the cavalry, stampeded their horses, and kept soldiers awake at night with loud commotion. Even though the Mormons got the better of the military contingent, they still seethed with rage over this invasion of Zion. Among the Mormon population in the 1850s, former Danites and Nauvoo Legion members, who had experienced the horrors of Missouri and been steeped in a military theology, were keen to channel their might and their ferocity against those they perceived had wronged them. Grudges burned like lye.

Isaac Haight was a constable in Nauvoo when, in 1844, he received news of Joseph Smith's murder. By 1857, he was living in Parowan, a town in the Iron Mission district, where he served as a major in the southern Utah militia battalion. As an early church adherent, he had been devastated by the prophet's death, and like thousands of others, he likely took the oath of vengeance before leaving Nauvoo. When Haight heard of the invasion, he vowed to fight with everything he had. "I have been driven from my home for the last time," wrote Haight. "I'm prepared to feed the Gentiles the same bread they fed to us. God being my helper, I will give the last ounce of strength and if need be my blood in defense of Zion."

It was the Baker-Fancher party—a group of unsuspecting Gentile emigrants from Arkansas—who were made to eat this bitter bread just for the act of crossing Utah Territory during this time of deep tension. The party, led by John Twitty Baker and Alexander Fancher, the latter an experienced wagon-train captain, included about a dozen wealthy farming and ranching families and several individuals traveling with somewhere between four hundred and eight hundred cows and horses. Being such a great procession, they were conspicuous. Throughout their journey, some families peeled off to join other trains—perhaps, according to Bagley, due to arguments over slavery—while other travelers had joined the Baker-Fancher team, seeking safety in numbers.

On May 13, 1857, mere days before the Baker-Fancher party headed west, Parley Pratt, the scout who had surveyed the Dixie region for Brigham Young, was shot and stabbed to death in Arkansas by Hector McLean. This jealous ex-husband of a woman whom Pratt had recently wed followed him for weeks, then murdered him during what happened to be the same month the US Army began its Utah campaign. Though this incident was completely unrelated to the Baker-Fancher party, the Pratt-McLean incident branded the families all the same. McLean killed Pratt in Arkansas, so the state was lumped with Missouri and Illinois as places whose residents the Mormon people most hated.

To be from Arkansas, to be Gentile, and to be wealthy were three things that earned targets on the backs of this group of travelers. Throughout their journey in the Utah Territory, the Baker-Fancher group found very few Mormons willing to sell them supplies. As they made their way south toward the Dixie and Iron Missions, things went from bad to worse. Locals began to spread lies and gossip, and these tales followed the group along the road. It was said that the Arkansans had poisoned a spring. Some Mormons accused them of pouring cyanide into the carcass of a butchered bull and giving the meat to the regional Indigenous people. And some said they had heard team members brag of killing Joseph Smith. Though these rumors were all untrue, the party did in fact commit one outrage. Their herds were very big and needed a lot of forage, a valued resource in a meager country. When a Mormon near Provo asked party members to get their animals out of his precious winter pasture, a member of the Baker-Fancher wagon train responded, "This is Uncle Sam's grass. We are his boys." Fighting words in Zion.

The Mormons had it in for the Arkansans. As the migrants journeyed west, Isaac Haight and John Lee gave local Paiute people weapons, with a promise that they could help themselves to the party's goods and cows in exchange for launching an attack. With these assurances, Native men joined the Mormon assailants, who had smeared their faces with dark paint (to appear as Paiute), awaiting their chance to pounce. When the Baker-Fancher party reached the last point of respite before their final leg of the California Trail, one that took them across the pitiless Mojave Desert, team members set up camp in a place called Mountain Meadows. It's a beautiful valley with good grass and water, in those days used by Mormons and non-Mormons alike. On September 7, 1857, after spending a peaceful night, some of the travelers woke early to tend the fires and prepare breakfast. That's when bullets began to fly.

Following the first rounds of gunshot fire, several party members sprang into action, some circling the wagons and digging foxholes while others returned fire. The women and children took refuge in shallow pits. By the end of the first assault, seven Arkansans, including a child, slumped dead in the early autumn sun. One Native man was killed and two others badly wounded.

Details regarding the attack plan are sketchy and still argued among historians, but it's clear that the Baker-Fancher party was targeted by Mormon militia, and maybe even Brigham Young himself. What's also clear is that the people behind the campaign to bring down the Baker-Fancher party did not count on their incredible tenacity. Behind makeshift fortifications, the Arkansans and their traveling companions spent the next five days fighting the attackers and their increasingly reluctant Southern Paiute partners. Over the course of the week, the Mormon aggressors launched many strikes, but the wagon-train party endured. Native people, who totaled between forty to a hundred during the raid, slowly abandoned the instigators. The Mormons grew panicky as the ordeal stretched on for days. The Baker-Fancher strike was supposed to have been surgical and pinned on the Paiute people. Instead it was a slow-motion massacre.

Carcasses, of both humans and livestock, lay rotting in the hot fall weather after days of attacks. The emigrants, who thirsted for the spring water that ran beyond the cover of their circled wagons, braved the volleys of gunfire to fill buckets and chop wood. John Lee, a leader in the raid, wrote in his autobiography, *Mormonism Unveiled*, that watching these men, women, and children throughout their suffering had brought him near to "dead from grief." Lee began to have second thoughts and wanted to let the Arkansans go, but by now the party had seen the Mormons and might have known they were somehow involved. Lee was tasked with bringing the massacre to a conclusion by William Dane, a commander in the Mormon militia, who ordered that there be no witnesses. A command was sent to Cedar City for militia members to come bury the bodies of the Baker-Fancher party, whom they were told had been killed by Indians. Nephi Johnson later recollected that "a company of men with shovels" had been dispatched "to bury the dead," but when they arrived at Mountain Meadows, he added, "they would find something else to do when they got there."

On September 11, Lee approached the beleaguered Baker-Fancher party with a white flag, offering a cease-fire, complete with safe passage to Cedar City and protection from further attack from—so he said—the Southern Paiute. Although the Gentiles were skeptical and still unclear about who had assaulted them, the last living members were out of choices, supplies, and ammunition. Demoralized and thirsty, after hours of negotiation they decided to trust the Mormon militia, come out from their shelter, and give up their weapons. The Mormons separated the Gentiles into three groups—the children and wounded were loaded onto wagons and able-bodied men and women walked, instructed to follow their "protectors," who took them about a half mile to a stretch of the trail. Then Major John Higbee shot his pistol into the air to signal an ambush and the members of the party, scattered along the short stretch of the California

Trail, were shot and hacked to death by the Mormons and the remaining Paiute—leaving all those over the age of six mutilated and dead.

This event, the Mountain Meadows Massacre, was one of the worst slaughters in the history of western settlements, along with the Bear River Massacre and Wounded Knee. Although many historians describe the tribe's participation, members of the Southern Paiute deny any involvement at all. White historical accounts could very well be inaccurate given how shrouded the event was at the time. The church denied involvement for decades and locals stayed tightlipped about any firsthand knowledge of the siege. Jacob Hamblin's wife Rachel cared for surviving children who had been spared because it was believed they were too young to testify as witnesses. Some later did.

It has been said that if Jacob Hamblin had been in the area, he might have prevented the bloodbath. But he'd been in Salt Lake City taking another wife, Priscilla. His biographer, Todd M. Compton, speculated that when Hamblin heard news of an Indian attack that left so many dead at the Mountain Meadows, he "considered the generally peaceful Paiutes to be incapable of such aggressive action. He was probably skeptical of the story." As would be so many others.

The event was chronicled decades later by Jack London in his 1915 novel *The Star Rover*. London renders it so compellingly that a leading Mormon historian, Richard Turley, noted for his own work on the Mountain Meadows Massacre, recommends *The Star Rover* as a very realistic narrative. Famous for his earlier novels *White Fang* and *The Call of the Wild*, London imagines a prisoner and his series of past lives, one as the nine-year-old son of wagon-train leader Captain Alexander Fancher. A science fiction novel, weirdly divergent from his other work, *The Star Rover* emphasizes the deep and abiding hatred that Mormons held for the Gentiles. But London also portrays the disgust that the Baker-Fancher party carried for the Mormons, and depicts a scene of mutual revulsion detonating in this lonely grassland on the Utah-Nevada border. Culpability for this horrendous event was denied by the church for nearly one hundred years. Leaders accepted no blame and gave little acknowledgment to the lives brutally taken in the name of Mormon homeland.

In the Utah Territory, the Baker-Fancher party massacre further ruptured relations between the Mormons and the Paiute people, as the Saints pinned the murders on their Native allies. The reality in our country in the second half of the nineteenth century was that of a place deeply divided along religious, economic, cultural, and political lines. The Civil War broke out three-and-a-half years after the massacre at Mountain Meadows, diverting the nation's abhorrence of polygamy and Mormonism toward the fight over slavery in many of its states.

Those traveling through Mountain Meadows saw in its aftermath wretched reminders of the men, women, and children who had paid grievously for being migrants in the wrong geography. James Lynch wrote of his experience the year following the event: "Human skeletons, disjointed bones, ghastly skulls, and the hair of women were scattered in frightful profusion over a distance of two miles." In the meadow today, monuments, plaques, and interpretive panels stand in tribute to the dead, but also as testament to what a people can do when they feel they are owed something and answerable only to their own laws.

The one assassin held to account for his role in the massacre was John Lee, who in 1877, twenty years after the event, was charged, convicted, and shot by a firing squad. Before he died, he denounced Brigham Young and accused him of masterminding the whole brutal affair. Young's direct involvement continues to be in dispute, but there is no question about the role he played in encouraging a type of vengeful insurgency.

In 1861, four years after the bloodbath, Young visited Mountain Meadows with a group of his followers. Two years earlier, US Army major James H. Carleton and his men had built a fifty-foot-wide cairn atop the mass grave and affixed a cross inscribed, "120 Men, Women, & Children, Murdered in Cold Blood Early in Sept 1857 From Arkansaw [*sic*]." They added a passage from Romans 12:19: "Vengeance is mine: I will repay, saith the Lord." When Brigham Young visited Mountain Meadows and saw the army's inscription, he told his companions, "It should be vengeance is mine and I have taken a little." Dudley Leavitt, Cliven Bundy's ancestor and a participant in the massacre, said Young then commanded the destruction of the stone cairn. "He didn't give an order. He just lifted his right arm to the square [Salt Lake City's Temple Square], and in five minutes there wasn't one stone left upon another. He didn't have to tell us what he wanted done. We understood." They left the monument in ruins.

At the time of Mountain Meadows, statehood was still nearly forty years in the future. And the people of Utah Territory were in no hurry to abandon polygamy, one step in becoming a state. Nephi Johnson himself had three wives. His first two spouses, Mandana Merrill and Conradina Mariger, bore him a total of twenty-six children. He had one child with his third wife, Bodil Margrethe ("Maggie") Anderson Johnson, who had also brought six of her own children from a prior marriage. As a dutiful husband, Johnson adopted all of them spiritually in a church ritual, sealing himself to her children so they would be bound together eternally after leaving this earthly realm. Among those adopted children was Johnny Jensen, who in his youth carried a passion for racing horses and went on to become the grandfather of Cliven Bundy.

Carol and Cliven Bundy lit up when we chatted about the Dixie Mission during my Bunkerville call. It continues to inspire pride in generations of Mormon families still fixed in this region, of which there are shockingly many. To descendants of the Dixie pioneers, the mission still represents resolve and steadfastness. The Bundys are quite proud of their connection to Nephi Johnson and of the fact that their family now lives in the southern end of the Dixie region (though their direct kin haven't been there continuously since Mormon settlement). Ryan Bundy asked if I knew of the Muddy Mission, an effort further south on the Muddy River. I had read about the first Muddy settlement in 1865, St. Thomas, Nevada, which today sits under the waters of Lake Mead, thanks to Hoover Dam. This dam is one of many indications that over the years, in spite of the ineffectual Utah War, the United States ultimately made its mark over Mormondom. And as the former residents of St. Thomas might attest if they were alive today, as the Bundys certainly do, some of these government policies affronted Zion.

Though Lee got scapegoated and was the only member of the Mormon militia who met with capital punishment, this hardly means that others were left untouched. Nephi Johnson, for one, spent his life troubled by his recollections. In later years, this once-handsome man with a trim dark beard appears rumpled in one photograph, his whiskers bleached and unkempt. He'd claimed adamantly that he had been against the atrocity, and that he never wanted "anything to do with the killing of emigrants." Nonetheless, he remained haunted by guilt. Eventually this burden led Johnson to Juanita Brooks, a young schoolteacher and the granddaughter of Dudley Leavitt, when he asked her to help him write his memoir. What he really needed was someone to hear his confession. Appealing to Brooks, he told her, "My eyes have witnessed things that my tongue has never uttered, and before I die, I want it written down. And I want you to do it."

Because of all the things that keep a young woman busy, Brooks didn't follow up for a while. When she finally got around to visiting him, he was in the throes of death. She sat with him, ready to hear his story, but by that time, he could no longer share it. He recapped no childhood memories of Kirtland, Ohio, about the temple, of the sort he had written in his journal, nor did he mention his joy in hearing voices raised singing his father's famous Mormon anthem, "High on the Mountain." He didn't brag about his 27 children (and adopted children), his 104 grandchildren, or his 54 great-grandchildren. Instead he screamed one word over and over: "Blood, blood, blood . . ." Lost in delirium, Johnson relived the slaughter of the Baker-Fancher party.

After Johnson passed away, Brooks got to work, researching the terrible incident, Johnson's role, and her grandfather's involvement as well. The result, *Mountain Meadows Massacre*, published in 1950, was the first account by a Mormon author who shined light on the church's complicity. Brooks wrote of the fury, perpetrated by Brigham Young, that catalyzed the massacre. Prior to her work, the church had not admitted the role Brigham Young played in helping shift the blame fraudulently to the Southern Paiute people.

Brooks later lamented that her book, revealing church members' roles in the massacre, had "branded me as an apostate." Her biographer, Levi Peterson, noted, "Although Juanita was not excommunicated for her history of the massacre, she resented bitterly the atmosphere of disgrace, which descended upon her and her loyal husband." Today she is lauded for her contributions to Mormon history, for daring to present anguishing truths about people she knew and cared about. She scrutinized her faith, uncovered an ugly history, and yet remained a faithful Mormon. Hers is a brave, careful, and incomparable voice in western history.

During Brooks's lifetime (1898–1989), the Dixie and Iron regions still smoldered. Nearly one hundred years after the death of Joseph Smith, she remembered that an officiant at her wedding, or sealing ceremony, had asked her to repeat the oath for blood atonement, swearing "to be strong in defense of Zion, and in avenging the blood of the prophet." In some corners of Mormondom, secrets and grudges have a half-life of forever.

PART 2:

American Zion

Silver

Can any good come out of Utah? We've heard of spiritual wives and materialistic husbands, of the conflict between Mormon morals and Gentile laws . . . let us consider the many things in Utah which interest without pain. We have for this survey an embarrassment of riches . . .

—*Harper's Magazine*, October 1876

After the Mountain Meadows Massacre, though locals blamed the Paiute people, it didn't take long for Americans to suspect Mormon involvement. Rumors, inconsistent testimonies, and recollections of the children who had been spared and finally returned to their families, all pointed to Mormon instigation. Forty summers, winters, springs, and falls would pass, seasons that baked and froze the lonely valley where it all took place, before Nephi Johnson had his final vision of the carnage on his deathbed. All the while, Brigham Young continued to build his kingdom. Mormon fathers dandled babies. Mormon women baked bread. Mormon apples ripened in orchards, and the stench, screams, entreaties, and betrayals of Mountain Meadows were left shrouded in lies.

In 1858, the year after the massacre, Young sent Nephi Johnson to survey suitable locations for settlement along the Virgin River, a small tributary of the Colorado that drained from southwestern Utah across a corner of Arizona and into southeastern Nevada. Johnson located several sites, which would meet with mixed success as settlement areas, due to the nature of the flood-prone Virgin. Over the course of his travels, he worked his way toward the river's headwaters, a narrow ravine in the snug clasp of red walls so high that the river bottom is often in deep shadow. He found the canyon too rocky and steep for settlement and farming, so he turned back to the promising stretches of bottomland downstream. Though this rock-walled stretch didn't seem to make an impression on him at the time, Johnson was the first Mormon settler to gaze upon what is today considered the region's crown jewel and the centerpiece of Zion National Park, Zion Canyon. It's a gulch visited today by millions of people annually, yet Johnson's walk along its contours didn't even merit a mention in his diary or autobiography. He couldn't foresee that a national park would one day be built around this spectacular formation, its name borrowed from Mormon nomenclature. Mormon Zion was not valued for its scenery. The beauty of the region would be for other Americans to discover.

By the 1860s, Brigham Young was dealing with an influx of miners looking for precious metals. Young's policy on land was egalitarian and in a famous statement, though its accuracy is debated, he said, "There shall be no private ownership of the streams that come out of the canyons, not the timber that grows out of the hills. They belong to the people, all of the people." This might sound like a vision of the American public ideal, but it wasn't. Young didn't really mean "all of the people." He meant Mormon people.

Unlike the elusive riches that Joseph Smith once tried to locate by staring into the bottom of his hat, the underground riches in the Utah Territory were real. An 1862 *Harper's New Monthly Magazine* quoted Abraham Lincoln: "Utah will become the treasure house of the nation." Though Young tried to keep the Mormons isolated from the corruptions of outsiders, these cultures mixed all the same. Young saw miners as men compelled by avarice, who took pleasure in drink and harlotry and knew nothing of the sacred work involved in building up God's kingdom. He did not want his people exposed to these profligates, who flocked to foothills of the Wasatch Range to pan and pick. In fact, Young discouraged his church members from chasing ore themselves, declaring, "Instead of hunting gold, we ought to pray the Lord to hide it up." Riches changed people and mining culture stained souls. Joseph Smith himself had set a counter-example: having come out of a culture of treasure-seeking, he eventually abandoned the pursuit of gold, forever, in favor of a religious life.

But the church needed money, and the prophet waffled. When news of valuable deposits near the Mountain Meadows region reached Young, his interest in building church coffers superseded his trepidations about mining culture. Historian W. Paul Reeve, in his excellent *Making Space on the Western Frontier: Mormons, Miners, and Southern Paiutes*, tells the story of a silver deposit that perfectly captures the realities of contested lands and resources in the region by the 1860s. Jacob Hamblin's brother, Bill "Gunlock" Hamblin, who settled near Jacob along the Santa Clara River thirty miles from the massacre site, was approached by a Southern Paiute man named Moroni (a self-chosen sobriquet, chosen as a gesture of friendship with neighborly Mormons) who brought him a nugget of silver from a nearby vein. Having spent two years in California as a prospector, Hamblin was still ore-hungry and this nugget made him twitchy to get his hands on more. Despite Hamblin's entreaties and despite his Mormonish name, Moroni refused to help. He remained mum, having promised his father to protect the site for fear that settlers would dig up traditional hunting grounds. But Hamblin persisted, continuing to badger Moroni for the secret location. Finally, with the gift of a gun, Moroni caved, taking Hamblin and a few others to the outcrop. There, the Mormons laid claim to Paiute silver, making Moroni's father's warning prescient.

Brigham Young gave his approval to the Mormon Church to stake claims. But operations were suspended in 1863 due to the Black Hawk War, a protracted altercation with the Southern Paiutes and other tribes. For them, this war arose from tangible grievances. Paiute homeland, which once offered a bounty of rabbits, roots, and wild grasses, now stood ploughed, irrigated, planted, and off-limits. Hungry and resentful over continued duplicities, including the lies about Mountain Meadows, Paiute warriors targeted farms and rustled livestock. Settlers responded by killing twenty-six unarmed Paiute people in Circleville, Utah, just north of the Dixie region, monstrously slitting their throats and leaving them—men, women, and children—to die. So little is known of this heartbreaking act, not even the names of the people murdered. In 2016, a memorial was built to commemorate their deaths, one hundred and fifty years after the fact. A gray stone marker in the town park reads, "To the memory of the Koosharem Band Paiute Indian Tribe of Utah. Massacred by local Mormon settlers, April 22–24, 1866." Residents in Circleville were so perturbed by the tribute and its indictment of their forefathers that, due to his support of its installation, the mayor was not reelected.

In Clover Valley, Nevada, a lovely little vale about thirty miles from Hamblin's claim, numerous Indian raids forced Mormon families to abandon their homes. In the nearby town of Panaca, Nevada, (the Paiute word for silver), Native raiders stole oxen from LDS people, spurring the colonialists to kill five men for their role in the theft. Periodic violence continued for years; fearing attacks, Gunlock Hamblin and the other Mormon men left the silver claim unattended. But rumors spread about the outcropping and, given the broad contagion of gold and silver fever in the West, an unwatched and unexcavated stake was too tempting, even amid Indian attacks.

Near the tidy Mormon settlement of Panaca, in 1868, a rough-and-tumble town of scattered cabins sprung up atop more silver. This place was named Pioche—for a French-man, François L. A. Pioche, who, despite having bought mining claims in the area, would never walk its muddy streets. He killed himself in San Francisco over money woes. In its heyday, the town became famous for being lawless. According to a report by a Nevada state mineralogist inspecting Pioche for the Nevada state legislature in 1873, "About one-half of the community are thieves, scoundrels and murderers. Hired gunmen were imported at the rate of 20 a day to fight mining claim encroachments. The sheriff's office could count on about $40,000 a year in bribe money. It was so bad 75 people were killed before one died a natural death." It was a town that festered with all of the depravity Brigham Young fretted over. In 1872, William Hamblin sold the rights to the silver, but because of ambiguities caused by his years of leaving the claims unattended during the Black Hawk War, two competing companies claimed possession to it. Hamblin was called to Pioche to testify in court, in order to determine who rightly held the title.

On the morning of the hearing, Hamblin went for coffee and breakfast with his lawyer. According to legend, after a sip or two, he lurched out of his chair and hollered, "I've been poisoned!" Three agonizing weeks later, the man who had traded a gun for Moroni's silver was dead, murdered by parties loath to give up their treasure.

Today William Hamblin's grave is fenced by sturdy white pickets, on a ranch in Clover Valley belonging to Kelton Hafen. Hafen calls himself Cliven Bundy's neighbor, a term that gives context to the way folks out west consider space and relationships. The Bundy spread lies some eighty miles south as the crow flies. Kelton is an old-time rancher, a descendant of the first Mormons to homestead the valley. His family had fled during the same conflict that kept Hamblin from mining his silver claim.

I met Kelton and his son Lyman over tacos in St. George at one of their favorite lunch spots. Kelton told me that his ancestors, while living in Clover Valley, had tried to doctor Hamblin after the incident in Pioche. But the ministering, and presumably the laying on of hands and the prayers, didn't work. He died from the poison and was laid to rest on the Hafen property. After lunch, we chatted about W. Paul Reeve's book, which I had in my car, and the complicated relationships among Mormons, Southern Paiutes, and miners—these disparate parties who shared the region for a volatile and deadly decade while trying to establish ownership to what each believed was theirs.

Kelton, in his eighties, is sharp and clear, although he needed the steadying hand of his son to navigate his walk back to the parking lot. He told me, "Brigham Young was right." About mining, he meant. In spite of Young's go-ahead over the Hamblin silver, the Lion of the Lord never did like the idea of mining. It was a primrose path, unwholesome for Mormons and counter to their values. Not like, say, ranching. The Hafens are descended from hardy folks who came to the Great Basin with endowments given by Joseph Smith, a stamina forged through surviving persecutions, and a longing to find and build a safe haven. As settlers turned new homeland into rangeland, ranching became fixed within the deepening grooves of Zion. To generations of Mormon ranchers, a cowboy livelihood stands as a celebration of decent work, proud heritage, and the Mormon triumph over its legacy of adversity. Ranching is an emblem of Zion.

Two Gods

Zion Canyon is an epic, written by Mother Nature in her most ecstatic humor, illustrated by Creation in its most majestic manifestations, published by God Almighty as an inspiration to all mankind. . . . On every side was crude but marvelous nature in bird and foliage and fish and rock and water. I stood there and gasped, though I had become almost familiar with the miracles of Zion. I gasped a prayer, for one may not behold what one beholds there without knowing that there is a God: that His ways are inexplicable to man and to be taken in faith alone. . . . it gives to one . . . a more profound impression of the wonderworks of God.

—Jack Lait, Union Pacific Railroad, 1917

It wasn't just the region's silver that brought outsiders into Mormon country, it was also the region's land. As Washington became increasingly interested in big, unsettled western spaces, university expeditions were dispatched to survey, map, assess, and report findings on lands, geology, and wildlife. The most famous trek during the late nineteenth century was undertaken by Civil War veteran Major John Wesley Powell, a man who went on to challenge many myths about the West and its resources, especially in regard to water. Powell, who lost most of his right arm during the Battle of Shiloh while fighting for the Union, visited Dixie and the surrounding region during his effort to chart the contours and rivers of the West for the federal government. In the summer of 1869, Powell, who had grown up boating the Mississippi, voyaged along the Green and Colorado Rivers and through the Grand Canyon with a team of ten men, in the first government-sponsored survey of the region. His boat, one of four in the fleet and named after his wife, Emma Dean, came specially equipped with a strap to steady someone with only one arm. Over the three months of the trip, across what are today the states of Wyoming, Colorado, Utah, and Arizona, members of the party were often miserable, some even mutinous. When they weren't portaging around what looked to Powell to be lethal rapids, the men crewed their crafts, cupped by the river's powerful flow, smashing into rock walls and pounding white water. They lost two boats during the journey, one down the river and the other, the *Emma Dean*, was left beyond repair due to her daily battering. Various supplies, including food, notebooks, maps, and barometers also vanished in high and roaring waters. The rations they did keep hold of—dried apples, musty bread, rotten bacon—were cold comfort.

Before it was over, four of the ten men abandoned the expedition. First, a month into the journey, John Goodman left the team; he found his way to the Southern Paiute people, lived among them for years, and later settled in Vernal, a rare Utah quirk of a town that was actually a Gentile outpost. Oramel Howland, his brother Seneca, and Bill Dunn also departed, two months after Goodman, taking their chances on foot across the desert rather than trying to finish the journey through rapids they feared would do them in. They were never seen again. Some said the Southern Paiutes killed them. Others blamed the Mormons.

Two days after the very cordial departure of the Howlands and Dunn, Powell's party pushed through the canyon and pulled out at the mouth of the Virgin River. Powell returned west in 1871 and 1872 for further data collection. This second expedition lacked some of the rigors of his initial foray, but nonetheless he saw moments of high adventure along the edges of Mormon domesticity. His team crossed paths with some of Dixie's most notorious members, including John Lee, Isaac Haight, and Nephi Johnson. In his classic book *Beyond the Hundredth Meridian: John Wesley Powell and the Second Opening of the West*, Wallace Stegner remarks that in spite of their notoriety, these Gentile-hating men came across as perfectly friendly to Powell's party. Haight, who had once vowed that he'd sacrifice blood in the defense of Zion, then did just that, was not only cordial to the interlopers but went out of his way to help them. When Powell's party became stranded in the Lonely Dell, a spot just north of where the Paria River meets the Colorado, Haight came to their rescue, hauling in food and supplies over some unforgiving country. It's ironic to consider that Powell and the findings he brought back to Washington were a much greater threat to Haight's Zion than the Baker-Fancher party ever was. With their charts and measurements, the survey team told the story of public domain in Mormon country, introducing the Utah Territory to an audience far bigger than the miners or the migrating Gentile wagon parties. It wouldn't be long before outsiders began to pour in with their own desires for these lands.

During the last decades of the nineteenth century, Brigham Young's people continued to be regarded as American pariahs, and this was wrapped into interpretations of their lands. One writer for *Harper's Magazine*, who visited the Dixie region a few years after Powell's return, wrote, "In the south there is a grandeur that is awfully suggestive—suggestive of death and worn out lands, of cosmic convulsions and volcanic catastrophes that swept away whole races of pre-Adamites." Little did this writer know—nor had Abraham Lincoln known, when he called the Utah Territory the "treasure house of the nation"—that the territory's vast mineral holdings would eventually be valued far less by most Americans than its scenery. These "worn out lands," were destined to become attractions that eclipsed the region's waning silver rush. Though Latter-day Saints had come to value their lands for the production values, America would fall in love with the rocks.

The lands of the Utah Territory weren't the only aspect of his trip that impressed Powell; so did the people. He and his wife camped near what is today the town of Kanab, and there they made good friends, attended dances, and even met the prophet himself, Brigham Young. Fredrick Dellenbaugh, an artist and topographer on the second Powell expedition, wrote, "As pioneers the Mormons were superior to any class I have ever come in contact with, their idea being homemaking and not skimming the cream off the country with a six-shooter and a whiskey bottle." Perhaps the relations between the Mormons and the rest of the country were thawing a bit since the days of the Utah War, but there was still plenty of bitterness to go around.

A new movement was in its infancy, one that blended patriotism and spirituality with the appreciation of wild places. This was American preservationism, a school of thought that later blossomed, diverging into the conservation and environmental movements. When Powell went west, he tread on lands acquired through colonization and treaty agreements with England, France, Spain, Canada, and Mexico—those places stolen from Native peoples. Lands left unlisted in state land grants or treaty agreements, unclaimed by individual homesteaders, or not snapped up by railroad companies became public domain. Americans were coming to value wild places, once seen as wastelands that were too remote for development, and politicians became keen on protection designations. Wild landscapes became important in distinguishing this country—as a place whose wild lands rivaled the wonders of the world. Points of jaw-dropping beauty, left unclaimed under the Homestead Act, became our first national parks. Yellowstone was established in 1872. Then came Yosemite in 1891, followed by Glacier in 1897 and Mount Rainier in 1899.

But, in addition to the wonders, those soaring peaks, geysers, canyons, and sandstone arches that might make a traveler rethink a European tour and come west, the federal government oversaw a lot of ground that was free-for-all rangeland. Though the Taylor Grazing Act was decades away, compilers of federal inventories were attempting to gather data and inform decision-makers in Washington on how to manage the public domain and its waters, forests, and grasslands. The government owned 47 percent of the West—if you count "the West" as those areas now constituting the states of Washington, Oregon, California, Arizona, Nevada, New Mexico, Utah, Wyoming, Colorado, Montana, and Idaho. To manage these vast properties, new governing agencies were established—agencies such as the Forest Bureau in 1905, later the US Forest Service. Over the decades, other managing agencies emerged, including the National Park Service, the Fish and Wildlife Service, and the Bureau of Land Management (BLM).

The conservation movement was forged out of a sense of awe. Members of Powell's team, first Frederick Dellenbaugh and later Clarence E. Dutton, brought with them ideas very much at odds with the Mormons they encountered. Inspired by writers like Henry David Thoreau and Ralph Waldo Emerson, Dellenbaugh and Dutton in their writings, and Dellenbaugh also in his paintings, channeled the spirit of transcendentalism. In the writings of Emerson and Thoreau, nature had become a place of spiritual significance, not a place to conquer, subdue, and civilize. American sensibilities were changing as people realized that a country once seemingly endless and boundless now seemed, to some at least, urbanized and overrun. John Muir, a big fan of Emerson, is known for his forays into deep backcountry, where he sought solitude and God. Muir was very involved in, among other things, protecting California's Sierra Nevada. He saw a need for wilderness as refuge, noting in 1901 that "thousands of tired, nerve-shaken, over-civilized people are beginning to find out that going to the mountains is going home; that wilderness is a necessity, and mountain parks and reservations are useful not only as fountains of timber and irrigating rivers, but as foundations of life." Today Muir's prediction of thousands seeking refuge is laughably paltry. In 2017, 331 million people visited American national parks.

In spite of their reverence for the land, though, many early conservationists did not recognize that these were homelands to others. The places that Muir wanted to protect as untrammeled "wilderness" had been in use for thousands of years by Northern Paiute, Ahwahnechee, Mono, and Sierra Miwok peoples and the Kawaiisu and Tübatulabal peoples. Like the Mormons, and the other white colonialists, activists of the early conservation movement ignored Native people and their rights.

Ralph Waldo Emerson and Joseph Smith were contemporaries, born two years apart, but while Smith died at the age of thirty-nine, Emerson died just shy of his eightieth birthday. Smith hailed from Vermont and New York, Emerson from Massachusetts. Both were driven to understand the divine, and they instilled their ideas within two distinct cultures that continue, even today, to clash over public lands. To Smith, land became sacred through human industry. When the Mormons reached the Great Basin, sacralizing a landscape was achieved by planting, irrigating, running cows, or, according to historian Jedediah Rogers, even the struggle to build routes across canyon country. God's blessings were manifest in the fruit-laden branches of trees growing in a carefully tended Mormon orchard, or in a trail blasted into rocks. To Emerson, by contrast, lands *without* the imprint of humans were divine. Holy places could be found in the jut of a mountain, the chop of a river, and the polished face of a sun-dappled stone. Still, though they disagreed on what constituted hallowed ground, Smith and Emerson did share a position that is not surprising, given their shared moment in time. Both agreed on the idea that slaves should be emancipated by compensating slaveholders with monies made in the sale of American public lands. That idea is a terrible one for a million reasons—Native lands being sold to white people in order to pay other white people to give black people their own bodies back? If it had been implemented, American history and landscape would have changed considerably. You might not even be reading this book.

A few years after Nephi Johnson's scouting trip along the Virgin River, homesteader and Mormon tobacco farmer Isaac Behunin moved into the canyon that had left so little impression on Johnson. Behunin named it Zion, not unusual given that the idea of a divinely promised homeland was everywhere in Mormondom. Like Johnson's family, Behunin was an original adherent of Joseph Smith, having followed the Mormons from New York to Ohio, then to Missouri and Illinois, and finally to Utah. Zion Canyon became a hideaway for this Mormon and his family, far from the miseries of the Midwest. But he had long since moved on, to another homestead elsewhere in Utah, when Captain Clarence E. Dutton visited Behunin's former spread, noting, "Nothing exceeds the wondrous beauty of Little Zion Valley, which separates two temples and their respective group of towers. . . . In its proportions it is about equal to Yosemite, but in the nobility and beauty of the sculptures there is no comparison. It is Hyperion to a satyr. No wonder the fierce Mormon zealot, who named it, was reminded of the Great Zion, on which his fervid thoughts were bent—'of houses not built with hands, eternal in the heavens.'" Though Dutton believed that he could relate to Behunin, that "fierce Mormon zealot," the two men had been shaped by wildly differing experiences, and carried wildly different purposes. Dutton, a geologist, came to measure and record the majestic features of the Colorado Plateau and to consider how they might be opened to the American people. Behunin was a religious refugee, seeking to farm in a beautiful but unforgiving land, who wanted it closed off to the rest of America. For

Dutton, God was in the majesty of the scenery; for Behunin, He was in its safety.

Both cultures saw God in the land. Historian and author William Cronon has observed that, to those in the thrall of Emerson, "God was on the mountaintop, in the chasm, in the waterfall, in the thundercloud, in the rainbow, in the sunset—Yellowstone, Yosemite, Grand Canyon, Rainier, Zion." But to the Mormon, God was in routine and the tasks of everyday life, not on some distant summit. When God gave the Latter-day Saints their Zion, He stuck around. And though He could challenge the faithful, He'd eventually come to their aid. Stories from journals and later oral histories describe God's constant involvement in Dixie lives—working miracles, sending premonitions, revealing Himself in various ways. There was no task too small and God was ever ready to help people out of jams or pickles. Just as He would one day do for Cliven Bundy. Or as He did with Lulu Waite.

Lulu Waite, born in 1910, spent her girlhood on the Virgin River, the same river that Bundy's cows walk across today. One day, so the story goes, God alerted her that the devil was messing with her horse, Old Blue. The nag stopped cold and refused to move. "I knew immediately what it was, because the Spirit said, 'Satan.' . . . I whipped him again, I thought this time I am not going to let anything stop me." She then addressed the devil directly. "Satan, get out of my way. You are not going to hinder me.' This horse went up [a hill] as if nothing was wrong. I knew that these powers were always around you."

Lulu Waite went on to become a romance novelist, writing on the passions of wholesome Mormon love. Her ex-husband, Glenn Waite, born in Bunkerville, Nevada, in 1906, talked of his own spiritual experiences. He called them "faith-promoting incidents." As he would explain, "We did not call them miracles because it was more or less an everyday affair. We prayed for things and we usually [received] them in a roundabout way."

The places where Lulu and Glenn grew up, got married, then divorced, were the places mapped by Powell and his team. It was a region that became coveted by an American public, many of whom, early on, equated natural beauty with God. With this recognition, Americans called for preservation, in part to protect His creation. But public sentiment ran up against the belief in another version of God, one disinclined to pay much attention to geology or ecology. Rather, this God got involved in the day-to-day of the people. He even pitched in to sort ornery livestock. This God was one of everyday human affairs, not focused on the trifling aspects of nature that didn't aid in the industry of His adherents. If the Mormons called Him in prayer, He was more than willing to jump in. If they had a fight on their hands, He was eager to enlist. And with God's backing, each event, and even battle, became another faith-promoting experience.

Welcome to Utah

Uncle Sam asks you to be his guest. He has prepared for you the choice places of this continent—places of grandeur, beauty and wonder. He has built roads through the deepest cut canyons and beside happy streams, which will carry you into these places in comfort, and has provided lodgings and food in the most distant and inaccessible place that you might enjoy yourself and realize as little as possible the rigors of the pioneer traveler's life. These are for you. They are playgrounds for the people. To see them is to make more hearty your affection for America.

—Franklin K. Lane, Secretary of the Interior, 1917

At this intersect of the Mojave Desert, the Colorado Plateau, and the Great Basin, a collision of convictions was in play. Tourists, beckoned by the tales of western beauty, soon boarded trains and, a little later, loaded up automobiles to see for themselves the glories of Utah and Arizona wilderness. In 1872, the same year that Isaac Haight came to Powell's rescue, President Ulysses S. Grant signed into law the Yellowstone National Park Protection Act. In contrast to the *Harper's* article's crabby description of worn-out lands, the stories brought home by Major Powell and his party spoke of Dixie's allure. During his travels down the Virgin River, Powell had observed in his journal on September 9, 1872, "cool springs, green meadows, and forest-clad slopes; below us stretching toward the south until the world was lost in a blue haze, was a painted desert—not a desert plain, but a desert of rocks cut by deep gorges and relieved by towering cliffs and pinnacled rocks, naked rocks brilliant in the sunlight." Mormon homeland held American wonderlands.

As outside ideas came into Zion, attitudes shifted, at least for a time. There was a period, roughly from 1910 to 1930, while the National Park Service was first looking to southern Utah for scenic opportunities, that locals opened their arms wide to the idea of preservation and tourism. The park promoters and the locals had very different beliefs, which would soon come to loggerheads, but for a while both groups were happy to tout the region's beauty and exploit economic opportunities that could be found in sightseeing. During this time, one Latter-day Saint emerged who pushed public land protection forward in Mormon homeland.

Reed Smoot was born in 1862, the year Isaac Behunin named his canyon Zion. One of twenty-seven children, Reed was the son of Anne, the fifth wife of Abraham Smoot. A dashing man with an impressive mustache, Reed won election to the United States Senate at the age of forty-one. But he didn't enter that chamber easily; his position was challenged by the Senate Committee on Privileges and Elections on grounds that his Mormon ties made him ineligible. For the next four years, the Mormon politician slogged through a punishing confirmation battle, facing bipartisan hostility toward his appointment.

Early on in the Smoot hearings, in 1904, Mormon Church president Joseph Fielding Smith, son of the first prophet's brother Hyrum, who was killed with Joseph in Carthage, was brought to Washington to give testimony on, among other things, the illegal practice of plural marriage. This Smith had become the sixth prophet and president of the church in 1901, twenty-four years after the death of Brigham Young. Prophet and president status was handed down to a new church leader after the death of the former. Though polygamy had been banned by the church, it was still practiced. When asked about his five wives back home, President Smith said, "Mr. Chairman, I have not claimed that in that case I have obeyed the law of the land." He spent six days under grueling questioning, but his most vexing position, to both press and committee members, was his doublespeak regarding the original prophet Joseph Smith's revelation on plural marriage, and the Woodruff Manifesto, a document from a more recent prophet/president, that revealed God had changed his tune and now forbade polygamy among church members. Which position did he believe? He replied that he believed both positions, Smith's and Wilford Woodruff's, as both were divinely inspired. The Woodruff Manifesto was issued at a time of heavy federal pressure, along with the government's promise of statehood in exchange for an end to plural marriage. Joseph Fielding Smith's confusing testimony and his own marital situation led to public speculation that Smoot's confirmation would be tanked.

Although polygamy was officially denounced and banned by the church in 1890 after the issuance of the Woodruff Manifesto, plural marriages persisted in Mormondom. (There are accounts that Nephi Johnson left Utah from 1889 to 1894, taking his wives to Colonia Juárez, a Mormon community in Mexico, in order to evade the law enforcement crackdown on polygamists.) Smoot was not a polygamist, but the practice continued to brand him and his faith in early twentieth-century America.

Over the months and years of the Smoot hearings, the committee addressed the church's pattern in holding revelation above the law, its history of Danite violence, secret oaths, and the Mountain Meadows Massacre. National media coverage and political cartoons provided daily reminders to a predominantly Protestant America of both the peculiarities and the ferocities of the Latter-day Saints. In Washington, onlookers jammed hearing halls and galleries, listening to the sensationalized testimonies and denunciations. Some members of Congress reported receiving over a thousand letters a day, notes of outrage from their anti-Mormon constituents. But finally, in 1907, Smoot was confirmed. After the years of grueling inquiry, which included 3,500 pages of testimony, the two-thirds majority necessary to block Smoot was not achieved. Reed became Senator Smoot and remained Senator Smoot for the next two-and-a-half decades.

His career was distinguished by two notable, though unrelated, pieces of legislation. He'll forever be remembered for coauthoring the Smoot-Hawley Tariff Act, a protectionist law that imposed a series of steep tariffs on foreign goods—a set of regulations that, many historians maintain, helped usher in the Great Depression. And yet Smoot was also one of the original architects of the National Park Service Organic Act, a law that institutionalized our park system and may have been "the best idea we ever had," in the words of western author Wallace Stegner. Smoot lost the election of 1932 nonetheless, most likely because of the Smoot-Hawley Act. But thanks to his preservationist activism, he remains celebrated as one of a handful of national Mormon politicians who have championed American landscape conservation.

The turn of the century was marked by passage of our earliest environmental laws. While in Washington, Smoot made the advantageous friendship of President Theodore Roosevelt, the ardent conservationist who first put the 1906 Antiquities Act to use. Roosevelt once told him, "Mr. Smoot, you are a good enough American, or Gentile for that matter, for me." Let old bygones be bygones. The Antiquities Act gave the president unilateral authority to designate national monuments, at a time when both natural and archaeological sites were threatened by overuse and looting (as they still are). Iowa Republican John F. Lacey, considered the legislative father of the Antiquities Act, was also involved in the Lacey Act of 1900, America's first law to protect threatened species. It was the Republican Party, in those days, that went to bat for the wildlands and wildlife of America, partially in response to having watched one species in particular blink out. The passenger pigeon once caught the eye of wildlife artist John James Audubon and he painted a pair: a drab female feeding her brilliantly plumed orange-and-blue-gray companion as he reached up toward her, his neck stretched, clutching at her beak for the food that she offered. The painting is exquisite, and shattering to see, now that they are no longer on this earth. This was a species once so prolific that its flocks blackened the sky; while roosting, the combined weight of the birds snapped branches off sturdy trees. By 1900, there were hardly any left. The last female, Martha, died at the Cincinnati Zoo in 1914, at the age of twenty-nine. The bison of western prairies nearly vanished as well, also in the late 1800s, the victim of hunters' pursuits of meat and hides, a campaign to starve Native people and entertain witless recreational shooting from trains.

At the same time, women's elaborately plumed hats came into fashion, sending shorebirds that nested along the Florida and Louisiana coasts toward extinction. In response to the vanishing bison, the extinction of the passenger pigeon, and the devastation caused by the plume trade, preservation of species and lands became an American priority. In 1908, President Teddy Roosevelt set aside an Oregon valley of flooded wetlands and high grasses for the hundreds of migratory bird species that stopped over there. It became the Malheur Lake Refuge. One hundred and eight years later, Ammon Bundy would take the place over with an armed militia.

Though the Park Service wouldn't come into being until 1916, national monument status under the Antiquities Act served as a precursor, in several key cases, to national park designations. Roosevelt himself designated eighteen monuments, fifty-one bird refuges, and five national parks; "wilderness" for tourists, once home to Native peoples. In 1909, President William Howard Taft used the Antiquities Act to designate Zion Canyon a national monument; known briefly as Mukuntuweap, it would officially become Zion National Park a decade later.

I was very interested to see, in Reed Smoot's journals, his take on the wrenching confirmation hearings of his earliest years in Washington. None of those journals were written during his trial—none available to the public, anyway—which prevents us from better understanding his emotional seesaw during what must have been one of the most angst-ridden periods in his life. It was a mean time, and Smoot was a dignified man who found himself subject to old prejudices that still plagued the Mormon people. For all the hard work he put into the development of the Parks Act (over the course of several years), Senator Smoot's political reminiscences are bare-bones and rather ordinary, free of animosity—though he did spill quite a bit of ink on his own maladies. Hay fever, insomnia, a neck boil, a raw throat, a "very sore eye," a terrible earache, tender feet, and a "stomach that was out of order" kept the senator uncomfortable and filled many a page. He wrote about meetings and committees, making mention of his children and the dinner parties he attended while Alpha, his wife, convalesced at their Washington home, dealing with the breast cancer to which she would eventually succumb. There are passages on his early conservation work, but he lacked the flourish of a Powell—though I think he was no less excited about the possibilities of western lands. While serving as a member of the Senate Public Lands and Survey Committee, he noted with typical brevity, "Wednesday April 10, 1912: Spent considerable time discussing my bill creating Bureau of National Park." Still just a gleam in the senator's eye, the National Park Service Organic Act did not pass for another four-and-a-half years, but he was nonetheless hard at work on America's best idea.

Just seven years after Zion Canyon became a national monument, the Department of the Interior reported that it had received roughly one thousand to twelve hundred visitors in 1916. One of these was Utah governor William Spry, another politician excited about public lands and new strains of revenue. With a reporter from *The Salt Lake Tribune*, the governor and a small party undertook an exploration of Dixie, both old and new, with visits to a derelict cotton mill long out of operation and to the ghost town of Silver Reef, once site of the largest silver mine in the state. Cotton farming and silver mining were no longer economically viable activities in the region, and the primary focus of this trip was to assess a fresh opportunity for the Dixie economy: the region's unparalleled scenery and the potential for tourist dollars.

The *Tribune* dispatches, three in total, recorded difficult stretches of travel that left many in the party "incapacitated." Zion Canyon was only accessible by horse and wagon. So the party grabbed up a rig and set off overland from the town of Virgin, pitching back and forth as wooden wheels dragged against rocks and the river's current. Getting to Zion was rough and those expecting the leisure of a European tour weren't going to find it in Dixie. Not yet, anyway. But the *Tribune* reporter wrote that, despite the hard miles heading into the canyon and the lack of developed roads and infrastructure, Utah's beauty was such that it "can't stay hidden from pleasure-seekers much longer."

Historian Jedediah Rogers, in his thoughtful book *Roads in the Wilderness*, puts forth that even the act of road building was, in part, a sacred hallmark of Mormon mastery over the environment. Governor Spry focused on constructing better roads in southern Utah, in many cases with convict labor, so that its splendors could be more easily accessed. Soon after President Woodrow Wilson signed the National Park Service Organic Act, sponsored by Reed Smoot and William Kent of California, into law on August 25, 1916, Stephen Tyng Mather became the first director of the US national parks. A borax tycoon inspired by John Muir, Mather, even before he was named director, had established relationships with the Union Pacific and the Santa Fe Railroads, convincing both companies to advance over a million dollars for national park development and publicity. His irrepressible zeal for protecting land was hindered by a periodic and debilitating despair. Soon after his appointment, Mather retreated to a back room at a parks conference, anguished and suicidal. At the time, he was said to have experienced a nervous breakdown, which today probably would be diagnosed as bipolar disorder. In his stead, twenty-seven-year-old Horace Albright stepped in to run the new Park Service. This son of a miner, who had abandoned his hopes to enlist in the US Army and join the Great War, instead went to work creating some of America's earliest parks, counting among his fans many Dixie Mormons.

After the designation of Zion National Park, its federal managers welcomed the steady trickle of tourists with open arms. But hospitality was not extended to farmers and ranchers, who were banned from running their animals across park boundaries. With the establishment of the park, the government suddenly deprived local people of lands they had used since settlement. Pigs that had foraged along the banks of the Virgin River were relegated to yards. Cowboys who once relied on the steep trail from the canyon floor to the pasture above for moving their cows got eighty-sixed (as did their cows). Drovers had to take their flocks elsewhere. The path through the park was no longer sheep- or cattle-friendly. Zion the park operated with different rules from Zion the homeland.

In 1923, Senator Smoot brought President Warren Harding to Zion National Park. In an exuberant journal entry, Smoot wrote of their arrival in Cedar City, Utah, where they met an enthusiastic crowd. Here an escort awaited to take the senator, the president, and their party to the park. Smoot noted in his diary that their route "was in fair shape. About two hundred men had worked for days on the road repairing it without compensation. There was very little dust." Local people were so excited for the visit that they spent hours, unpaid, to improve sixty-three miles of notoriously bad road to the canyon, in order to impress the visiting president and show off their backyard. Upon entering the park, Senator Smoot and President Harding mounted horses and, with a small entourage, rode up the famous canyon. It must have been rough going for poor President Harding, a middle-aged man with a bad heart, riding on a giant chestnut mount. Locals still recall with amusement that he struggled with a painful case of hemorrhoids during his visit. He died a few months after visiting Utah, though, it should be noted, not from piles.

When the road was finally paved, Mormon homeland had become officially transformed from remote to accessible. The culmination was the Zion-Mount Carmel Tunnel and an improved route connecting Dixie to the Grand Canyon. At the tunnel's opening, held on the auspicious day of July 4, 1930, governors from twelve states came to see the impressive engineering feat. Utah's then governor, George Dern, announced to a large crowd, a mix of locals and visitors, that the park and this grand highway leading to it were now available for the "use of the people of the United States on its birthday. It is also fitting that this ceremony should be held in the presence of the governors of so many of Utah's sister states. It is as if the people of the whole nation were here this morning to see this marvelous undertaking placed at their service." At the time, local Mormons felt a great pride in seeing others come and appreciate the majesty of their landscape. Among them was John Lewis Crawford, a man who became an unlikely champion for Zion National Park and the Park Service as a whole.

JL, as he was known, wore many hats in the making of the park, taking a turn cooking dinners for park tourists; working on the construction crew for the Zion-Mount Carmel Tunnel; and helping build additional park infrastructure with the Civilian Conservation Corps. He was an amateur park historian and a lifelong friend of Park Service personnel, a few of whom were involved in its founding. He was also the son of the last homesteader in Zion Canyon. In 1932, he and his family were forced to leave their property as the land turned from farmland to tourist attraction. Still, in spite of this, JL spent his many years (he died at ninety-seven) as a champion of the park, lecturing on its attributes, interviewing its main players, and researching its stories.

William Lewis Crawford, JL's father, had been a sheepherder in Dixie as a young man, and during his long days alone, he entertained himself by taking pictures, often inserting himself into the image. His son explained that his father "would take a picture of scenery, but frequently get in the picture by carrying a spool of thread in his pocket." He'd rig it so he could hop into the frame, then "trip the shutter and get in his own pictures." William left behind photos of himself climbing natural bridges, honeymooning in Zion Canyon with his wife, Mary Jane Bean Crawford, and standing on a ledge overlooking the North Rim of the Grand Canyon. He also left a love of the land to his son.

On their farm along Oak Creek, now the site of the Zion National Park Visitor Center, the Crawford family grew McIntosh apples, three varieties of Winesap apples, banana apples, quinces, several varieties of peaches, and plums. JL remembered his childhood home as a place of God-given abundance. During each nightly prayer, his father asked God to "bless the water and elements." When he was young, JL misheard, mistaking this appeal, rather, as one to "bless the watermelons." At the time, he surmised that "the Lord must have heard it too because as long as we lived at Oak Creek [my father] grew great melon crops."

The family ached over leaving their gardens and orchards, but also felt great anxiety in the possible sacrilege involved in abandoning their place in Zion—not the park, but the homeland. The first superintendent of Zion National Park, Eviend T. Scoyen, told JL, years after the family was ousted, about a last-minute hitch. "I was trying every way I could to get the best possible deal that was satisfactory to them [your family], and I thought I'd done that. Everybody agreed to the deal." Then William, JL's father, told Scoyen, "Mister, we've been talking about it, and we can't sell you that property." The park superintendent asked him if the price was fair. "Yes," William replied. "The price is all right. And the conditions and everything are all right. But Brigham Young called us to settle here, and we can't go until we are released." Scoyen ended up traveling to Salt Lake City to request that the church president, Heber Grant, officially release the Crawford family from "the call." Brigham Young's "call" to Dixie had been a religious mandate to settle and build homeland, and even some eighty years after the mission was launched, the Crawford family still felt bound.

JL and Horace Albright, the former Park Service director, became very good friends, as Albright had spent a great deal of time in Utah, especially in the Dixie region. In 1986, Crawford visited Albright, who was ninety-seven and living in a senior facility in Van Nuys, California. JL found his friend, so integral to the founding and building of the American park system, in a miserable state. Albright's wife, Grace, had passed and he was left alone feeling helpless and dispirited, so far from the lands he loved and long past a career in stewarding them. After the visit, JL was deeply troubled over the state of his friend's well-being and petitioned the superintendent of Zion National Park to ask for "funds to purchase a suitable home [for Albright], give him domestic help, including nurses and make him comfortable for the rest of his days." He went on to explain, "I believed the nation owed him much more than that." Sadly, it didn't happen. JL Crawford, whose family had been evicted from their home in part due to the ambitions of Horace Albright, still viewed Albright and his services as a gift to the nation. He was among those locals who believed that the conservation of landscape fit, though unconventionally, within the bounds of Mormon homeland.

Other Dixie residents felt weary when they realized that the state of Utah was composed mostly of federally owned land and therefore subject to further designs for national parks.

Two-thirds of Utah was (and is) public, meaning that Latter-day Saints operated on space administered by their old nemesis—the rest of America. Though Utah's first national park was a place of unlikely syncretism—a combination of Emerson's philosophy, Roosevelt's zeal for setting aside wild places (though the park bears President William Howard Taft's signature on its establishment decree), and the name of Mormon homeland—this cultural unification wouldn't last. As federal officials continued to ponder further park opportunities in the region, they schemed on seismic ground. With plans for new designations, and the requisite federal land regulations, Dixie began to judder, making way for today's modern quakes. At their epicenters were—and still are—Mormon cows.

A Collision of Convictions

One wonders what would have been the condition of this isolated people, with a background of rough and ready frontier life in which the cowpuncher was the predominating type, had it not been for the influence of the church.

—Nethelia King Griffin

As bridges, tunnels, and roads were built in Utah, engraving and opening the lands, railroads and hotels worked to lure tourists. In the keening and flowery prose meant to draw people and their dollars to the region, God was used as one device. Tour packages offered more than just beauty—marketing materials went so far as to offer a brush with the divine. One early brochure declares that Zion Canyon was "published by God Almighty as an inspiration to all mankind." Continuing breathlessly, the author wrote, "I gasped a prayer, for one may not behold what one beholds there without knowing that there is a God: that His ways are inexplicable to man and to be taken in faith alone." The pamphlet further promises that a visit to this southern Utah wonder would offer a lucky soul "a more profound impression of the wonderworks of God." But if this was God's country, then whose God?

There was hardly an inch in southern Utah that wasn't gorgeous, exotic, and stirring to gaze upon. And once the Park Service was up and running, Zion National Park was just the first stage in an ambitious effort by the leaders of that agency, along with their allies in Congress, to protect large areas in Utah and the Southwest. America wanted more. Roads now opened the region and it was only a matter of connecting Zion, on a great southwestern park tour, with other wonders such as the Grand Canyon, Cedar Breaks, and Bryce Canyon. With roads, these extraordinary places could be visited from the comfort of an automobile, available to an emerging middle class. Pack the car, hit the road, and see America!

Though plans to establish more tourist destinations shared support among both federal agents and many residents, disagreements between the two groups began to crop up in regard to both scope and restricted uses. Locals grew alarmed over Park Service ambitions when it seemed like the government wanted to limit the use of regional resources. They were keen on drawing tourists to regional attractions, but did not support the prohibition of other uses, such as logging, grazing, and mining. Cedar Breaks became a national monument in 1933, after a prolonged fight between the Park Service and the Forest Service over its management; the former wanting areas protected without invasive development, the latter wanting lands available for multiple uses that included logging the large stand of timber within its boundaries. Timber wouldn't be the only bone of contention in a federal drive to designate parks. Any land-use restrictions in parks were unpopular, but perhaps the most detested idea was that of grazing limits.

There were reasons that the Park Service did not want livestock traipsing across delicate vegetation and over fragile rock formations. In southern Utah, it was evident that overgrazing in the early nineteenth century had devastated the land. One rancher who ran eight thousand sheep on public commons near Price, Utah, recalled plentiful antelope, deer, and buffalo in the San Rafael desert before they were displaced by his own and other ranchers' livestock. Another remembered that "a man could ride for miles through the tall grass.... Some valleys were covered with white sage, in which a herd of sheep would be entirely hidden. . . . It was a blooming flower garden as far as one could see. Now tumbleweeds, Russian thistle has taken the place of the . . . luscious grass and other rich forage." Cows had trampled the desert, bringing with them an invasion of weeds, which further unraveled a delicate mosaic of native plants. Independence Taylor, a rancher near Kolob Canyon (now part of Zion National Park) recalled the dramatic erosion and "the time when there was not so much as a wash between New Harmony and the highway. Now there are many and some from 10 to 20 feet deep." He continued that, due to several mild winters "between 1875–1890, thousands of cattle were driven from Cedar City, Parowan, Beaver and Wilford for Dixie." In a place prone to floods, thousands of cows moving up and down riverbanks trounced the land, damaging riparian areas that had helped mitigate swollen waters and protect bottomland.

Cows were most certainly hard on the place, but the place too was hard on cows. Scorching temperatures, thorny cactus, and hazardous terrain proved unfriendly to European stock animals, and buffalo historic range does not include what is now Nevada, nor sections of western and southern Utah. Israel Bennion, an early Mormon settler who was a part of the Southern Dixie Mission, wrote of a cattle drive near the Muddy River, just below Bunkerville, Nevada. Though someone had shouted to the party, "Don't let your animals stop and drink," it was too late. The cows walked onto the wet sands "and then . . . calamity!" recalled Bennion. "Teams, chains, men frantically dragging cattle out onto the bank. Soon, very soon, as the cattle sank lower, their legs and then their necks broke under the strains of the tugging teams. Further struggling was worse than useless. Friendly pistol shots rang down the curtain." The land remains the same today, its mudflats potential deathtraps for lumbering, ill-adapted bovines.

All the same, some local families had made a living for generations in this region running livestock and they did not want to lose grazing access with new plans for national parks. Historian Karl Jacoby has spent his career determining how federal conservation measures confront the cultures that depend on lands that get protected as people get ejected. In his book *Crimes Against Nature: Squatters, Poachers, Thieves, and the Hidden History of American Conservation*, he wrote, ". . . the most notable feature of conservation was the transformation of previously acceptable practices into illegal acts: hunting or fishing redefined as poaching, foraging as trespassing, the setting of fires as arson, and the cutting of trees as timber theft." This targeting, of course, was practiced against Native peoples too in Yellowstone, Yosemite, and Glacier. The Park Service wanted its parklands to appear "unpeopled," as they outlawed traditional uses. Federal officials did try to reach compromises in some of their park efforts; with Bryce Canyon, designated a national monument in 1923 (and a park in 1928), they made an exception for cows, and grazing continued, with a long-term plan for eventual elimination. In 1964, livestock was abolished entirely from Bryce and a thirteen-mile fence was built to keep cows from trespassing.

Records regarding the creation of Zion National Park contain little evidence of discord, but there is one exception. John Winder, a Latter-day Saint who had lived above Zion Canyon before the park was designated, was very much put out by the Park Service, according to his son. Described by a neighbor as energetic yet stooped, Winder made his living ranching, farming, and bootlegging. Though he did not leave behind any documentation regarding his opinions on the park, his son Dan Winder offered insight on how the family regarded the park regulations. When asked about the prohibition of cattle grazing in the park, the younger Winder opined, "I think people were better off financially before they ever made it a park. Because everyone had a few head of cattle and if you needed something you could sell a few cows. I'm not a lover of the Park Service." He added that "it's [the Park Service] just a dictatorship as far as I can see."

Milton Twitchell lived in the town of Escalante, a tiny hamlet on the edge of one of southern Utah's most beautiful features, an area also known as Escalante. In 1936, the Park Service held a town hall meeting in Price, Utah, to roll out plans for turning the Escalante area into a 6,968-square-mile national monument. There was even talk of making it a giant national park. To put this in perspective, the feds wanted to turn 8 percent of the state of Utah, a chunk roughly the size of New Jersey, into a destination managed for tourism rather than for local livestock producers. Needless to say, the sheer enormity of the proposal did not sit well among the Mormons who ran their cows and sheep along huge rock faces and slot canyons of that area. Twitchell summed up the sentiments of his fellow cowboys when he testified that "you might just as well go out and take the property as to take their grazing rights. You can make it legal, but you can never make it moral." The next decades would see folks bring their own moral compasses with them onto public lands, and those compasses would be pointing in very different directions.

Named after Silvestre Vélez de Escalante, a Franciscan friar who in 1776 wandered the area looking for a route from Santa Fe to California, this zone of backcountry north of the Colorado River was settled by Mormons a hundred years after the Spanish missionaries came through. Described by geologist Clarence Dutton as an enormous staircase, the sandstone formation emerges from the Grand Canyon as a series of chocolate, vermillion, white, gray, and pink uplifts. These cliffs frame coral-colored sand dunes, striated plateaus, a precious few springs, and a desert so colorful that sixteenth-century explorer Francisco Vázquez de Coronado thought it looked like a painting in pastels. But it was, and remains, a dry and difficult country for livestock. After the Mormons drove thousands of sheep and cattle up through its canyons in the late 1800s, resident Nethelia King Griffin recalled "several years of drought that naturally intensified the evil of overgrazing." Forage was scant and many animals starved to death. "By 1905," King remembered, "the rich meadows on the mountain plateau had turned to dust beds. Sheep, bedded in the headwaters of the mountain streams and dying in the water ditches, so befouled them that ranchers' families could hardly get a decent drink of water. Cattle bones bleached on the dry benches and around mudholes and 'loco' patches, these poisonous weeds seeming to grow after other forage was dead and to attract starving animals with the promise of food." Escalante offered a ton of acreage but was woefully inadequate in climate and topography for large ranching operations. Still, they happened.

During that town hall meeting in Price where Milton Twitchell questioned the morality of the Park Service, Charlie Redd of La Sal, Utah, representing the newly created advisory board of Utah grazing districts, shared his own objections over making Escalante into a protected tourist destination. Noting the Park Service's track record in their dealings with regional ranchers, he observed that the agency "is not very promising to the livestock industry because they are not satisfied as long as there is a cow or sheep left." If the service had its way, Redd feared that he and others might suffer the dire economic consequences of grazing restrictions in the region. His testimony was testy, despite conceding that he was "not diplomatic and maybe a bit strong, but that's the way I feel about the situation." As a grazing district advisor, a role that had become available with the new Taylor Grazing Act, he wanted to help alleviate historic overgrazing but he did not want rangeland made into a park.

Congress had passed the 1934 Taylor Grazing Act to deal with the millions of acres of public lands hammered by decades of unregulated herds of livestock. This law, creating grazing districts and ten-year leases, stipulated that new lease agreements would set the number of "animal units," cow and calf pairs, within each grazing allotment. The law also established the Grazing Service, which later became the dreaded BLM. The Grazing Service initially recruited ranchers, like Redd, rather than bureaucrats, to serve as district advisory board members and oversee permittees, stock limits, and range improvements. To come in and pile on additional restrictions just as the district's boards were up and running was, in Redd's estimation, poor timing, superfluous, and absolutely not in the ranchers' best interests, which included his own.

Born in 1889, Redd was the child of early church adherents. At the age of thirty-four, he took charge of his family's ranching business on land that spread from northern Colorado across the La Sal Range and through southeastern Utah. Bad investments and fluctuating prices put the family business over a half-million dollars in the hole, but after the death of his father in 1923, with diligence and parsimony, Charlie and his brother brought the foundering operation back. There was a reason Charlie felt protective of livestock grazing at the meeting in Price. He had just come out of the Great Depression (courtesy of, to some degree, Utah Senator Reed Smoot) and was understandably loath to see public land access taken from him. Bills, bank failures, and plummeting prices for cows and sheep tested his will and nearly lost him his business. But he persevered.

One thing he did lose was some confidence in the Mormon Church. Among his father's financial records was a promissory note for future collection written for a whopping sum of money to a man well-established in the hierarchy of the church. In the process of settling the estate and the large debts that their father had incurred, Charlie and his brother approached the signatory for collection. The Mormon elder was vague and disinclined to pay back his obligation, so the Redd boys forgave it. But Charlie did not forgive the church. He held this act of squelching against his own religion.

Growing up in the tiny community of La Sal, Utah, a town just west of the Colorado border, Charlie was the sixth child of his polygamous father Lemuel's first wife, Eliza Ann Westover Redd. Before Charlie was born, Lemuel and Eliza were selected to accompany other families heading out on the San Juan Mission, an undertaking directed by Brigham Young in his goal to expand Zion. Their task was to colonize an eastern front to Mormon homeland and create peaceful relations with its Native residents, the Navajo and Ute. Their trip across the Escalante region is famous in Mormon history, most notably for their descent through the famous Hole in the Rock. Their blasting and chiseling into a sandstone wall from Glen Canyon's rim to its base left a lip scratched across the rock that seemed to hang in the air. Though precarious, it was steady enough to carry 250 people, including Charlie's parents, along a precipice just wide enough for the wheels of a wagon. The mission bounced through country sliced by cliffs and gulches, and their safe passage became yet another faith-promoting miracle in Mormon homeland.

Redd's grandparents came into the church through the missionary efforts of John Lee, ten years dead by the time Lem and Eliza headed toward the San Juan. Lee converted the Redds and prompted their move from Tennessee to the Utah Territory. Charlie's father, Lem, a taciturn man, never got over the severities of the San Juan Mission's journey from Dixie to Bluff. It wasn't the terror of coming down Hole in the Rock, that perilous catwalk, but another memory that haunted him throughout his life. Lem recalled the "spasms and near convulsions" that his horses underwent as they labored under the crack of a whip up the last pitch of the San Juan Mission. According to Charlie, "by the time most of the outfits were across, the worst stretches could easily be identified by the dried blood and matted hair from the forelegs of the struggling teams. . . . Whenever in later years the full pathos of San Juan Hill was recalled either by himself or someone else, the memory of such bitter struggles was too much for him and he wept." Zion was a struggle not just for the Mormon people but also for their animals.

Milton Twitchell and Charlie Redd were joined by others who shared grievances at the Price meeting. Though not in attendance, the director of the Grazing Service, Farrington Carpenter, asked that his own apprehensions, sent within a memo, be read aloud at the meeting so they might be part of its permanent record. Carpenter did not like that the Park Service banned grazing in its parks and monuments. He conceded that exceptions were made and the Park Service did permit cows in some cases, for those already grazing within designated areas, but he believed these were inadequate because they were only given "for a specified term of years, and in some cases for the life of the present owner." He did not approve of canceling permits or any denial of their transferal with the sale of a property. As with Bryce Canyon, the Park Service was open to grandfathering grazing permits, but only for the life of the individual permittee, and not to next of kin. This was extremely unpopular. Livestock operators did not want to see what they interpreted as grazing entitlements evaporate upon their deaths, denying them the ability to pass along those rights or sell them. Federal grazing permits added value to private ranches, and without them, a family could lose their operation. With parks and monuments came the potential demise of Mormon family ranches.

A representative from the Utah State Planning Board, George Staples, gave his two cents in Price as well, declaring the proprietary rights of the Mormon people. During his testimony, he reminded the committee that this was Mormon homeland, "as it was when Brigham Young stuck his staff in the ground and said, 'This is the place.'" Thus Staples stamped Brigham Young, and this most-likely apocryphal (but no less powerful) statement upon the written record of grazing debate—the statement Young had made (or not) when he arrived in the Salt Lake Valley recovering from Rocky Mountain spotted fever and claimed Zion. The Park Service, Staples continued, should "let our livestock go on and graze the areas that they have always been grazing." By the time the meeting took place, in 1936, "always been grazing" meant about fifty years.

The Park Service representative, Dave Madsen, also a Latter-day Saint from Utah, surely understood the resentment the ranchers expressed over further protections on public lands, but nonetheless explained his agency's perspective. In spite of the feelings of a small clutch of livestock producers, he said, "there are a great many people in the United States who want public lands devoted more and more to recreation and wild life [*sic*] and less and less to the use of the livestock." All the same, the attendees of this planning meeting voted unanimously to oppose the Park Service proposal, and Escalante got shoved to the backburner.

Then, with the outbreak of World War II, the national focus shifted to matters in the European and Pacific theaters, far from Utah's backcountry. But the American public did not abandon its love affair with American lands while otherwise engaged with troubles overseas. And in the decades after the war, more voices emerged to further champion wildlife and wildlands.

Cows in the Wilderness

And I think God must be a cowboy at heart.
He made wide-open spaces from the start.
He made grass and trees and mountains
  and a horse to be a friend.
And trails to lead old cowboys home again.

—Dan Seals, "God Must Be a Cowboy"

Charlie Redd and Cliven Bundy are Mormon ranchers born fifty-seven years apart. They've both scorned government overreach in places that felt proprietary. But beyond this, the two men could not be more different. Redd's life stretched along a timeline that saw a reshaping and redefinition of the public domain, from the largely unmanaged western commons to a place of increasing regulations and various federal designations. He was born into an isolated population of Mormons that ran their livestock as they pleased, but with the reconfiguring of the federal lands during Redd's time on earth, his world changed. He witnessed the first waves of tourists, non-Mormons who came to his homeland seeking pleasure in lands he knew as his workplace. He lived through the era of an emerging conservation community, which would bring with it a change in the demographics of southern Utah, most particularly around Moab, attracting new people and causing deep shifts in the cultures of that little Mormon town. He was erudite and law-abiding, and though he wasn't always crazy about the changes happening in his state, he focused his advocacy on the creation of a program at Brigham Young University, the Charles Redd Center for Western Studies, dedicated to western "history, geography, sociology, anthropology, politics, economics, literature, art, folklore, range science, forestry, and popular culture." He had a love for learning, a deep intellectual curiosity, and unlike Bundy, did not wrap church culture into his ranching business. In fact, he had mixed feelings toward the Mormon Church that lingered throughout his life.

After Redd passed away in 1975, non-Mormons just kept coming, either visiting or buying residences in St. George, Kanab, Torrey, Moab, Escalante, and Hurricane. The new population brought new ideas on land use. This was due in part to the 1964 Wilderness Act, the most restrictive conservation land law to date, which was passed by Congress and signed by Lyndon Johnson, a cynical populist from Texas. In the years after the first go-around with Escalante, there came a grumbling among preservationists over the roads and cars now clogging up the parks. Markers of tourism became eyesores. Promotional billboards, neon signs, and curio shops were antithetical to what Emerson and John Muir had imagined. Aldo Leopold was among those who yearned for big landscapes without permanent buildings or roads. He worried that scenic places like the Grand Canyon, on Escalante's southern flank, had become blighted by the clutter of industrial tourism—roadside attractions, hotels, cafés, and ticky-tacky summer cottages. Leopold, who wanted wild places that weren't easily accessible to humans, free of cheap souvenir shops, parking lots, and too many people, was the first person to label this idea "wilderness." He was also among the first voices in the conservation movement to raise concern about predators, particularly with regard to the wild animals killed to protect livestock.

As a ranger for the US Forest Service, Leopold had spent his early career ridding public lands of animals seen as varmints. These included coyotes, mountain lions, and wolves, wildlife that threatened cows and sheep. In his posthumously published *A Sand County Almanac*, Leopold recounts his own epiphany concerning these "varmints," during a moment watching life drain from the eyes of a wolf he had wounded. In witnessing the ebbing mortality of this animal—an animal viewed by ranchers as garbage—Leopold bore witness to the wolf's sentience and its inherent dignity. Although he was not anti-ranching, he came to understand that western lands were much bigger and more substantial than what cattle operators viewed as a pasture scrubbed free of wolves, bears, and coyotes. If his idea of untrammeled wilderness was ultimately mythic (American "wilderness" lands bear many footprints!), his fear of vanishing wildlife was not.

Embracing Leopold's wilderness concept, post-World War II conservationists shifted their focus to large landscapes, not just pretty geological features. They wanted big wild lands, where people seemed inconsequential in relation to the magnitude of the great outdoors and the "forest primeval." This dream passed into law with the enactment of the Wilderness Act. Written primarily by Howard Zahniser, executive director of an early conservation organization, the Wilderness Society, the bill incorporated the popular definition of wilderness at the time, uninhabited, unroaded, untamed. Born the son of a Methodist minister, Zahniser was a man whose Christian love of nature and a sense of stewardship for wild places steered the direction of his career as well as his incredible contributions to American conservation. His ethical sensibility prompted him to create legislation that would safeguard millions of acres of protected ecosystems and wildlife habitat within the most stringent public land designation so far, "wilderness areas." He shared his zeal with preservationist Teddy Roosevelt, who had been president when Zahniser was born in 1906. Zahniser's bill laid out his definition of wilderness, which "in contrast with those areas where man and his works dominate the landscape, is hereby recognized as an area where the earth and its community of life are untrammeled by man, where man himself is a visitor who does not remain." It also invented a new category of protected area—"designated wilderness," or as some came to think of it, Wilderness with a capital W. Each such wilderness would be created by special action of Congress. The Wilderness Act captured the thinking of mid-century environmental activists, which diverged mightily from Mormon worldview. Preservationists, conservationists, and those later known as environmentalists regarded wild places as immeasurably precious and finite, essential habitat for wildlife, and refuges for the human soul. With that view came the ethical imperative to defend them.

While Leopold and Zahniser are noted for their roles both in the emergence of wilderness preservation and in environmental ethics, another influencer in post-World War II America also established himself as a voice for the wild. Writer and activist Edward Abbey, who came to Utah in the 1950s, was an irreverent charmer who infuriated locals with his somewhat facetious contempt for humanity and his no-holds-barred campaign for land protection. He resembled a more mirthful but perhaps no less ardent Orrin Porter Rockwell, and as so many white men before him, Abbey claimed the land. Just as Brigham Young had declared the place Zion, Abbey planted a new flag, and the land became Abbey Country. His works and passions inspired a new generation of environmentalists, firing up activism in a spirited defense of the earth. His most notable work, published four years after the passage of the Wilderness Act, was *Desert Solitaire*, a memoir of his years serving as a ranger in Arches National Monument and a meditation on transcendentalism. Like Leopold, Abbey loved unsung critters. He celebrated rattlesnakes and ravens. Extolled the magic of sunsets and moon risings. Eulogized desert winters and the recrudescence of spring. *Desert Solitaire* called to young activists, agitators, and dirtbags who came to Mormon homeland prepared for battle in protecting the red desert West.

During his seasons as a ranger with the National Park Service, Cactus Ed, as he would become known, worked in Arches National Park, land that had been part of the original Escalante proposal, and where the Redd family had once run their cattle. He spent his days checking on tourists, picking up trash, and giving directions to the wayward. While assisting and collecting, he also admired the landscape, and he wrote in a style that was both tetchy and ribald, an irreverent departure from the breathy and purple prose of the early nature writers. In addition to being a good writer, he was polemical, insensitive to Native peoples, and a rake.

While Abbey was living in this corner of the United States, uranium mines were cropping up along the plateaus. The Bureau of Reclamation, a branch of the Interior Department charged with water "development," was in the process of building a dam to block the mighty Colorado River at the downward end of a majestic split in the rocks, a place called Glen Canyon. The resulting reservoir was to be named after Major John Wesley Powell: Lake Powell. But Abbey's followers, disgusted by the damage the impounded water flooding had on a labyrinth of irreplaceable side canyons, renamed that big, dammed body of water Lake Foul. Abbey cursed federal agencies that focused on exploitation rather than on protection. Unlike the Mormon ranchers who accused feds of overreaching, Abbey saw the government as woefully deficient in its responsibilities in land conservation. He believed that the BLM, for instance, which he cantankerously called the Bureau of Livestock and Mines, was far more interested in ranching and development than it was in protecting lands and species. He was anti-development, anti-anthropocentric, and anti-automobile. Add to this very anti-public-land-ranching. With typical cheek he made his case when he said that those who run sheep on public lands rightfully gripe about their lambs getting eaten by coyotes. "This is true, but do they eat enough? I mean, enough lambs to keep the coyotes sleek, healthy and well fed. That is my concern. As for the sacrifice of an occasional lamb, that seems to me a small price for the support of the coyote population. The lambs, accustomed by tradition to their role, do not complain; and the sheepmen, who run their hooved locusts on public lands and are heavily subsidized, most of them as hog-rich as they are pigheaded, can easily afford these trifling losses."

Charles Redd, once one of the wealthiest and most successful ranchers in the state, had a son familiar with Abbey. Robert Redd grew up ranching with his father in southern Utah and western Colorado, when cattle were still rounded up and moved from one seasonal pasture to another by cowboys on horseback. Although Robert now lives in Provo, his own sons live in the family's old stomping grounds. One sells curios in Monticello to tourists visiting nearby petroglyphs, wilderness areas, and the new monument, Bears Ears. The other works cows with his mother, Robert's ex-wife, on the Dugout Ranch, one of Charlie Redd's old properties now owned by the Nature Conservancy. Matthew, his oldest, still calls his dad for advice on cattle, Robert told me during a phone conversation. We chatted about his father—he's one among several who describe Charlie as smart and worldly.

Charlie had been married and divorced, but when he wed his second wife, Annaley Naegle, he found his match. Together they had nine children, and when those children were impish or naughty, Robert told me, his father lovingly called them "muggings." Charlie had chafed against the federal proposals that restricted grazing, because according to Robert, he was focused "on dollars and cents." Robert certainly understood his father's perspective, but he embraced his mother's point of view as well. She loved the look of the land. A rancher and a lessee of public lands for many years, Robert has had good relationships with federal managers and bad ones. We talked about his ranching days and riding with his father over the broad, broken country of western Colorado and southern Utah. He was particularly fond of the La Sal Mountains that rise along the border of these two states.

He told me that the anti-conservation attitude that proliferates in rural Utah and has spread into Nevada and Arizona is irrational. "I'm embarrassed for the way the locals are so negative," he remarked. "Public land has not been treated like it should be treated." When I asked him about Cliven Bundy, this cheerful and effusive man suddenly turned sober. He said flatly, "I am so deeply prejudiced against the Bundys. He [Cliven] is really the worst example I know of." Robert paused and added, "He makes all of us ranchers look bad."

I asked him if he'd ever met Ed Abbey. He practically giggled when I mentioned this name. "He was a wonderful, wonderful writer." Yes, Robert said, he met Ed Abbey twice. The first time, Robert was at a friend's home when Abbey pulled up in a Cadillac with a girlfriend. According to Robert, the woman had been working a good job as a receptionist, but something had happened and Abbey had been driving her around to collect a monthly unemployment check. Robert went out to look at Abbey's fancy rig, peering in through the window. "It had air-conditioning," he told me. Abbey twice makes snide remarks about air-conditioning in *Desert Solitaire*, a book that Robert read and adored. So Robert called Ed over, pointed at the unit, and said, "I thought you didn't like air-conditioning." "It's not mine," Abbey said of the car. "It's a rental."

Robert had a second encounter with Abbey that was a little more edgy. The writer was running low on gas, and at the time this was an empty country where opportunities to fill up weren't as readily available as they are today. So the writer pulled into Redd's Dugout Ranch, near the Needles District of Canyonlands National Park, where Robert lived at the time with his first wife, and where she and his son still run cows. Redd had recently read another of Abbey's paperbacks and did not like what the book suggested. "I said that I was very angry about *The Monkey Wrench Gang*," a story about a group of unlikely men and one woman who together, through a variety of means, obstruct the industrialization of their cherished red rock country. Abbey told Robert to relax and explained, "It's just a novel." But it was a novel that didn't win him many Mormon rancher friends in southern Utah, because it romanticized sabotage and vilified multiple uses of public lands. Abbey had stirred a band of passionate activists to carry out actions modeled on those enacted by his characters, which included burning down billboards, disabling heavy machinery, pulling survey stakes, vandalizing industrial sites aimed at road building, mining, logging, or developing on public lands, and throwing beer cans out of car windows.

Like Roosevelt, Abbey felt a deep sense of morality in his position. Like Muir, he insisted that wilderness was imperative, though not in its usefulness to humans. Abbey saw the wild as much more important than any human society, no matter who those humans were or what had befallen them. And he saw little need to thank God for wilderness experiences. In *Desert Solitaire*, his ode to Emerson, he wrote of the virtues of canyon country. In the Escalante region, for instance, "there are enough cathedrals and temples and altars here for a Hindu pantheon of divinities." If a man's imagination were not so weak and easily tired, Abbey added, "if his capacity for wonder not so limited, he would abandon forever such fantasies of the supernal. He would learn to perceive in water, leaves and silence more than sufficient of the absolute and marvelous, more than enough to console him for the loss of the ancient dreams." Echoing Muir, Thoreau, Leopold, and even Zahniser, Abbey recognized that humanity would lose something much bigger than themselves with the loss of wilderness.

In *Desert Solitaire*, he was dealing in myth—the myth of empty wilderness—because there is no such thing as American land without humans. In fact, Abbey was never solitary in Utah;

he was with ranchers and miners and tourists and federal government employees on lands that Pueblo, Southern Paiute, Ute and Navajo peoples had used for thousands of years. He also neglected to mention that he was living with a wife and child during the "solitary" desert days he described in *Desert Solitaire*. Another irony is that, by writing so beguilingly of the desert, Abbey played no small role in increasing the allure of—and therefore also the traffic to—these remote lands. Today millions of people come to southern Utah seeking the elusive solitude that this writer publicized. There they are met with both crowds and cows.

Drums of War

Not wanting to convert to their beliefs is not a particularly good excuse for hanging in effigy, vandalizing, threatening or any other cowardly ways used to harass them [environmentalists].

—Gwendolyn Zeta, Letter to the Editor,
Garfield County News, 1999

In 1976, eight years after the release of Abbey's famous book *Desert Solitaire*, Congress passed the Federal Land Policy and Management Act (FLPMA), effectively ending the Homestead Act and the opportunity to stake a claim on public domain. The frontier was closed, and federal land was to remain in the public trust. This law required the BLM to survey its jurisdiction and find places with special "scientific, scenic, historical, ecological, environmental, air and atmospheric, water resource, and archaeological values."

The BLM's mission, from its founding in 1946, was to manage the "leftovers" of federal land—all the places not identified as scenic attractions, such as those managed by the Park Service, or sources of timber, such as those managed by the Forest Service. The agency oversaw almost three times as much land as the National Park Service, a great deal of it leased to livestock interests. Until the new directive in 1976, the BLM had maintained cozy relations with ranchers and the mining industry. It had an old-boys-network reputation, and the protection of species and landscape was not a big priority in BLM culture. But with the passage of FLPMA, the agency was now responsible for protecting ecological integrity, a concept that was rather foreign and deeply unpopular in the places where the BLM managed lands. The law demanded the review of BLM roadless areas, parcels of five thousand acres and greater that lacked developed routes, to be assessed for wilderness characteristics. "Wilderness" was the strictest designation applied to public lands. This meant no vehicles. No mines. No logging. And potential restrictions on grazing. In other words, great expanses of public land that westerners had been using with little oversight and regulation— these BLM roadless areas—were on the verge of being what locals considered "locked up."

FLPMA, along with the National Environmental Policy Act (1970), the Clean Water Act (1972), and the Endangered Species Act (1973), reflected attitudes in a nation more and more concerned about its environment. And this changing national sentiment, bringing the new laws and regulations, created a backlash. If Ed Abbey combined both fiction and nonfiction in his work, the people of the rural West could also create, elaborate, and act upon their own mythologies—that outsiders were out to take their lands. With FLPMA came, in prompt reaction, the Sagebrush Rebellion, a war in the West. Off-road vehicle enthusiasts, ranchers, and miners began committing their own acts of defiance, employing a variety of tactics to make their points to Washington bureaucrats who had no business being in their backyards. Western state legislators devised schemes to wrest public lands from federal control altogether, passing bills to cede acreage to the states. In addition to asserting states' rights, these so-called sagebrush rebels demanded less environmental oversight, more sovereignty for states and counties that would thwart federal authority. Oversight infringed on their personal freedoms! they yelled. Dust-ups and demonstrations erupted across Utah, Nevada, and other western states. The quakes had begun.

The same year that FLPMA was signed into law, a $3.5 billion coal-fired generation project on BLM lands, atop the Kaiparowits Plateau in the Escalante region, was shelved. Had it gone through, the plant could have provided power to major cities such as Los Angeles and San Diego, giving jobs to residents in southern Utah's Garfield and Kane Counties. Due to legal complexities and their consequent costs, imposed on the Southern California Edison Company by new environmental regulations, backers abandoned the project. With the desertion of those financial backers, the promise of mining jobs vanished too, prompting a mob of five hundred people in Kanab, Utah, to target one particular vocal opponent to the project, actor Robert Redford. A part-time resident of Utah, Redford was an outspoken environmentalist, and in April 1976 he was burned in effigy. His likeness, topped by a telltale blond wig, was set afire by angry Kanabians who, in what sounds like a scene straight out of *South Park*, roasted hotdogs over the flames. As one protester, John Nelson, put it, "This is the time and day that we, the people of Kane County, have chosen to put a torch to skunkman Redford, self-proclaimed voice of the hypocritical obstructionists." Redford was famous for work filmed in Dixie—parts of *Butch Cassidy and the Sundance Kid* were shot in the beautiful ghost town of Grafton next to Zion National Park. (The real Butch Cassidy, by the way, was the oldest of thirteen children born to a Mormon family living in Circleville, Utah. His criminal career began by rustling cattle from Parowan, the town founded by Isaac Haight, about three decades after the slaughter at Mountain Meadows and ninety-two years before Mormons torched Redford's stuffed dummy.)

Now things were turning nasty in these little southern Utah towns. A year after the riot in Kane County, rumors were out of control. Some residents of Moab even accused the BLM of amassing weapons. Gene Day, the regional BLM supervisor, pleaded with the local paper, "There are many malicious rumors being circulated particularly in the Moab area that the BLM is stockpiling firearms and engaging in similarly frightening activities. These are absolutely untrue and apparently the result of some people's effort to discredit everything that the BLM is doing because of their own fears." At the time, no one in the Moab District was authorized to carry firearms, he said, adding that he and his agents were even prohibited from carrying personal firearms in government vehicles. "However," he said confidently, "I am sure that will eventually change." A year later it did, when the agency appointed thirteen armed law enforcement officers to deal with illegal off-road activity in California.

But in the few years after Robert Redford's effigy turned to ash, bitterness still abounded. A place call Negro Bill Canyon, now known as Granstaff Canyon (both iterations referring to William Granstaff, a mixed-race rancher and bootlegger who lived in a beautiful ravine near Moab in the late 1870s), was being assessed as wilderness by the BLM. In his day, Granstaff had made a living between the cows and the hooch, before the Mormons (according to local legend, at least) ran him out. A primitive track made the canyon reachable by recreationists on off-road vehicles. Hundreds of mining claims were also accessed by this undeveloped route. In order to determine if the canyon was eligible for wilderness status, the BLM closed motorized access, and thereafter locals hit the roof.

A group of protesters drove heavy machinery into the canyon to cut more roads. On July 4, 1980, demonstrators sent a bulldozer emblazoned with a sign reading "I'm a sagebrush rebel," to slice a road into nearby Mill Creek Canyon, circumventing Granstaff Canyon, where BLM officers and federal marshals were set up in anticipation of the protest. Because they had thrown off the cops, the rebels achieved a publicity coup—their road-building protest splashed across headlines—but they faced no legal actions. When asked about this act of vandalism, Debbie Sease, then of the Wilderness Society and later of the Sierra

Club, said, "The Sagebrush Rebellion's true intent is not to give the lands back to the states. It is to emasculate BLM and to stop the management of these lands."

Locals did not want the feds to make decisions for them. They wanted local and state control. Giving federal lands to the states was a popular notion and remains so even today. But managing land was and is expensive, and states and other municipal bodies—counties in particular—would be hard-pressed to afford upkeep if the lands came to these jurisdictions. Whether or not the transfer of land was desired by all the rebels, it certainly was by some of them, and today the Bundy family, their supporters, and many Mormon politicians follow suit. Emasculating the federal government, I'm certain, is always part of it, too. The sagebrush rebels, the Bundys and their supporters, are engaged in a macho cowboy contest to show the feds that when you mess with the bull, you get the horns.

Mormon residents felt absolutely justified in their pushback on environmental regulations, including any restrictions to what they perceived as traditional ways of using the land. This was no longer the cordial, if testy, interactions of Charlie Redd, David Madsen, and Milton Twitchell during the 1936 Price meeting. In 1979, two years after he was named Outstanding Elected Official of Utah while serving on the San Juan County Commission, Calvin Black roared at BLM agents who were in the process of assessing areas east of Escalante for their wilderness attributes. Black was a heavyset man and well known for his lack of diplomacy, who over the years had mined uranium, owned two radio stations, and acted as mayor of Blanding, Utah. Today, if you fly into Halls Crossing, Utah, you'll taxi on the Cal Black Memorial Airport runway. Like Brigham Young, Black was not one to mince words. "We've had enough of you guys telling us what to do. I'm not a violent man, but I'm getting to the point where I'll blow up bridges, ruins [antiquities], and vehicles. We're going to start a revolution. We're going to take back our lands.

We're going to sabotage your vehicles. We're going out in twos and threes because we are going to take care of you BLMers," he warned. The same year of Cal Black's threats, *The New York Times* reported that westerners felt the "most abused by the federal government and least understood." This was a place unaccustomed to regulation from a government seen as fettering cowboy culture.

Ed Abbey and Black had values that were uncompromising and wildly divergent. And yet they maintained a rapport. Upon hearing about Black's diagnosis of cancer—a cancer that would eventually kill him—Abbey wrote Black a note on December 1, 1988. "I hear rumors that you've come down with a serious illness. If true, I hope you beat it. Although you and I probably disagree about almost everything, you should know that I have never felt the slightest ill will toward you as a person. Furthermore, you still owe me an airplane ride. Good luck and best wishes." Sadly, Abbey himself died a few months after these tidings. Black succumbed the next spring.

In spite of Abbey's gesture toward Cal Black, an early civility seen in the creation of Zion National Park between conservation interests and regional Mormons had collapsed. And the sagebrush rebels weren't just aiming their anger at the government; they were now targeting local opponents, too. In the town of Escalante, residents hanged three relatively new residents in effigy. Stuffed dummies of Robert Weed Weinick, Clive Kinkaid, and Grant Johnson, the founders of the new organization Southern Utah Wilderness Alliance, were finally cut down after being strung up for three days, and then dragged behind cars. But this wasn't just silliness.

Escalante is a town of 750 people, most of whom come from long-established Mormon families. It's part of Garfield County, which Clive Kincaid described as "one of the least inhabited counties in the United States. Two hundred miles long and just four thousand people." He added: "You could live here twenty years and never belong. This was one of the last Mormon outposts of the 1880s and outsiders are not made welcome." After the effigies, someone buried wooden boards, punctuated with long, sharp nails, in Weinick's driveway. His wife hit this booby trap while taking their children to school, blowing a tire and causing her car to fishtail dangerously along a sheer roadside cliff. The family was shaken, but unharmed. The vandals also contaminated the family's well and broke its pump, leaving behind a sign that chided, "IF YOU WANT WILDERNESS THEN CARRY YOUR WATER." Following the incident, Escalante's mayor, Mohr Christensen, suggested that Weinick himself had staged both the break-in and his wife's accident, adding that Weinick was nothing but a government-funded parasite.

But it wasn't just the Mormon residents menacing conservationists. In 1990, Arthur Lyman of Boulder, Utah, a tiny town next to Escalante, found fifteen of his cows and six of his calves shot to death on an Escalante River grazing allotment in the Glen Canyon National Recreation Area. The perpetrators also burned down three of Lyman's cabins. Around the time of this incident, Lyman discovered a sign posted nearby that read "Stop Destructive Welfare Ranching." To call the men and women who run their livestock on public lands "welfare ranchers" was the ultimate dig against a culture convinced of its own rugged individualism. The people of southern Utah were bootstrappers who had settled a desert and thrived amid its severity. To suggest that their success was in part due to government subsidies was a giant affront. Though ranchers paid the government pennies on the dollar (compared to contracts with private landholders) to lease public lands for grazing their animals, they did not view themselves as federal dependents.

A reward of twenty-four thousand dollars was offered for leads on the people who slaughtered the cows and set the Lyman properties ablaze, but no one was ever caught. Two years later, the Lyman family agreed to relinquish rights to their 54,825-acre allotment, which had supported 360 animals, in exchange for undisclosed compensation from the Richard King Mellon Foundation and the Conservation Fund. The superintendent of the Glen Canyon National Recreation Area explained that ridding the area of livestock would eradicate "user conflict and enhance recreational opportunities for hikers and other park visitors, while protecting our water quality, wetlands and streamside habitat." Although he was offered reparation, Arthur Lyman was melancholic when faced with abandoning his livelihood and all that it meant. He told *The New York Times*, "It makes no difference to the big old United States if this ranch goes under and goes to sagebrush. But this is my way of life." It's a pervasive sentiment in the region—to be a cowboy is a lifeline to ancestry, identity, and a claim to the land. But others think differently. To some, subsidized public land ranching is the very height of white privilege.

The Southern Utah Wilderness Alliance wanted Utah's back-country protected as wilderness and sought to whittle down cattle numbers and prevent mining operations and road-building on public lands. Utah representative Jim Hansen and Utah senators Jake Garn and Orrin Hatch introduced their own "conservation" bill in 1992, entitled the Canyons of the Escalante National Conservation Act. It masqueraded as protective legislation but opened the Escalante country to a "showcase of multiple uses." Their bill underscored the vast cultural differences in land-use proclivities between Garfield County locals and those coming to the region seeking the solitude of Abbey Country. Rep. Hansen gleefully pointed out that only stuffed shirts wanted to safeguard wild places. "In a park, you have rangers in Smokey Bear hats telling you to look but not touch," he said. "In a resource area you can have cattle roundups like in the movie *City Slickers*, you can have rodeos, wagon rides, cookouts, and walks." Ken Rait, then a young man from the East Coast who'd moved to Salt Lake City to work for the Southern Utah Wilderness Alliance, countered that Hansen, Hatch, and Garn's bill "would do nothing more than turn the Escalante country into a three-ring circus for cowboys, miners, and road builders. It's a proposal that would rob the American public of the highest and best designation for the spectacular Escalante country, which is wilderness."

God and Guns

In a sluggish economy, never, ever f*ck with another man's livelihood.

—Guido the Killer Pimp, *Risky Business*

With the presidency of Ronald Reagan and his appointment of the notoriously anti-environmental James Watt to interior secretary, the Sagebrush Rebellion cooled down. Reagan was elected in 1980, but even before being sworn in, on January 20, 1981, he sent a telegram to an oversight hearing of the Subcommittee on Mines and Mining. It read, "Please convey best wishes to all my fellow sagebrush rebels. . . . I renew my pledge to work toward a 'sagebrush solution.' My administration will work to ensure that the states have an equitable share of public lands and their natural resources. To all good luck." Rebels were apparently placated by support offered by President Reagan and Interior Secretary Watt, as their rage settled down for a time.

According even to certain conservative voices, including some from the American Enterprise Institute, the Sagebrush Rebellion was a wild goose chase. From the ranchers' perspective, if the western states had taken ownership of public lands, the grazing fees, substantially lower on those lands than on private lands, would have likely increased. Today public land is leased at $1.87 per cow-calf pair per month, as compared to an average of roughly $22.00 on private land. If state legislators suddenly controlled public lands within their boundaries, many states would be forced to deal with dramatic financial burdens and burgeoning budgets. If such transfers had occurred, rebels and critics alike would have seen a painful outcome as states scrambled to pad their budgets with increased fees from hunters, anglers, recreationalists, and ranchers in order to manage the massive amounts of land. State control of lands would likely result in their sale.

When Republicans lost control of the presidency in the 1990s, the bugbears of the sagebrush rebels, such as over-regulation and environmental strictures, were wrapped into the less incendiary and more judicious-sounding, but no less rancorous, wise-use movement. Again, like the sagebrush rebels, this was a coalition of ranching, timber-harvest, and oil and mineral interests, but it was funded mainly by the mining industry. They focused on opening up federal lands for resource extraction free of regulations. The reemergence of that effort was fueled by George Bush Sr.'s aggressive anti-environmental response on the campaign trail to Al Gore's emphasis on what at the time was known as global warming, now called climate change. Bush, who lost to Bill Clinton in 1993 in his bid for a second term, warned voters that environmental efforts came at the expense of jobs.

In the 1990s, conspiracy theories were rife, proliferating nationally through rumors spread at gatherings, activist workshops, and on AM radio. Even the televangelist Pat Robertson wrote, in his book *The New World Order* of global forces intent on running the world's economy. Robertson and other heavyweights alluded to dark global forces, such as Jewish bankers and New-Agers, who in pursuing globalism were taking the world down a destructive and decisively anti-Christian path. Wise-use folks became saturated by these ideas, and their theories began to focus on environmentalists. At a 1995 rally in Spokane, Washington, wise-user Troy Mader of Wyoming, a representative of both the Common Man Institute and the Abundant Wildlife Foundation, explained to his audience, "Most environmental groups, with no regard for truth, use misinformation to further their agendas and are anti-God, anti-American, and anti-gun." Tree huggers were lying, godless globalists who were out to snatch away Second Amendment rights.

The most broadly ramifying conspiracy, in the minds of wise-users, was Agenda 21, a plan put forth at the 1992 United Nations Earth Summit to address sustainability in the twenty-first century. Wise-users grabbed onto this proposal, conceived in Rio de Janeiro, which had recommended nonbinding ways for local governments to make their own action plans for sustainable development. Conspiracy-mongers twisted that call into the idea that the United Nations wanted to usurp US sovereignty and private property rights. They also came to believe that it had at its root a design to move rural people into urban areas in order to control them. This United Nations proposal was, among other things, a model for combating poverty, deforestation, and the marginalization of Indigenous people. But to the wise-use movement, Agenda 21 was a blueprint for local government takeovers and, with that, a plot to take American land and rights. Environmentalists, wise-users decided, were in cahoots, and groups like the Southern Utah Wilderness Alliance, the Sierra Club, and Grand Canyon Trust came to be considered, over the years, fronts for takeovers. It wasn't just conservation laws making public lands less accessible to family ranchers and the extraction industry—it was a global cabal intent on grabbing American lands from rural people in the quest to take over the world. Or something along those lines . . .

By the mid-1990s the wise-use movement began to intertwine with an emerging militia movement, or patriot movement—a loose consortium of white supremacists, survivalists, libertarian eccentrics, and religious cranks who saw a rot growing within the United States government. Various forms of ideological flotsam drifted along with these campaigns—anti-environmentalism, religious fundamentalism, militarism, and sedition. Together they imagined a battle between good and evil—an event to bring corruption, in all its many imagined manifestations, to an end. A contagious distrust and fury over federal powers spread to broader and broader audiences, after two events rocked the United States and galvanized widespread anti-government sentiment.

The first event took place on August 21, 1992, when Randy Weaver of Naples, Idaho, saw his teenage son shot by federal agents during a siege at Ruby Ridge. Six US marshals had been surveilling the family's home in order to approach the elder Weaver with a bench warrant when the Weavers' dog, Striker, started barking. Sammy Weaver, age fourteen, and his friend Kevin Harris came out of the house to check on the disturbance, and a gun battle ensued. The feds later claimed they were attacked and the Weavers claimed the agents shot first. Sammy was killed, shot twice in the back. Deputy Marshal William Degan was shot dead and so was the dog. The Weaver family had no idea what was happening as night fell and hundreds of FBI and state police amassed in the dark to create a militarized zone all around the compound. A "shoot on sight" rule was implemented and officers were given the go-ahead to target anyone who appeared to be armed.

On August 22, while attempting to take his son Sammy's body to a shed, Randy was shot and wounded. While standing on the porch holding her ten-month-old infant, Elisheba, Vicki Weaver ordered everyone inside just before she was shot in the face and killed. Her infant daughter survived. Kevin Harris was also wounded, and for days the two men and the Weavers' three surviving children didn't leave the house or answer appeals to negotiate with the FBI. Members of the Aryan Nations, a group that Weaver was himself affiliated with, and radical right-wing protesters from all over the West arrived on the scene to demonstrate against the horrific and mishandled government actions. On August 28, a man named Bo Gritz helped bring the standoff to an end. After visiting the Weaver's property, he told FBI negotiator Jim Botting, "Boy, you guys really screwed that one up. Vicki's dead. Randy's been shot. Harris has been shot. Dog's dead. Sam's dead. You damn near killed the whole family." The FBI apparently had no idea how much damage they had done.

James Gordon "Bo" Gritz, a beefy silver-haired ex-Green Beret and twenty-year Army Special Forces veteran, ran for president with the Populist Party in 1992, the year of Ruby Ridge, under the slogan "God, Guns and Gritz." He spoke against globalism and the New World Order. Before his own presidential run, Gritz had been on a ticket as running mate to the former grand wizard of the Ku Klux Klan David Duke in 1988, though he later denounced him. Gritz had been baptized into the Mormon Church in 1984, but eventually parted ways with the Latter-day Saints. He taught survival skills in Idaho for those anticipating end-times and became a hero for his role in Ruby Ridge.

How did Randy Weaver and his family end up in Idaho? God told them to go. Like Randy, Vicki grew up in Iowa. She and her family had attended the Reorganized Church of Jesus Christ of Latter-day Saints, a branch of Mormonism that splintered off from the main church after Brigham Young came to power. After the Weavers married, they settled in Cedar Falls, west of Dubuque, where they both became convinced of the imminence of the world's end. Vicki had a vision that God wanted her and her family to head west and await the event. Once in Idaho, they'd live off the grid, homeschool their children, grow vegetables, read the Bible, and picnic at Hayden Lake with members of the Aryan Nations.

At these neo-Nazi get-togethers, just sixteen miles down the road from the family cabin, the Weavers mixed with members of the Christian Identity Church, another apocalyptic religion with anti-government underpinnings, one that emphasized whites as the chosen people. The roots of this sect can be traced to nineteenth-century British anti-Semitism, and to its spillover into a few American religious fringe groups in the early twentieth century. Weaver had been selling guns for extra money when an undercover FBI agent posing as a member of the Hayden Lake group approached him in 1989 to buy sawed-off shotguns. He agreed to sell.

After the deal went through, the FBI contacted Weaver and threatened him with a weapons charge, while promising the whole affair would be dropped if he consented to act as an informant. He said no. A few months later, Weaver was pulled over, shoved in the snow, frisked, cuffed, and thrown in jail. He posted bail, went home, and didn't attend his later hearing. There had been a mix-up in regard to the date, but he was anyway reluctant to appear—he'd been told by the magistrate that if he was found guilty he would lose his property. That was false, but nonetheless he took it as truth and it terrified him.

The Ruby Ridge siege became a rallying event for the militia movement, filling its ranks primarily with rural white men outraged by what they deemed a miscarriage of justice. After his surrender, Randy Weaver served eighteen months in jail, and the family was awarded more than three million dollars in a civil suit against the feds. Kevin Harris was awarded $380,000. The man who coordinated the FBI actions at Ruby Ridge, E. Michael Kahoe, was sentenced to eighteen months in prison for destroying internal analysis that was unfavorable to the FBI response and lying to investigators. A manslaughter charge was dropped against FBI sniper Lon Horiuchi, who shot and killed Vicki Weaver.

In her gripping memoir, *Educated*, Tara Westover points to the time when her Mormon family used the Weavers' story as a cautionary tale, her father, Val, convincing the family to anticipate the day when they would face their own government siege. In preparation, her dad made his seven children stuff what he called "head for the hills bags" full of "herbal medicines, water purifiers, flint, steel," with "several boxes of military MREs—Meals Ready to Eat." Each family member added a sleeping bag and weapons to their kit. Her brothers packed guns while Tara carried a small knife, weaponry necessary to withstand the attack sure to come. She grew up believing that the siege was imminent, the specter of the Weaver family becoming the very backdrop of her life, as it did for so many would-be insurgents and fundamentalists across the country.

The next episode that added to the uptick in the American patriot movement took place a year later, in Waco, Texas. Branch Davidians were a religious cult led by a self-proclaimed prophet of God, David Koresh. This handsome, magnetic Bible teacher instructed his followers to, among other things, hunker down in their New Mount Carmel Center compound and await the end of the world. Koresh practiced polygamy and stockpiled weapons. In February 1993, agents of the Bureau of Alcohol, Tobacco and Firearms (ATF) arrived at the compound, intending to search the property and arrest the self-proclaimed prophet. Shots were fired by both the agents and the cultists, but who fired first is still debated. Ten people in total were killed, members of the Davidians and of the ATF. After the failed first assault, Texas law enforcement and FBI agents surrounded the Davidian property, spending weeks in unsuccessful negotiations with Koresh, trying to encourage his surrender. On April 19, the FBI rolled tear-gas canisters into the facility. A fire broke out and the entire compound burned to the ground, leaving seventy-five dead, including children. Koresh was found dead after the fire from a gunshot wound to the head.

Militia activity exploded in the United States, and zealots of various stripes went to war with the government. Timothy McVeigh blew up the Alfred P. Murrah Federal Building in

Oklahoma City in 1995, killing 186 people. The Montana Free-men declared they were no longer part of the United States and in 1996 sat holed up for eighty-one days in Jordan, Montana, during a standoff with the FBI. The Bureau had been sent in with eight arrest warrants stemming from financial impropri-eties such as counterfeiting. Militia contagion also infected rural Mormon communities whose members had a long familiar-ity with religious oppression and were disposed toward anti-government feelings.

The wise-use and militia movements were creating a cam-paign of attrition against law and order, breaking codes of civil society and taunting government officials to try and make them stop. Some continued to question whether the federal govern-ment, or the public, could legally own land in their states. Dick Carver, an official in Nye County, Nevada, claimed the federal government had "no authority to own, hold, or accept dominion over public lands," and to prove his point he bulldozed open a road that the Forest Service had closed, as Cliven Bundy cheered with a gathered crowd. Carver, a buddy of Bundy's, believed in county supremacy over federal authority, and pledged to "end apartheid in the West." At a 1995 rally in Alturas, California, Carver told the audience that he had refused to stop his bull-dozer despite a Forest Service ranger having commanded him to do so, when "all it would have taken was for him [the ranger] to draw a weapon." Smugly, Carver added, "Fifty people with side-arms would have drilled him."

Wise-use and militia circles had guns, but the environmen-talists had their own tools. And in Utah, one tool was the Antiq-uities Act. In the 1990s, bills proposing large-scale wilderness designations were a near impossibility to get through Congress due to intractable Republican politicians from western states. But the Antiquities Act allowed a president to move unilater-ally to protect lands in spite of any congressional opposition. In 1996, President Bill Clinton did just that when he made the

Grand Staircase-Escalante region a national monument, sixty years after Charlie Redd had expressed concerns that Escalante would become a national park. Though some Utahns applauded Clinton's designation, there was fury among many people who lived in southern Utah. Protesters in Kanab carried black balloons and shook "Shame on You, Clinton" signs. Kanab realtor Dale Clarkson called Escalante "the finest energy field we have in the United States," but said that the "monument won't have a dime's influence on tourism. . . . It's not even second-class scenery—it's third or fourth class. It's such marginal ground that part of it was used in the motion picture *Planet of the Apes*." This was a far cry from the 1930 Zion-Mount Carmel Tunnel celebration, when Utah's governor announced before a jubilant crowd of locals that the lands of Utah were open for the "use of the people of the United States . . ."

At the time Grand Staircase-Escalante was designated, Utah Republican Chris Cannon announced his candidacy for Congress. His opposition to the new monument was the perfect issue for engaging a furious electorate, and Cannon soon dropped a bombshell advertisement comparing the new monument's declaration to the federal government's nineteenth-century incursion during the Utah War, when the westbound Baker-Fancher party was caught in the crossfire of the Mormon rebellion. In Cannon's 1990s television ad, he told viewers, "I feel like I'm back in the 1850s again, with the federal government encamped all around us. Now Clinton takes our land." The ad was intended to spark 150-year-old memories of multi-generational Mormon oppression at the hands of the federal government. Cannon expertly fanned the flames, reminding voters that the last time "the federal government encamped all around us," a lot of blood was spilled. The message was clear: Dixie knew what to do with outsiders who trespassed on Zion. And with his menacing message, Cannon won the race and served in Congress from 1997 to 2009.

A Cowboy Named Mary

Yep, there's nothing like being a cowboy in the middle of society, is there?

—Mary Bulloch

President Clinton surprised a lot of people with his designation of Grand Staircase-Escalante National Monument in 1996, blindsiding many Kanab residents, including Shawna Cox. The Cox family has lived in Dixie for five generations, some even working for the government. Shawna's great uncle was Walter Reusch, the first custodian of Zion National Monument (its designation before becoming a park), who coincidentally was tasked with rounding up the last cattle trespassing in Zion Canyon in 1918. Though she likes the idea of Zion National Park, Cox does not like further environmental efforts or the changes that outsiders, lured by her region's natural beauty, have brought to her town of Kanab—changes, she tells me, like pedestrian sidewalks. She especially does not like Grand Staircase-Escalante Monument.

Cox was among those who protested the monument back when Clinton created it. She is a longtime friend of the Bundy family and grew up in the small town of Fredonia, Arizona, seven miles south of Kanab. In the 1990s she became involved in People for the West!, a wise-use group that sponsored workshops in rural communities aimed at opposing the agendas of "extreme environmentalists." It was a well-funded front for corporate mining interests, cloaked in a cowboy ethos, with the ultimate purpose of keeping public lands open to extraction. People for the West! (yes, with an exclamation point as part of its name like its nemesis Earth First!) held forums serving as founts of right-wing ideas, Mormon resentments, and anti-government activism. Cox, a ruddy, round blond with intense blue eyes, became secretary for the local Kanab, Utah, chapter. At its height, this lobbying group (by then known as People for the USA!) had over 120 chapters nationwide. The organization consisted primarily of members who shared conservative Christian values, rightwing passions, and crackpot notions. Under various names, it was active from 1988 until its shutdown in 2001.

As wise-users grew more adamant about their positions on public lands and their rights to use them, they, like Shawna Cox and Cliven Bundy, flouted constitutional interpretations of laws and statutes. Many treated their protests as a religious calling, stemming from their righteous obligation to stand up to "overreach" by an interfering and shadowy global community. The Mormons tied this imperative to prophecy and, like the militias, to duty. Together they shared particular constitutional suppositions and conspiracy theories at gun shows and rallies, encouraging one another to learn the Constitution (or rather a misconstrued interpretation of the document), while assuming the moniker of "we the people," a rallying cry that Cliven Bundy and his family use to this day.

The wise-use movement was showing mounting signs of anti-government radicalization. Political scientist William Chaloupka pointed out in 1996 the increase in western states being influenced by the militia movement, a fringe that supported "federalism, constitutionalism and sovereign legitimacy," emboldening rebels to question federal authority over public lands.

In addition to constitutional analysis, they dabbled in reviving obscure old laws, such as the Posse Comitatus Act as understood by William Potter Gale. Gale, who died in 1988, was a minister in the Christian Identity Church, the sect whose ideas Bo Gritz, Randy Weaver, and the Aryan Nations followed. A white supremacist and anti-government agitator, Gale emphasized decentralizing federal authority and building power in local governments. In his 1972 Christian Posse Association newsletter, he wrote "a county (or parish) government is the highest authority in the land." This rejection of federal authority came in response, on Gale's part, to his ongoing fight with the IRS over taxes, one that led him to note the Internal Revenue Code was one of constitutional abuse. Further, he believed that any official deemed to be in violation of the Constitution should be removed from office using posse comitatus, or power to the county. Gale recommended this device to allow sheriffs to recruit militias to keep the peace, in lieu of federal law enforcement. If a county sheriff refused a citizen's request for help, then a militia could take charge with force and stand against federal law enforcement.

In the aftermath of the American Civil War, the US Congress borrowed this posse comitatus idea from England, to disastrous effect, as a way of appeasing angry Southerners who resented federal forces sent by President Ulysses S. Grant to protect African Americans during Reconstruction. In 1878, President Rutherford B. Hayes signed the Posse Comitatus Act, outlawing interference by federal law enforcement with local affairs, in principle, and giving county sheriffs the authority to push back on what they regarded as government overreach and unlawful aggression. The principle of posse comitatus has been used to justify the evils of mobocracy and lynching in corners of the country ever since.

The Constitutional Sheriffs and Peace Officers Association is a militia-backing, posse-comitatus-supporting group of elected officials who have sworn to take on federal government forces, should the need arise. Joe Arpaio, David Clarke, and Richard

Mack are examples of its membership, numbering about five hundred. *Politico* reported in 2017, "In Utah, 28 of 30 sheriffs went even further, warning that '[n]o federal official will be permitted to descend upon our constituents and take from them what the Bill of Rights—in particular Amendment II—has given them.'" In other words, even if the United States ever implemented comprehensive gun control laws, as of 2017 twenty-eight sheriffs in the Beehive State would not enforce them. Or if, say by extension, a sheriff felt that federal grazing restrictions were capricious, he or she might oblige federal officials to back off.

Although the militia movements, apocalyptic prophecies, and anti-government outrage swirled over the West in the 1990s, most livestock producers on public land weren't driven by doomsday narratives or conspiracy. And although the Bundys have tried to position themselves as archetypal public land ranchers with their backs to the wall, facing intolerable federal rules, many others out there present different stories. Like the story of Mary Bulloch. Hers is a sad one that demonstrates how changes in the West and its cowboy myth do break hearts.

In her self-published book, *Last Rancher Standing: The Cliven Bundy Saga, A Close-up View*, a sort of memoir/biography of Cliven Bundy and constitutional primer, Shawna Cox wrote she "spent 20 years trying to open the Kaparowitz [*sic*] coal mine," and after working through all the paperwork she and her partners were ready to sink the first shaft in the coal-rich region. Then Clinton created the Escalante monument. Its designation distressed Cox for two reasons: her own lost opportunities of mining the Kaiparowits, and the question of what the monument status would do to her friend Mary Bulloch, a rancher with a permit to run cows in the monument's backcountry. A stunningly beautiful woman with a face etched by years of cigarettes and the withering Dixie sun, Bulloch ran about one hundred cows through some of the roughest landscape in Garfield County. She called herself a cowboy.

Bulloch was the oldest of eight siblings raised in a Mormon ranching family outside Cedar City. Her first husband, a handsome tomcat from a wealthy family, left her and their two babies soon after they married. She would be a bride on two more occasions before she met Boyd Rucker, a man forty years her senior who ranched longhorns out of Escalante.

Mary's lifestyle had gotten her booted from the Mormon Church, so every Sunday she joined Boyd on the four-plus-hour round trip from the town of Escalante to Kanab to attend services and prove her devotion to both this man and the faith of her childhood. The couple's religious resolve so touched church leaders that her excommunication was revoked and, at the age of thirty, Mary was married to Rucker at the St. George Temple. This meant sealing themselves to one another for all eternity—remaining together beyond the veil of death.

Theirs was a happy marriage, a ten-year period of stability in Mary's chaotic life, according to Marti Hulet, Bulloch's daughter. She quit drinking and brought her two children, Marti and a brother, into a situation of relative constancy. But Bulloch was first and foremost a cowboy. She'd leave her kids at home with some food and a wringer washer during the school year, and go out with Boyd for weeks at a time to Fifty Mile Mountain—the Fifty, as locals called it—and together they'd tend their herd. In the summers, Marti and her brother joined them, living in a remote cabin on public lands where Boyd had dug a well. Even in the backcountry, Marti remembered, Mary dressed every morning in a crisp white shirt, adorned with turquoise jewelry that set off her aquamarine eyes. In spite of the red dust, flies, and grime of the trail, her daughter recalled with a smile, Mary remained impeccably turned out for her husband, her kids, and their semi-feral cows.

Boyd was still going strong at the age of eighty when he went up to his allotment one day to check on things. Something spooked his horse, sending the old rancher headlong into the wooden bars of his pack saddle. Though his forehead turned black from the tremendous collision, he refused to go see a doctor. Not to worry, he told Mary, he was fine. But while the two were out on a ride some weeks later, Boyd fell off his horse, then lingered in a coma until he died.

She continued to work the Fifty and the Mudholes, a hundred-thousand-acre area for which the BLM allowed 175 AUMs (the acronym for animal unit months, a term conveying the amount of forage needed for a cow and calf pair). Mary and Boyd had run unbranded, stray cattle, and her feral herd was notoriously difficult to round up. With Boyd gone, hers was a big operation for just one person.

In 2000, the BLM asked her to get her cows off her allotment due to a drought plaguing the region. She didn't. They asked again. The cows remained. It became a public fight between two tenacious women both trying to do their jobs. Kate Cannon, the Escalante monument manager, was tasked with keeping the land healthy during the dry spell. She explained that "it's the job of the BLM to be the caretaker of the land, to manage grazing so the land remains healthy for all uses." Although Cannon told the press that "I don't want to be in the roundup business," Bulloch's cows were not permitted to be on the monument. As a recourse, the BLM fenced Mary's cows off the ecologically sensitive areas—and the precious little water that was available.

Dixie ranchers feel they know the land far better than land managers, who spend a few years at one position, then get transferred to another regional office. Locals familiar with running stock in this desert believe that they have a special sensitivity to their cattle's use of sparse regional vegetation. Their cows, they claim, are quite healthy in this arid country and can survive on the scrubbiest of browse. But studies suggest otherwise. With no historical presence of grazing herbivores, the region is not suited for livestock at all. The Grand Staircase-Escalante

Monument, like so much of this region, is covered in what is known as biological soil crust, the cyanobacteria, lichen, moss, and microfungi communities that act as an epoxy to thin soils. These layers provide adhesive that gives resistance against wind and water erosion. They are fragile formations and can easily be broken up when trampled by humans or cows, causing erosion that's especially damaging in drought years. Conservation groups were calling for the closure of monument allotments, including Mary Bulloch's, citing overgrazing, erosion, and the spread of weedy non-native plants, such as cheatgrass. During Mary's fight, the Grand Canyon Trust offered fair compensation to Bulloch in exchange for retiring her grazing permits. "She should have taken it," daughter Marti told me.

But her identity superseded her practicality. Marti believed that her mother's public land cattle grazing was too fundamental to who she was; to contemplate being bought out was to lose herself. "She wanted to be a cowboy, and everything that got in the way . . ." Marti paused and swept her hand across the table where we sat talking, demonstrating that Mary swiped any and all obstacles aside. The cowboy identity is embodied in these folks—any alternative feels akin to dismemberment.

One day during the conflict, Bulloch coerced Shawna Cox to ride out on her allotment and shoot footage of how her animals were faring under BLM management. She wrote a letter to the editor of the *Garfield County News*, claiming that the BLM "choked over 20 heads of cows and calves to death!" She added, "I personally watched three heifers lay down and their calves walk off; they were so delirious for water." She further bemoaned that "the worst part is, before I can get her [Kate Cannon] stopped, I'm afraid all my cattle will be dead." Both Bulloch and Cannon were unrelentingly determined. Cannon to uphold the laws governing public lands and Bulloch to keep her cows on her allotment. Unlike Cliven Bundy, Mary Bulloch continued to pay her grazing fees and even paid trespassing fines, but her longhorns got seized in November 2001 all the same. The BLM was in the roundup business after all.

Cliven Bundy himself, summoned by Cox, drove up from his spread in Bunkerville, Nevada, to join a posse that gathered to grab Bulloch's cattle back from an auction house in Salina, Utah. The BLM had the cows housed at a livestock market and were planning to auction them off the following day. Mary accused the BLM of cattle-rustling and now she had backup. "I knew a confrontation was coming," said the Sevier County sheriff, Phil Barney. Aware that this group would look to him to sort it out, by evocation of posse comitatus, he chose to defuse the situation and let Mary reclaim the animals, in spite of the federal confiscation order. The sheriff said he wanted to avoid a "Waco situation."

Though it had been expensive and exhausting, the event rather thrilled Mary, and she described the affair to reporters as "pretty western." She recalled, with some satisfaction: "Police lined up on one side and us cowboys were on the other side." By his presence and statements there, Bundy started to distinguish himself in the press as a spokesperson both for ranchers and for the posse comitatus stance. He said that ranchers "have been beaten down by the BLM's heavy hand. I have a sheriff who understands my rights and who stands up for me and helps me protect them." Further, he accused, "The BLM simply bypassed the law and stole her cattle." But they hadn't. Mary's cows were in trespass.

While being transported back and forth between the monument and the auction yard, a few cows had panicked in the confines of the trailer, and some had to be put down as the result of injury. Mary butchered one of the dead cows, hung its head on the side of her truck, and parked the vehicle in front of the BLM office with a sign that read: "DIRECT RESULT OF KATE CANNON'S GRAZING MANAGEMENT PLAN." Pretty western indeed.

Mary died in 2009, and there are many who say that the BLM killed her. No, said Marti, it was the cancer, myeloma that had formed in her back and spread to her brain. As a child, Mary had been exposed to the same radiation that killed her father's sheep herds along the Arizona Strip during nuclear testing in Nevada. Still, there are people who blame the government for her death. She—like her beloved cowboy, the mythic one, not Boyd Rucker—has been mythologized, made a symbol of the Old West, whose freedom was manacled by regulation. There was even a song written in her honor by the folk singer Curly Musgrave, who crooned that while riding in Escalante, "with luck I'll see Mary a' chasing a wild cow, cross the arroyo, my, she's one fine hand. Somewhere in the shadows of Fifty Mile Mountain, alone she's a' trying to hold to the land."

Meanwhile, the broader battle raged on. Shawna Cox's People for the USA!, unlike the sagebrush rebels, had shifted their focus—away from agitating for the transfer of public lands to state control, and onto a better story. They emphasized the economic woes of the rural West, including the loss of jobs, pinning these hardships to overbearing environmental regulations. This change of tack presented better optics and created broader support. The public could feel sympathy for the poor rancher "trying to hold to the land" to feed and water her cows, or for the logger out of work due to protections of old-growth forest. People for the USA! blamed the conservationists and the liberal elite, accusing them of caring more about spotted owls than rural families and land more than jobs. Shawna Cox found her calling within the confrontation over lost liberties, constitutional entitlements, and the appropriate use of public land. She, like so many others, embraced the People for the USA! motto fully: "Fighting to Keep America Strong by Keeping Public Lands Open."

Rural folks indeed suffered and natural resource jobs did dwindle, and some of this could be pegged to enforcement of environmental regulations, but it mainly had to do with economic downturns, foreign competition, and advances in extractive mechanization in the 1980s and 1990s. Family farms and coal-mining jobs weren't disappearing due to new wilderness areas and the Endangered Species Act; those sectors of the economy were collapsing under the steady march of modernity, the bust end of boom cycles, and at the expense of further extraction.

I visited Shawna Cox, Mary's bosom pal and a longtime friend of the Bundy family. At her office inside a manufactured-home building just south of downtown Kanab, she made me feel welcome. Shawna's office is her classroom and it was clear that there had been many a student before me. Upon my arrival, she gave me a handbook on the evils of Agenda 21. And during my ninety minutes with her, she diagrammed, on a white dry-erase board behind her desk, her fervid ideas of freedoms and rights. She talked mostly about life, liberty, and property and the government's obligation to provide rights to "we the people"—that iconic and universal identity to which some westerners feel an exclusive right—emphasizing that the federal government can't own land, nor can they prevent people from making a living. During her firehose lecture, Shawna's husband brought us bowls of chopped fruit.

Shawna blames the Chinese for Clinton's interest in Escalante and thinks he sold it to them in order to get reelected. The conspiracies around conservation measures in southern Utah are as dense as kudzu in Georgia and just as impenetrable. She told me that the Grand Canyon Trust, the conservation group that wanted to compensate Mary Bulloch to retire her grazing allotment, was in fact a "company" making money from Chinese nationals intent on taking over public lands. When I asked her to show me substantiation, she changed the subject, going with a favorite old chestnut: rancher stewardship.

Environmentalists don't need to pursue further protections on public lands, she told me, parroting what so many public-land livestock producers attest. "The best environmentalists you have are going to be ranchers," she said, because they know the land best. She told me that an outsider who comes in and tells ranchers to "get your cows off" is not conservation-minded. "All the ranchers respect life and take care of them and it's a really good balance and it's beautiful just like someone taking care of a garden, you know?" Again, this goes back to Zion, a place made through cultivation. Mormon homeland is crafted by human hands, and, it seems, by cows.

Prophecy and End-Times

Prophecy is like a half-trained mule. It looks as though it might be useful, but the moment you trust in it, it kicks you in the head.

—George R. R. Martin, *A Dance with Dragons*

This story began with the divining of Joseph Smith and traveled west with Nephi Johnson. Now it's time to meet another of Cliven Bundy's inspirations, Willard Cleon Skousen. He was a wide-ranging man who, notwithstanding his resemblance to a bespectacled Elmer Fudd, had a two-thousand-page FBI file. Born into a Mormon community in Canada in 1913, he moved to California at age ten and later to Washington, DC, and then Utah. In 1967, he founded the Freeman Institute, which became the National Center for Constitutional Studies, an organization that merged Mormon and American patriot movement ideologies and today produces the little Constitutions popping out of breast pockets at Bundy rallies. He spent his career broadcasting the tenets of the John Birch Society, the right-wing organization established, in part, by Fred Koch, the father of the archconservative, public-land-privatization advocates Charles and David Koch. Skousen was a fervid anti-communist agitator and New World Order conspiracy theorist. In the 1970s and 1980s, he focused on government overreach, also feeding into Sagebrush Rebellion assumptions by spinning his own special "understanding" of the illegality of federal land ownership. A prolific writer and orator who played fast and loose with the truth, he engaged a passionate fan base as well as a large stable of critics.

Skousen called himself an international expert on the global communist threat, citing his eleven-year, largely clerical tenure at the FBI, and often bragged that he was one of three agents authorized to speak publicly on communism if J. Edgar Hoover was otherwise engaged. The FBI begged to differ; Skousen's claim was discredited by Hoover himself. "I welcome the opportunity to make it perfectly clear that former Special Agents of the FBI are not necessarily experts on communism," wrote the Bureau's director in 1962. "Some of them have sought to capitalize on their former employment with this Bureau for the purpose of establishing themselves as such authorities. I am firmly convinced there are too many self-styled experts on communism, without valid credentials and without any access whatsoever to classified, factual data, who are engaging in rumor mongering and hurling false and wholly unsubstantiated allegations against people whose views differ from their own. This makes more difficult the task of the professional investigator." Hoover added, "Mr. Skousen is no longer associated with the FBI and his opinions are strictly his own and do not represent this Bureau in any way."

Skousen's resumé was not the only place to find his penchant for fabrication; he had a lifelong pattern of misrepresentations and falsehoods. These he brought both into the workplace, such as his stint teaching at Brigham Young University, and into the seminars that he held all over the country, teaching participants his own version of history, culture, and politics. His propaganda fed on Cold War dread, accusing the Russians of stealing US plans to produce their designs for Sputnik and claiming that FDR's advisor Harry Hopkins gave secrets to the Soviets along with half of America's supply of enriched uranium. His conspiracies were often tangled with his racism. Slavery had been a happy condition for African Americans, he offered in his book *The Making of America*, and quoted historian Fred Albert Shannon, who wrote that slaves "were usually a cheerful lot, though the presence of a number of the more vicious type sometimes made it necessary for them all to go in chains." He asserted that the founding fathers never envisioned separation of church and state, but that rather, in their conception of the Constitution, they dreamed that each state would be sovereign and embrace its own version of theocracy.

Skousen's Mormonism influenced both his politics and his Weltanschauung. In *Prophecy and Modern Times*, a book not as popular as his others, such as *The Naked Communist* or *The 5000 Year Leap*, he presents the Book of Mormon as an actual history of America, and the Bible as a literal account of Palestine and Israel. Everything in these sacred texts either happened or will happen, he writes, including the predictions of Joseph Smith and those of other church prophets who repeated and reaffirmed Joseph's revelations. The book focuses on the importance of America within a global context, God's most sacred land on earth, and the singular role of Mormon people in America's redemption. The Mormon sense of morality, when not wavering, Skousen maintains, is impeccable. As the world's modern prophet, Joseph Smith gave his people the most up-to-date information on God's will. In addition to encouraging Mormons to follow the commandments, to act charitably (within reason) and to love their neighbor (also within reason), God, as detailed in Skousen's work, promised the latter days, an event that could be brought about through defending the Constitution against its multitudinous enemies.

Skousen, like Joseph Smith and many other Mormon prophets, held that God had always been a big fan of America's founding document. Church presidents, generation after generation, extolled the importance of the Constitution, further reiterating Smith's position that this American civil document is actually part of the Latter-day Saints' sacred canon. Eleven years after Smith's murder (or martyrdom, depending on how you look at it), Brigham Young roared, echoing the famous White Horse Prophecy, "When the Constitution of the United States hangs, as it were, upon a single thread, they will have to call for the 'Mormon' Elders to save it from utter destruction; and they will step forth and do it." Young also mused, "Is the form of the Government ruined? Has its form become evil? No; but the administrators of the Government are evil. As we have said many times, it is the best form of human government man ever lived under; but it has as corrupt a set to administer it as God ever permitted to disgrace his footstool." The government is good. It's the federal agents who are corrupt and Mormon people need to set things right.

Two-and-a-half decades later, in 1879, the church's third president, John Taylor, foretold, "The day is not far distant when this nation will be shaken from center to circumference." He added, "The people shall have torn to shreds the Constitution of the United States," and it will be up to the Latter-day Saints to right this wrong. Apostle Melvin Ballard declared, during an annual church leadership conference in 1933, "I believe that it is the destiny of the Latter-day Saints to support the Constitution of the United States." And he continued, echoing generations of prophets, that it was incumbent upon the Mormon people to uphold the Constitution, "maintain it and defend it and support it by their lives and by their vote. Let us not disappoint God nor his prophet. Our place is fixed."

Ezra Taft Benson, the thirteenth president of the Mormon Church, didn't just warn of the approaching battle over the Constitution, he announced that "Satan is anxious to neutralize the inspired counsel of the Prophet and hence keep the priesthood off-balance, ineffective and inert in the fight for freedom." Benson said that Satan was ever ready to convince the unobservant that there was "no need to get involved in the fight for freedom—all you need to do is live the gospel." But no, clean living wasn't enough—a truly observant Mormon embodied the militant theology redolent of the early church and might well take a page from Danite history. A Latter-day Saint fought for the Constitution in what was a clash between good and evil. Both Benson and Skousen believed this battle could be launched by a devout and valiant effort informed by prophecy and a zeal for freedom, securing the sacred Constitution and perhaps ushering in the Second Coming as foretold in the White Horse Prophecy.

The vision of the inevitable apocalypse may have amplified Skousen's focus on law enforcement and its role in controlling a mayhem bound to occur. In his 1966 book, *The Communist Attack on US Police*, he warns of weak police forces both diminished by communists inciting race riots and compromised by an increasing influx of federal funding that made departments dependent upon and acquiescent to the government. These concerns are similar to the fears that have spawned the uptick in county sheriffs embracing posse comitatus, like former Sheriff Richard Mack, a man hugely influenced by Skousen.

Skousen himself served as Salt Lake City's chief of police before Mayor J. Bracken Lee fired him, after he caught the mayor gambling in 1960. The sacking caused Skousen's supporters to retaliate by burning a cross on the mayor's lawn, with a placard that read: LEE, YOU ARE A FOOL. The mayor, who was also an archconservative, had come to regard Skousen as heavy-handed, two-faced, and a spendthrift. "The man is also a master of half-truths," Lee wrote in a letter. "In at least three instances I have proved him to be a liar before the City Commissioners and the newspaper reporters. To me, he is a very dangerous man because he preaches one thing, practices another, does not tell the truth, and cannot be relied upon. He also was one of the greatest spenders of public funds of anyone who ever served in any capacity in Salt Lake City government."

After Skousen died, his ideas and writings were largely ignored. That is until Glenn Beck, the leaky-eyed, right-wing former Fox News commentator, became an enraptured devotee of Skousen's religion, political points of view, and half-baked ideas and then gave them new life. In the book *Common Nonsense*, journalist Alexander Zaitchik writes, "The biggest factor in the development of Beck's conspiratorial world-view was his midlife Mormon conversion." Zaitchik continues, "After joining the church in 1999, Beck aligned himself with the religion's ultraconservative strain, in which paranoia thrives." This strain was nourished by Cleon Skousen, whose fearmongering infuses the fringe of the church today. Beck can take credit for Skousen's influence on the Tea Party and the militia movement. Thanks to Beck encouraging his followers to embrace Skousen's publications, Skousen became an Amazon bestselling author in 2009, though by then he'd been dead for three years.

"My uncle was the optimist," said Cleon's nephew Joel Skousen when I visited him in Spring City, Utah. He shares a modest home with his son Andrew, a daughter-in-law, and four cherubic grandchildren in one of the most eerily idyllic communities in Mormondom. It's perfect. The whole town is on the National Register of Historic Places. The Confectionary and Firehouse. Sandstrom's Dance and Pool Hall. The Relief Society Granary. The Chester School and Meeting House. White picket fences hem manicured lawns. Town dogs drink from a spring where the Mormon settlers once baptized new converts and children. We like it here, Andrew told me, standing alongside his tow-headed kids as they crowded in the entryway sweetly gawping at me, a stranger in their midst. Spring City is full of like-minded people, he said. They're folks like us, survivalists. He added, "Some artists have started moving to town, too." I picture a very awkward potluck.

Joel's own underground bunker is off-site. As are those of his six children, each of whom has his or her own. I forgot to ask if his wife, who resides in St. George for health reasons, has her own fallout shelter too. His daughter-in-law prepared a late dinner, vegetable soup, under the benevolent gaze of a very European-looking Jesus in a framed portrait on the wall, while Joel and I moved into his office and began our talk. Joel is a fit man with a military-style haircut, born the same year as Cliven Bundy, though he seems much younger. His father died at forty-six, after which his widowed mother and her ten children moved to Provo to be near Uncle Cleon. Joel remembered driving into town and stopping to ask for directions. When locals heard they were related to the elder Skousen, he said, they ended up getting a police escort. "Everyone loved him," Joel noted fondly. Then quickly added, "—but the liberals." He reminisced about the dinners Cleon presided over—his uncle's stories, prayers, and help in shaping a family that Joel's father's demise had left without strong male leadership.

Then our conversation turned to territory that left me feeling a bit at sea, shifting without much introduction to "homosexuality in Yale's Skull and Bones Society," the New World Order, pseudo-Christians, and "kowtowing to Republicans." We got on the topic of "deep state," the idea that the government is compromised by disloyal operatives who have infiltrated each branch and agency. "Even Cleon didn't understand the dark side of the government," Joel said. "It took me until the year before he died to convince him. All his books were optimistic." But, Joel added grimly, "I'm a realist."

Cleon and his nephew have built professions on the proliferation of evil in the world. Cleon pointed to communism as its source, famously in the book *The Naked Communist*, but Joel identifies many other wicked forces in the world, the most threatening of which are certain international cabals. Globalism, he told me, is the devil's plaything, and if I didn't believe so, he had "scientific evidence." Globalists and their international networks, families, and entities have controlled the power and money for over a hundred years, he said. "In the mafia, a family can maintain control for one, maybe two generations," then the power structure shifts. That's how things work. One mafia network might spend thirty or forty years in charge, then power is usurped by another family. But, according to Joel, globalists can maintain power for several generations because the devil himself is pulling the strings. "God allows Satan to control power for testing purposes." It's all part of the Lord's plan—to let bad guys control governments with deep-state networks in order for the righteous to recognize them, and not directly confront them but rather wait them out. Which, in Joel's case, means getting ready for a coming nuclear war.

Like Uncle Cleon, who was thirty-three when his nephew was born, Joel spent some very formative years in Washington, DC. He worked as a political consultant and an editor at the *Conservative Digest*, following six years in the Marine Corps as a pilot during the Vietnam War. Although he grew up with his uncle, it was only after reading *The Naked Communist* that Joel became aware of the dangers that lurked across the globe and the threat to America and our society. "They crucified McCarthy," he told me, and "painted him as an extremist." Unlike his uncle, Joel doesn't believe that a battle against the government can happen right now through direct defiance. Cleon felt that patriots could fight against international evils using the Constitution as their bludgeon. Joel thinks this is naïve.

Although Joel Skousen and Cliven Bundy are on friendly terms, the old rancher is more in Cleon's camp than in Joel's. Just months before Ammon and Ryan Bundy organized their takeover of Malheur, Cliven explained to me why the Constitution is so important to him and why he so depends on its influence in his fight. "As a Mormon we believe in inspiration," he said, and "the Constitution was inspired." Then, in a very typical Bundy rhetorical device, such as he and his sons often adopt, he took on the role of a teacher schooling a pupil, and he asked me what this might mean. "If it's inspired, who is the author? Who is the author of the Bible?" He prompted me by asking, "Don't we believe that Jesus Christ is basically the author of most of the things that are written in the Bible? Well, if the Constitution is inspired, who is the author? Wouldn't that author be Jesus Christ again?"

Although Cleon Skousen has since left this world, his organization, the National Center for Constitutional Studies (NCCS), continues to be active as the clearinghouse for Skousen's annotated pocket Constitutions. The current president of the organization is Earl Taylor, an elderly Mormon gentleman, like Skousen, Bundy, and Benson, who likewise anticipates a fight in saving the Constitution. "I fear that the United States is going to have to go through the wringer," Taylor told a *Washington Post* reporter in 2010. "It's gonna be rough. When the time comes, when the people who are in power for the power and the glory, and there is no more power and glory left, they'll probably be looking around asking, 'Can anybody help?' And you'll say, 'Yeah, I've got some ideas. Come on over and eat a little something.' Because there probably won't be much food anyway, but if you're wise, you'll have some. We're gonna win this thing. I've read the last chapter, like you have, and in the end, we're gonna win this thing." He added, "Isn't that great?" Taylor, Skousen, the Bundys, and their many followers believe they need to prepare for a knockdown, a drag-out battle, as depicted in Revelation, the final book of the Bible. And according to Revelation, this "last chapter" that Taylor referred to, a reckoning for "dogs, and sorcerers, and whoremongers, and murderers, and idolaters, and whosoever loveth and maketh a lie" is in store. I assume this also includes communists, federal agents, and conservationists.

Meeting Skousen in 1978, Earl Taylor had found his inspirational man who embraced the supposed religiosity of the US Constitution and understood that in its preservation lay the key to the salvation of America, the world, and humanity. Taylor became a libertarian darling in the late 2000s with the emergence of the Tea Party, touring the country, giving eight-hour seminars, lessons created by Skousen. Taylor and the NCCS impart Skousen's own constitutional interpretations, sharing "historical" anecdotes about the founding fathers, such as how Thomas Jefferson was loath to free his own slaves because they were so well cared for that "they just didn't want to leave." Taylor's Skousen-inspired lessons have attracted not just Tea Party audiences but also militia fans, including the Three Percenters, a militia group similarly committed to protecting the Constitution. So with Taylor, Cleon Skousen, and the NCCS, a strain of radical libertarianism, apocalyptic prophecy, and racist revisionist histories has flowed into the militia movement, reinforcing in those people their own embrace of white supremacy and end-times.

Of course, this is far from the first time that religious fanaticism has held hands with heavily armed militants, but with Taylor's organization, we see an esoteric Mormon worldview seeping into larger militant circles. When Taylor made his statements suggesting an imminent Revelation-type event that will harken a change in government and the nation, when our country "goes through the wringer," he was challenging his followers' pluck, their ability and vigilance, as have generations of Mormon prophets. And like his mentor Cleon Skousen, Taylor is sanguine about the outcome.

Like Joel, his uncle, and some other members of the Mormon Church, many militia members are also motivated by apocalyptic narratives. According to Morris Dees, the founder of the Southern Poverty Law Center, an organization that tracks hate crimes, some neo-Nazis and militia groups practice a "postmillennial religion that believes Jesus Christ will return once God's Law is established on earth, following the Battle of Armageddon. Identity adherents are preparing for that battle. They are advocating a well-stocked arsenal and survival gear at the ready." Believing in the inevitability of the world's end, lots of people have grown reckless and dangerous. After all, what do they have to lose in their unbending and erratic convictions?

Grazing rules, road closures, resource development regulations, wilderness studies, and Endangered Species Act restrictions have been piled onto lands that Skousen and others refuse to believe are even subject to federal oversight. Conservation measures have contributed to feelings of helplessness, fear, and oppression—spurring the idea that an overreaching government is malevolently focused on their rural culture and their "independent cowboy" lifestyle. According to a 1999 study published in *Political Psychology*, "Some ranchers and loggers of the American West believe that the government threatens their way of life, and they think there is a conspiracy to deprive them of their lands, livelihood, and rights." They have imagined an Orwellian order, where the government is intentionally disrupting their existence through public land management. When conspiracy is rife, an unstable social order appears, wherein "truth" becomes just an image in a funhouse mirror. And such "truth" becomes perpetuated among the paranoid and mistrustful. Amplified by the internet, social networks of conspiratorial theorists built unified communities to share their own realities and delusions of grandeur. It's within this dangerously distorted, petulantly subjective, endlessly reechoing environment that the writings of Cleon Skousen, the conspiracy theories held firmly by his nephew Joel, the rage over land grabs, and the idea of being a Latter-day Saint in the latter days provide a febrile context to the lives and actions of the Bundys.

Before he died, Cleon Skousen was on the brink of excommunication by the Mormon Church for his agitating. In 1979, President Spencer W. Kimball sent a carefully worded letter rebuking Skousen's activism. Addressed to "All Stake Presidents, Bishops, and Branch Presidents in the United States," it reads:

It has come to our attention that in some areas announcements have been made in Church meetings of lectures to be given by those connected with the Freemen Institute. This is to inform you that no announcements should be made in Church meetings of these, or other similar, lectures or events that are not under the sponsorship of the Church. This instruction is not intended to express any disapproval of the right of the Freemen Institute and its lecturers to conduct such meetings or of the contents of the lectures. The only purpose is to make certain that neither Church facilities nor Church meetings are used to advertise such events and to avoid any implication that the Church endorses what is said during such lectures.

Skousen remained well-regarded by the church's right-wingers in their fight over federal bogeymen, public land ownership, state sovereignty, and the Constitution. Paul Skousen, Cleon's son, mentioned the close relations his father had with church presidents like Ezra Taft Benson, David O. McKay, Thomas S. Monson, "and others," mentioning in a letter defending his father against criticism that he maintained "close, warm and cordial" relations with church leaders.

Joel continues in his battle and believes that, as things stand, warfare against government corruption is impossible until we experience a major disruption. Cleon believed that the federal government could be brought to heel with awareness, vigilance, and good Mormon devotion, but Joel thinks evil forces are just too pervasive. Republicans, Democrats, and globalists are involved in such massive corruption, he told me, that even our current president, Donald J. Trump, who has the best of intentions to fight all the layers of deep state, is out of his league, he believes. "A secret combination of powers is running the government," and the world. They concoct spectacles to throw Americans off their trail—diversions like the Enron scandal,

9/11, and the 2017 Las Vegas massacre (the mass shooting that left fifty-eight people dead). All of these are fabricated, he said.

It's going to take a global thermonuclear war to bring about an opportunity to weed out all of the satanic cells in the global network, according to Joel Skousen—a war that he thinks is about ten years away. "If you are going to fight the deep state, you're going to have to fight the war." War on a global scale that annihilates current institutional and power structures. Over the years, Joel has been involved in the design of hundreds of secure homes (average installation runs about $100K) to withstand the day when a hostile country will launch nukes at the USA. Due to compromised and complicit politicians and agents and an intentional weakening of our defenses, the United States won't retaliate, he said, and our military bases will be destroyed. Then, in post-war desperation, America will appeal to an outside, militarized western government, "not the UN, but something new," he said, trailing off. The EU? Maybe. "Brexit is a fraud," he added. The trick, he said, is surviving the war. Then the real fight will begin. This is what Cleon did not understand—you can't take on the devil until half the world lies in ruins.

The Bundys, he said, they too are optimists. They think they can challenge the government, save the Constitution, and emerge victorious. But they can't win, according to Joel. The government is too powerful, for now at least. In the meantime, armed challenges are a waste of time. When I asked him about Malheur, Joel wasn't keen on the whole Oregon takeover. He also expressed sadness over the death of Robert LaVoy Finicum, the man shot and killed at the roadblock during the occupation.

A message had hung in Finicum's home written on a note card that included a few patched-together statements from prophet Ezra Taft Benson, Cleon's good friend. It read, in part, "The fight for freedom is God's fight. So when a man stands for freedom he stands with God. And were he to stand alone, he would still stand with God. A man will be eternally rewarded for his stand for freedom." Benson was a prophet who both rebuked and provoked. He, Finicum, and Bundy believe that in fighting government forces, they're fighting for God.

"LaVoy was a great man," said Joel, and he thinks that Finicum's death shifted the optics around the occupation. After all of the initial bad publicity, that shooting put the Bundys back on what Joel called "high ground." It gave their cause a martyr and brought them more public support. But in Joel's estimation, this position isn't where any sensible person should be right now. If you want to survive end-times, find cover. High ground is for optimists, but realists will be in their bunkers.

Range War

*Praise the Lord, stockpile the ammunition, & keep Cliven
Bundy free.*

—James Conner's Flathead Memo (satire),
April 24, 2014

Keith Allen Nay had been dead for four years by the time
Cliven Bundy went up to Salina, Utah, to help spring
Mary Bulloch's longhorns. But this neighbor of Bundy's
left behind a talisman for Cliven's range war, known as *The Nay
Book*, a cache of quotes and scripture that felt like validation for
the family's crusade and worked to gird their sense of righteousness. The introduction is written by Cliven, who enthuses, "Dear
friends, I'm excited about sharing this book with you." He tells
the reader that Nay had worked to establish a rationale, as put
forth by the founding fathers, the Constitution, and Mormon
prophets, that defended "my rights and my ranch against the
tyrannical government's usurpation." Pages of *The Nay Book*,
which have been copied and shared among Bundy's supporters, are chock full of constitutional interpretations woven with
prophecies from Mormon leaders such as David O. McKay and
Ezra Taft Benson. McKay is quoted as saying, "Next to being
one in worshipping God there is nothing in this world upon
which the Church should be more united than in upholding and
defending the Constitution of the United States."

The Bundy war began in 1989, when the desert tortoise was listed under the Endangered Species Act (ESA). After that listing, the BLM began implementing a tortoise recovery plan on public lands, including Gold Butte, a section of the Mojave Desert that stretches through Bundy's former allotment. Gold Butte abuts the Lake Mead National Recreation Area, where the Hoover Dam blocks the Colorado River. The BLM informed Bundy that the new restrictions affected his grazing leases—most notably, limiting the cattle he could run in impacted areas. They also offered to buy him out.

A program had been established in Clark County, home of the Bundy family and Las Vegas, which would serve as a compensatory system whereby developers were given the go-ahead to build in tortoise habitat if they contributed to a fund used to remunerate ranchers who agreed to retire their permits. But Bundy didn't want the money. He wanted a right to graze. He wanted his lifestyle. Like Mary Bulloch, he's a cowboy. This was his land, and his claim upon it went back to Nephi Johnson, buried just up the road. Nephi's spiritual son, Johnny Jensen, married Cliven's grandmother, Abigail. Their daughter was Cliven's mother, Margaret Bodel Jensen Bundy, who raised Cliven and his siblings at the ranch where he and Carol now live. In her obituary, Abigail was lovingly commemorated by her family: "She taught them the value of hard work, keeping them busy gardening, irrigating, sheep herding, working cows, and growing Bundy Melons. Anyone who came to visit was well fed and loved. When you are a rancher, a farmer and an irrigator, plus a mother of 7—the words 'shit,' 'damn,' and 'hell' are NOT swear words!" Was she slightly abashed by the salty eulogy? In the photo accompanying her death notice, she's smiling broadly—and literally clutching her pearls.

Kelton Hafen, living in nearby Clover Valley, Nevada, took the federal compensation package and gave up his grazing permits, though he continued to raise cattle on his own spread.

Unlike his infamous neighbor Cliven Bundy, Hafen obeys the law, though he dislikes federal regulations. Although Hafen supported the Bundys in their fight, he believes the militia supporters undermined Bundy's credibility.

The whole tortoise issue is absurd, Hafen told me and maintains that there is no compelling evidence to implicate ranching in the tortoise population decline. Lyman, Kelton's son, also believes the tortoise issue is a sham, arguing that the reptiles disappeared from their habitat because Mormon families driving back and forth from Las Vegas grabbed them for children's pets. Some parent would see one lumbering down the asphalt, crawling slowly along under the weight of its heavy shell, and pull over, grab it, and drive the critter home. Over time, such "pets" escaped or were let go. The tortoises and their descendants can now be found farther north, near St. George, says Lyman, and blaming cows for their dwindling numbers in southern Nevada and southern Utah is environmentalist propaganda. But cows erode tortoise habitat, trample burrows, and compete for forage, and so, under NEPA and the ESA, no cows are legally allowed in the million-acre recovery area.

Lyman Hafen, a warm and generous man in his sixties, wrote in one of his books, *Roping the Wind*, "The environmental movement was trying to dull the luster of the cowboy myth by targeting public land ranchers as the enemies of the environment." Lyman straddles the worlds of cowboys and conservation, multi-generational Mormon ranchers and slack-jawed tourists. In addition to helping his dad on their ranch in Clover Valley, he is the executive director of the Zion Natural History Association, in Zion National Park, which he founded in 2007. Although he is deeply connected to the park, he is quick to point out that he is not a federal employee—his work is privately funded. This is a big point of pride. Lyman is no government guy.

Compensation for retiring grazing allotments, like that received by Kelton Hafen, came from a deal Clark County made with the US Fish and Wildlife Service in the early 1990s. Las Vegas was one of the country's fastest-growing municipalities, so developers agreed to pay $250 to $500 per acre into this mitigation fund, as they expanded into fragile tortoise habitat surrounding the metropolitan area. Some of this money was used to compensate public land leaseholders for retiring their allotments in order to avoid ESA violations, and some went toward tortoise recovery. The result was more development in urban Clark County, and bitter public land livestock producers. Even those who took the money, like Kelton Hafen, felt resentful.

Reuters wrote, "When the US government declared the Mojave desert tortoise an endangered species in 1989, it effectively marked the cattle ranchers of Nevada's Clark County for extinction." When the BLM ordered cows off the range, Bundy, his cousin Kelly Jensen, and Keith Nay took the feds to court and won, twice. But the BLM and Clark County were intent on moving cows out of the area. In the end, most leaseholders accepted the buyout, and nearly eight thousand cows, belonging to around fifty ranching families, were eliminated from public lands in the Mojave Desert. Cliven Bundy just ignored the federal protection efforts and continued to graze his herd. To date, he is the only rancher with cows on public lands in the one-million-acre desert tortoise recovery area. And he still owes over one million dollars in grazing fees and fines.

In the 1990s, Cliven started to make himself into a spokesperson. In Mary Bulloch's case, he helped grab up her longhorns before they were auctioned off. He became the Clark County director of the Nevada Livestock Association, showing up at rallies, denouncing the heavy hand of the BLM, and raging that the agency was contemptuous of ranchers' rights. He claimed that those rights were God-given and unalienable, and that the feds were in "direct conflict with the Constitution." He believed in the prophecies in *The Nay Book* and the power of posse comitatus—the idea that the county sheriff was the highest-ranking authority, superseding the power of the BLM and the FBI. And though Bundy's position is not shared by the Mormon Church, he did have support among its ranks. The *Garfield County News* reported in 2001 that of the $250,000 in legal fees Bundy paid in his fight against the federal government, "a big chunk was coming from the LDS church."

Other Nevada ranchers, including Cliff Gardner and Wayne Hage, were also embattled over control of public lands. Like Bundy, they claimed that their actions were mandated by their "sovereign state," that the government did not actually own public lands in the state of Nevada, and that therefore federal officials were not entitled to manage them. Gardner, a member of the Nevada Committee for Full Statehood (a group that likewise denied federal ownership or control over Nevada's public lands), lost his Forest Service permit in 1994 after allowing his cows to graze in an area that was recovering from fire damage. He simply refused to believe the scientific studies that indicated lands in recovery were fragile, or that certain species are especially vulnerable in fire-impacted areas.

As the Clark County director of the Nevada Livestock Association, Bundy echoed Gardner's position, disparaging research on the habitat needs of imperiled species. "Now they are claiming more of their 'lynx and spotted owl land grab science' that 25 to 30 cows, all a man has left, are somehow going to cause harm to the tortoises and willow flycatcher," he said in 2002 in the *Garfield County News*. "We don't believe it and we are not going to allow further impoundment of cattle. It's rustling pure and simple under the color of law. They'll probably kill more tortoises and willow flycatchers running over them with souped-up motorcycles and hired henchmen trying to run down some poor cow and her calf."

After his father's death in 2006, Wayne Hage Jr. continued the family tradition of running cows without permits on BLM and Forest Service lands in Nevada. In 2013, in what looked like a victory for public land ranching after years of fighting, US District Judge Robert Clive Jones, a member of the Church of Latter-day Saints, ruled that Hage could continue public lands grazing, permit or not, because of his existing water rights. When the decision was overturned three years later, and the cattle were considered to be trespassing on federal property, Wayne Jr., a wiry redhead, was incensed. "It looks to me that the Ninth Circuit just swelled the ranks of the militia," he railed. Wayne Jr. appealed to the US Supreme Court to overturn the Ninth Circuit decision, but in June 2019, the highest court in the land refused to take his family's case.

In 2013, the United States ordered Cliven Bundy—for the third time—to remove his rogue cows from the Southern Nevada Grazing District. In addition to the ecological damage his herd presented to habitat and fragile desert crusts, federal agents now declared the animals to be a public safety issue. According to court documents, the cows were nuisances, causing car accidents and even charging federal workers and tourists. They were also a danger to the rich cultural heritage of Gold Butte and its archaeological sites and petroglyphs.

In 1998, the government had won its first case against Bundy, with a penalty of two-hundred-dollars-a-day trespass fees for each offending cow. When neither Bundy nor his herds budged, the fines added up quickly, soaring into the seven figures. Bundy appealed the court's decision and lost, but the cows stayed put. His growing herd was spreading into areas vacated by neighbors who had agreed to the government's buyout. Every time the BLM strategized cattle removal, they were met with threats of violence. And so they delayed. Throughout the 1990s and 2000s, things became very tense in Nevada for federal workers. Two pipe bombs were found, one in a BLM office and another in a Forest Service building. The escalating tensions allowed Bundy, Hage, and Gardner to further defy federal laws, and to graze cattle with impunity.

Finally, on June 9, 2013, US District Judge Lloyd D. George, a Latter-day Saint appointed by Ronald Reagan, ruled, "Bundy shall remove his livestock from the New Trespass Lands within 45 days of the date hereof, and that the United States is entitled to seize and remove to impound any of Bundy's cattle that remain in trespass after 45 days of the date hereof: United States is entitled to seize and remove to impound any of Bundy's cattle for any future trespasses, provided the United States has provided notice to Bundy under the governing regulations of the United States Department of the Interior."

In early 2014, the BLM sent a letter notifying Cliven Bundy that his "trespass cattle" would be impounded. On March 15, it notified Bundy of plans to remove his cows and close off roughly six hundred thousand acres of remote public land. Clark County Sheriff Doug Gillespie earlier refused to help the BLM because he saw their strategy as being reckless and fraught. But he didn't show up to help Cliven Bundy, either. Federal agents went to work securing the ninety square miles where Bundy's cattle roamed, stretching into parts of Mormon Mesa, Bunkerville Flats, and Gold Butte, after establishing patrols to ensure the safety of officials and contract cowboys involved in the controversial roundup. The Bundys had a network of militia contacts, and these "patriots," as they called themselves, soon rallied their own networks. The idea of an actual confrontation with the federal government generated widespread excitement among insurgents who had long dreamed of just such a battle—along the lines of Ruby Ridge or Waco—and Bunkerville attracted anti-government zealots of all stripes.

The drama unfolded slowly, at least among the demonstrators. The cattle roundup started on April 5. Federal agents, some with sidearms, began patrolling the area. They were aggressive, following strangers' cars and parking their own large unmarked SUVs in the center of backcountry roads. Officers designated areas for protest behind orange plastic fencing, like pens to sequester protesters. The mood remained temperate for a while, with local supporters, mainly friends and family, trickling in; but on April 6, Dave Bundy, another of Cliven's sons, was arrested while taking pictures and, in BLM parlance, "refusing to disperse." Law enforcement officers tried to clear a group of protesters from the highway, but Dave stood his ground. It won him a night in detention, complete with a tuna sandwich in a paper sack.

Before Dave's release, Cliven had sounded the call on social media, proclaiming his son a political prisoner. More demonstrators arrived and the tenor changed dramatically. Online video clips over the next few days document an intransigent mob mentality, with people screaming, waving phone cameras, and challenging law enforcement. Agents held back dogs that strained on their leashes, menacing protesters. When Ammon Bundy kicked a barking dog repeatedly, he got tased. There was a palpable animosity as deep anti-government rage moved toward an outlet in a protest concerning cows. "The Bureau of Land Management and National Park Service support the public's right to express opinions peacefully and lawfully," BLM spokesperson Kirsten Cannon told one reporter. "However, if an individual threatens, intimidates, or assaults another individual or impedes the impoundment, they may be arrested in accordance with local, state, or federal laws."

On April 8, a BLM officer grabbed Cliven's fifty-seven-year-old sister, Margaret Houston, and threw her to the ground as she tried to stop a government vehicle. The video went viral. Although the BLM maintained that the officer was simply trying to get Houston out of the path of a moving truck, hundreds of people were now in Bunkerville or en route. Bringing with them indignation. And with this indignation, some brought AR-15s.

RVs clogged local routes and piled up onto interstate shoulders. National and even international media were covering the events. Amid flags, pickups, cowboys on horseback, and sagebrush along the roadsides, a sign near the Bundy compound beckoned: "MILITIA SIGHN IN." In the days leading up to the standoff, the Bundys and members of various supporting groups—the Three Percenters, the Oath Keepers, the Praetorian Guard, the White Mountain Militia, the Constitutional Sheriffs, the Peace Officers Association, and others—urged people to join the increasingly tense situation in Nevada. This included Ryan Payne, a former army ranger living in Montana who headed a militia group called Operation Mutual Aid, and who assumed a tactical role in the standoff. He would later go to Oregon with Ammon and Ryan Bundy.

Stewart Rhodes, the founder of the Oath Keepers militia, sent a message entreating his followers: "We need Oath Keepers to also show up and stand vigil and support this family and the patriot legislators and sheriffs who are taking the lead in defending them. This is critical. The goal is to stand vigil to prevent another Waco or Ruby Ridge. . . ." Rhodes continued, "We need numbers—boots on the ground. The more the better." He advised his followers to bring "no open-carry rifles" and not to wear military camo. "This is a protest by rural Americans," he emphasized, so "dress accordingly." Implicitly, he meant: this is a photo op for the cause, not (necessarily) a battle. Firearms must stay out of sight, but Rhodes implored his followers to "BRING CAMERAS." The more video footage, the better.

The no-open-carry/no-camo advice didn't sit well with some militia members. One Oath Keeper, calling himself WarriorClass III, an online pseudonym, wrote in the comment section after Rhodes's post, "Seems very strange that Oath Keepers doesn't want rifles after saying they were 'going operational' and all. Can you imagine if the colonists at Lexington met on the green without their rifles? What's the point?" Despite Rhodes's admonishment, guns were very much on display during the Battle of Bunkerville.

The standoff took place below an overpass of Interstate 15 where Carol and Cliven, their children, and dozens of grandchildren prayed to God for protection. Ryan Payne was in charge of the militia sharpshooters, whom he placed in strategic positions. "We locked them [the feds] down. We had counter-sniper positions on their sniper positions. We had at least one guy—sometimes two guys—per BLM agent in there. So, it was a complete tactical superiority." This he told Ted McDermott, reporting for the now-defunct *Missoula Independent*. "If they made one wrong move, every single BLM agent in that camp would've died." While the snipers lay flat, other insurgents marched toward the police, screaming obscenities, waving golden Gadsden flags emblazoned with coiled rattlesnakes and the words "Don't Tread on Me."

Although it's remembered as the Battle of Bunkerville, there was no battle. After a tense two-hour standoff, the BLM called a halt to the roundup, and police and government agents left. Not one single shot was fired. But all that fury, indignation, and adrenaline had sent some participants into reveries of anni-hilation. Some seemed to yearn for it. Retired Arizona Sheriff Richard Mack, an Oath Keeper and the founder of another mili-tia group, the Constitutional Sheriffs and Peace Officers Associ-ation, marched with the insurgents and later told Fox News, "We were actually strategizing to put all the women up at the front. If they are going to start shooting, it's going to be women that are going to be televised all across the world getting shot by these rogue federal officers." Still later, in an interview with right-wing journalist Ben Swann, Mack said, "I would have put my own wife or daughters there [Bunkerville], and I would have been screaming bloody murder to watch them die." He continued, "I would've gone next, I would have been the next one to be killed. I'm not afraid to die here. I'm willing to die here."

Mack, sixty-seven years old, with a full head of jet-black hair, believes that sheriffs, who are elected, not appointed, should not enforce laws they view as unconstitutional. He has said that while "state police and highway patrol get their orders from the governor," as a sheriff, "I get my orders from the citizens in this county." He's a devout Mormon, a former Eagle Scout, and an unsuccessful two-time Republican congressional candidate who reveres Cleon Skousen. After hearing Skousen speak in 1984 at Brigham Young University, Mack said he didn't know about the other attendees, but of himself, "this one was converted." Like Skousen and Bundy, he has taken the Saints' old anti-government animus, which long ago twined itself into the fabric of his faith, and projected it into modern protest.

Much of this goes back to Skousen and the radical prophecies he espoused. It was Skousen, after all, who brought forward into the late twentieth-century the idea that the federal government cannot own public lands. Not national parks. Not national forests. Not wilderness areas. Skousen also believed that the BLM should be abolished. For Mack and Bundy, by way of Skousen, the defense of Mormon homeland—American Zion—is a holy war over public lands, state sovereignty, and a distorted understanding of the Constitution. Whether the militia knew it on April 12, 2014, or not, whether Ryan Payne knew it or not, they were characters in a radical religious scenario, one that might have gotten a lot of people killed. As soldiers in the Battle of Bunkerville, willing to die and take many others with them, these belligerents were committing their lives, not just to the ideals of Patrick Henry or of James Madison, but to the dreams of Joseph Smith.

The Bird Refuge

I'm going to give all the credit and my ability to my Heavenly Father and your prayers that have come to me and my family. I have, without a doubt, felt His presence in my decisions.

—Cliven Bundy

After the agents retreated, Cliven Bundy, his voice hoarse from shouting, demanded the Clark County sheriff hand over the BLM officers' weapons. "We want those arms delivered right here under these flags in one hour." The presumption of that order, even now, is astonishing. After twenty-one years of legal violations, the government had finally tried to hold Cliven accountable for his illegal use of public land. Yet he was insolent enough that, when the BLM backed down, he actually directed law enforcement to bring him a pile of federal weapons. Cliven believed in his own story, one validated by his success and his conviction that his victory was God's victory. Three months after the event, he asked a reporter at *The Spectrum*, the St. George, Utah, newspaper, "If the standoff with the Bundys was wrong, would the Lord have been with us?" The Battle of Bunkerville is what early Dixie settlers might have called a real faith-promoting experience.

Cliven wanted Sheriff Gillespie to embrace the power of posse comitatus and disarm the tyrants. If they were allowed to keep their weapons, he prophesized, "We the people will have to face these arms in a civil war." He was at the apex of his powers—

he was certain of his own "truth," his favor with the Lord, and he commanded his own army. Perhaps he had been recalling the King Follett sermon, one of Joseph Smith's last, in which Smith encouraged men to think of themselves as gods. Watching the video of Bundy's demands after the standoff, I find myself wondering if, at that moment, he imagined himself immortal.

Cliven Bundy, like other visionaries such as Joseph Smith and Brigham Young, believes he is acting at the urging of God. There have been examples since forever of people, mostly men, believing that God speaks and tells them what they should do. Take old Abraham of the Old Testament, who barely escaped what he thought was God's command to kill his own son Isaac as a test of his loyalty. Or Noah, whom God told to build an ark and fill it full of animals, two by two. There have been many, within many faiths, who've acted on what they supposed was a divine revelation or instruction—engaging in deeds that ranged from odd to homicidal. And among those receiving prophecy have been quite a few Mormons.

Tara Westover, who grew up under the shadow of the Ruby Ridge horror in a tiny Mormon community in Idaho, wrote in her 2018 book, *Educated*, that her dad talked to God. On one occasion, Mr. Westover told the family that it had occurred to him that dairy, or maybe honey, was evil and needed to be purged from the family larder. But he'd been unclear as to which substance was the odious one. So he sought guidance from God, who pronounced dairy the offender. Tara Westover missed the milk on her breakfast cereal, though this deficiency is innocuous when compared to the results of other divine directives.

In the 1920s, Alma Dayer LeBaron, an Arizona man, was told by God to move to Chihuahua, Mexico, and establish a polygynous community, a haven full of fruit-laden trees, fine schools, cheerful adherents, and glorious churches. His son Joel LeBaron later took over that Mormon fundamentalist sect and the shabby, derelict community of impoverished women and children. The original vision never manifested as the one divinely promised. Family infighting and jealousies led another one of Alma's sons, Ervil LeBaron, to order Joel's murder. Ervil died in jail in 1981.

In *Under the Banner of Heaven*, Jon Krakauer tells of Mormon fundamentalist Ron Lafferty, who received God's order to kill his sister-in-law, Brenda Lafferty, and her infant, Erica, in 1984. He and his brother Dan, acting on the demented vision, carried out the directive, and left them both with slit throats. Today Dan sits in prison, and in 2019 Ron died on death row.

Ammon Bundy, named after a Nephite hero in the Book of Mormon, also heard directly from God. In 2015, the Lord told Cliven's son to head to central Oregon for another fight with the feds. In a YouTube video that Ammon uploaded a day before his armed occupation of the Oregon wildlife refuge, he sat dressed in a plaid flannel shirt, with a Skousen Constitution in his pocket, and explained his God-directed rationale for his actions. Plainspoken, with a neat beard going gray at the chin, he talked, hands folded, about God's wishes for a father and son by the name of Hammond.

Steven and Dwight Hammond are ranchers who, like the Bundys, hated the constraints placed on them by federal land managers. Ranching is not easy, and being beholden to rules on lands you think you know better than any government guy must feel infuriating and even emasculating to a western cowboy. Over the years, Dwight Hammond, the father, and his son Steven had many brushes, some vicious, with federal officials. The ranchers violated their grazing permit by running cows across sensitive wetlands. They also menaced refuge staff and, in four incidences, made death threats. In 2001 and in 2006 they set illegal fires—one to cover up evidence of having poached several deer. The other fire was a backburn, set to keep a larger fire at bay. Backburning is a common technique and in this case, the Hammonds claimed, they had used it to protect the family's property as another fire raged nearby. Both of the Hammond fires were unauthorized and spread to public land. Steven's nephew and Dwight's grandson, Dusty, was a key witness who detailed the first fire, testifying that his uncle and grandfather ordered him to help start it but told him to keep his mouth shut. This fire almost engulfed the boy, sixteen at the time, who had been forced to hunker down in a nearby creek amid the flames. The second fire, which the Hammonds set during a burn ban, put BLM firefighters camped nearby in mortal danger.

In 2012, the Hammonds were tried under the Antiterrorism and Effective Death Penalty Act for "maliciously damaging the real property of the United States by fire." The act became law in 1996—one response to militia member Timothy McVeigh's bombing of the Oklahoma courthouse, his own campaign in protest over Waco. Though the charges aimed at the Hammonds carried a mandatory five-year sentence, a judge thought the required punishment was too harsh and ordered Dwight to serve only three months and Steven a year and a day. They were also fined four hundred thousand dollars. After their initial release, another judge reversed the first decision and ruled that they serve the mandatory five years.

The Hammonds' plight was the first among many confused reasons for Ammon's takeover of the Malheur National Wildlife Refuge, a refuge for 340 species of birds among other animals, where the Hammond's once grazed their cows. As he goes on to explain on his YouTube post, "I begin to understand how the Lord felt about the Hammonds. I begin to understand about how the Lord felt about Harney County and about this country." He sniffs and continues, "I clearly understood that the Lord was not pleased." He tells us, on camera, what God had told him: that if the situation wasn't rectified and the Hammonds weren't freed, actions such as those taken against the ranchers would continue to happen to people all over the country. Getting on his knees and asking God what he should do, Ammon became convinced that he had to intervene on the Hammonds' behalf and restore to them "their God-given rights." He further explains that he is certain God will hold him accountable if he doesn't act. "It became very clear and I had a hard time," he says of when he understood what the Lord expected of him. He wrestled with God's order to go sort things out in Oregon but came to understand that he couldn't shirk a God-given duty. "It was like exactly what was happening at the Bundy ranch. We were getting guided and directed in what we were supposed to do. That's how it was." God wanted Ammon to round up a bunch of patriots who "understood that our Constitution was being violated. That it was hanging by a thread," he says, in reference to the White Horse Prophecy, the revelation attributed to Joseph Smith revealing the Mormon role in protecting the Constitution within the unfolding of the apocalypse.

On January 1, 2016, Ammon and Ryan joined Richard Mack and his organization, the Constitutional Sheriffs and Peace Officers Association, along with members of the Three Percenters, supportive neighbors, and friends of the Hammond family, at the Harney County Fairgrounds to protest the ranchers' resentencing. Then Ammon peeled off with a magpie crew and drove out to the wildlife refuge. Together they moved into the handsome stone refuge buildings and issued a list of demands. Bunkerville was dangerous and charged, and in comparison, Malheur seemed like a cross between a ragbag and a revival. First, these occupiers called for charges to be dropped against the Hammonds. Then they insisted that the federal government relinquish ownership of public lands, giving those lands "back" to miners, loggers, and ranchers. Further, they called for nullifying the system of federal grazing permits and returning to historic grazing practices, with no government interference. And finally, they wanted the wildlife refuge handed over to the county where it was situated. Altogether, Ammon's demands were both unclear and contradictory. Outside the refuge, the occupiers planted a sign rechristening the parcel of federally owned land "THE HARNEY COUNTY RESOURCE CENTER."

The media captured the madness of this uprising, with its outlandish cast of characters, religious pageantry, and military-style posturing. The occupiers were vivid and vehement, but not abundant; it was a scant turnout compared to Bunkerville. For weeks Ammon held the refuge while dozens of men and some women milled around with guns. *Forbes* and *New York Magazine* called them the Bundy Militia. Others called them Y'all Qaeda, Vanilla Isis, TaliBundy, the Redneck Caliphate, Infantada, YeeHawdists, and Yokel Haram. Although the FBI kept a low profile near the refuge, the town of Burns was astir with unmarked vehicles and G-men. Ammon was star of the show, conducting press conferences in which he railed against tyranny and constitutional abuses. Inside the occupation, participants fought among themselves. Some got drunk. Some rode around in government vehicles and rifled through files. Some prayed and sang and awaited signs from God.

Invocations, spiritual cleansings, and the blasts of a shofar (an ancient-style trumpet, made from the horn of a ram and used in early Jewish rituals) piercing the frigid Oregon air were as much part of the occupation as guns and pocket Constitutions. Occupier Dylan Anderson went so far as to take the title Captain Moroni, a hero in the Book of Mormon who fought to protect liberty among his people. In photographs, this clean-cut thirty-five-year-old man from Provo, Utah, appears in a camo jacket and baggy pants, wearing a dark version of the hat Bob Denver wore on *Gilligan's Island*.

Brand Thornton, who claimed to be related to the Bundy family, told Scott Carrier, a journalist who covered the Malheur takeover for his radio program *Home of the Brave*, that he was using a cursing ritual on federal employees. This practice, an artifact of the early Mormon Church, had stopped being widely practiced by the 1900s. In the past it was exercised primarily in response to rebuffed missionary efforts—for instance, against those Gentiles who slammed doors on Saints during their house-to-house proselytizing. Curses had also been used in the expectation of the Second Coming, combined with ritual washings to cleanse earth in preparation for God's return. In Malheur, Thornton had revived the process. After petitioning the government with a gripe without receiving satisfaction, he explained, it's time for a priesthood curse. "You start off by raising your arm to the Square [like Brigham Young had done when he inspired his companions to topple an early Mountain Meadows Memorial], calling upon the Lord through his priesthood, and then you specifically tell Him the oppression that is taking place and even the people's names who are doing it, and ask the Lord that they will remove this oppression. And then you pour the water over your feet and when you're done, you say, 'Amen.'" In addition to casting curses, Thornton was also blower of the camp shofar, similar to the instrument blown when Joseph Smith led Zion's Camp on their exercise of futility back in the Missouri days.

Although the Mormon Church condemned the actions at Malheur, several Latter-day Saints participated. Thornton, Anderson, and Ammon and Ryan Bundy were joined by other members, including Todd MacFarlane (one-time attorney for Mary Bulloch), LaVoy Finicum, Shawna Cox, and Wesley Kjar. Brian "Booda" Cavalier was also there, so nicknamed for a very rough tattoo of a Buddha on his belly. At the Bundy compound, he'd shared with me that he too had converted to Mormonism after serving as Cliven's bodyguard.

Ammon and his crew were on a mission from God. They were a religious army sent to address government abuse, and, he said, oppression wouldn't stop at Harney County, but would continue in "all the counties across the United States. And go into all ends of the earth if there was not a stand made." He told the press that the refuge had been stolen from its rightful owners, the ranchers, miners, and loggers. Refuge land was indeed stolen, but not from those he mentioned.

The Malheur National Wildlife Refuge was historically part of a 1.78-million-acre reservation "given" to the Northern Paiute people by the US government in 1872, even though it had been theirs already. That same year, irrespective of the reservation, one Dr. Hugh Green, of California, sent his henchman Pete French up to grab as much land as possible around Malheur Lake, for his cows. When the government failed to honor the reservation agreement, and ranchers ignored Native claims, frustrated members of the Northern Paiute Tribe rebelled, in an 1879 uprising known as the Bannock War. In response to the revolt, the government marched five hundred Paiute people involuntarily through deep snows onto Yakima lands in Washington, 350 miles away. With the Native people gone, ranchers swept in, setting up large cattle operations over the next decade.

Less than a decade after the Northern Paiute people were banished to Yakima, a range war over land entitlements left Pete French dead, shot by a neighbor angry at the cowboy's habit of fencing off public domain. In 1908, nine years after French's death, Teddy Roosevelt used the Antiquities Act to create the Malheur National Wildlife Refuge in reaction to the devastation of bird populations caused by the plume trade. Meanwhile, another line of federal protectionism had begun in parallel. The first species-protection act was passed in 1900, about the same time when the Mormons largely abandoned their cleansing rituals, to respond to bird slaughter. Feathered hats had come into fashion at the turn of the century, leaving bird species vulnerable to extinction. Americans were discovering that the great bounty they imagined their lands would always provide was in fact finite. And so began calls for the protection of wildlife and the public domain.

But this Oregon refuge was declared atop Paiute land. The Burns Paiute Tribe, descendants of the people who were marched from that land, received back a mere sliver, 760 acres of the original reservation, in 1933. (Today the tribe owns over 13,000 acres.) What Ammon Bundy failed to fathom was that basic fact: that Malheur National Wildlife Refuge is a place that ranchers took from Native people, just as Mormon people had taken Native homeland when they settled on Southern Paiute land. This made likewise no impression on Ryan Bundy, who told a reporter during the takeover, "Native Americans had the claim to the land, but they lost that claim. There are things to learn from cultures of the past, but the current culture is the most important."

Neither Ryan nor Ammon would let the particulars of history and ownership get in the way of God's plan. They said they were determined to dig their heels in deep at the refuge. "We're planning on staying here for years, absolutely. This is not a decision we've made at the last minute," said Ammon. But the Bundy militia seemed to have been weirdly ill-prepared. They didn't bring food. Or other supplies. They lacked a strategy. When asked how they wanted to see their demands implemented, Ammon said, "We could put more thought to that."

Though it got tons of press, the takeover at Malheur was a great deal less supported from outside, and attracted fewer participants, than the standoff at Bunkerville for several reasons. Ammon acted without building local support. The Hammonds did not condone their actions, and the Hammonds' lawyer, W. Alan Schroeder, issued a statement saying, "Neither Ammon Bundy nor anyone within his group/organization speak for the Hammond Family." The occupation was ill-conceived, seemingly improvised, and sloppy. Whereas Bunkerville attracted between six hundred and eight hundred protesters, estimates put participants at Malheur around fifty. This in spite of all of the public appeals, issued by participants, to join the cause.

Blaine Cooper, whose real name is Stanley Blaine Hicks, had been in Bunkerville two years before. Up in Oregon, he pleaded on the alt-right website *Signs of the Times* for others to join the Malheur rebellion. "It doesn't have to stop here. This could be a hope that spreads through the whole country, the whole United States. Everybody's looking for this hope because the government has beat us, and oppressed us, and took everything from us; they will not stop until we tell them no."

Stewart Rhodes, founder of the Oath Keepers, the anti-government militia that had been instrumental in Nevada, appealed directly to Ammon on his public website telling him of his ambivalence. "I believe you know that I respect you as a man of great, inspirational courage and conviction. And like-wise for your brothers," he wrote. The Bundy family's courage was what inspired him "and many other groups and individuals to come from all over the nation, rifles in hand, to protect your family and back you up, shoulder-to-shoulder, as you took a strong stand for your rights and for the Constitution against a clear and present danger of military trained snipers and Special Forces veteran 'contractor' mercenaries." Rhodes was more than willing to protect the "ranching family from being 'Waco'd.' It was a profound honor to do so, and it was a stand that will go down in history." But, he continued, "we oppose what you have chosen to do by occupying the wildlife preserve there in Oregon, specifically because it is not being done with the consent of the locals or at their request, without the request of the Hammond family, without even their knowledge of what you were going to do, until you did it, and because it is not in direct defense of anyone."

But LaVoy Finicum disagreed. He too had been involved in Bunkerville, and he came to Oregon ready to die in defense of freedom and God. In spite of the convoluted campaign and circus atmosphere, Finicum was there to take a hard stand. A fifty-four-year-old Mormon rancher from Cane Beds, Arizona, less than five miles south of Colorado City (where the notorious Warren Jeffs oversaw the Fundamentalist Church of Jesus Christ of Latter-day Saints), Finicum served as a spokesperson during the occupation, and came across as sympathetic and earnest. He ran a cattle ranch that made no money, but he pulled in over one hundred thousand dollars a year in compensation for taking in troubled foster children, his only source of income. He had long been involved with the Bundy plight and was deeply distrustful of the federal government. Before joining the Bundy brothers in Malheur, he self-published an apocalyptic novel, *Only by Blood and Suffering: Regaining Lost Freedom*. On the dedication page he warns, "It is my belief that freedom will rise again in this land, but only after much blood and suffering. This is my witness and my warning." The book imagines a societal and technological breakdown and a self-sufficient Utah ranching family, the Bonhams, who fight to survive a dystopian age of cannibalism, rape, murder, robbery, and the collapse of the monetary system and the federal government. Automobiles no longer run, and travel is done on horseback. Food is raised or hunted. Corruption is rife, so "natural law," or vigilante justice, is employed. In its final scene, Finicum's hero, a cowboy, is killed while defending his family and his freedom.

Finicum died in an encounter with law enforcement during an arrest attempt on January 26, 2016. He and several others were en route to a town hall meeting in John Day, Oregon, about one hundred miles from the refuge, to meet with a sheriff sympathetic to the idea of posse comitatus. Finicum was driving a white pickup in a convoy along with FBI informant Mark McConnell, who drove a Jeep. The two vehicles were pulled over by FBI and Oregon State Police, and Ammon Bundy and Brian Cavalier, both of whom had been in McConnell's Jeep, were arrested. Finicum attempted to leave the scene, whereupon Oregon state troopers fired off pepper-spray cartridges; one of Finicum's passengers, the former army ranger and Bunkerville tactician Ryan Payne, jumped out of the truck and was taken into custody. Video footage shows Finicum screaming at the officers, "You want a bloodbath? It's going to be on your hands." Pulling away, he drove about a mile down the Harney County highway with his remaining passengers, Ryan Bundy, Shawna Cox, and eighteen-year-old Victoria Sharp, before crashing into a snowbank, where the vehicle sat stuck as the Oregon State Police and FBI arrived. Both Cox and Bundy attempted to call the Pacific Patriots Network for backup, but the roadblocks had been set up intentionally in places with bad cell service. Finicum lurched out of the driver's side, alternating between holding his hands in the air and reaching for his pocket. He yelled, "Just shoot me," and was fired upon and killed by two officers. Other shots hit the truck. Ryan Bundy was wounded, and he and Cox were arrested. Officer 6, as named in the police report, noted that as Cox was apprehended, she asked him "if he believed in the Constitution." He found it "irritating" that she did not inquire about her friend LaVoy, lying bloody in the snow. It's hard to imagine what was going through her head right then, but the account certainly speaks to Cox's unwavering resolve.

Before LaVoy Finicum was killed, the Malheur takeover was dismissed as half-baked. But his death somehow served to legitimize the cause, at least in many anti-government circles, because it "proved" that the government really was out to get Americans. Joel Skousen said it gave the Bundys their "high ground." This time, in the eyes of the Bundy family and their supporters, someone had indeed been "Waco'd." Militia ambivalence thawed, and a great many more supporters came to regard the death of Finicum and a subsequent investigation as a murder and a cover-up, providing retroactive validation for the grievances behind the Bundys' occupation. The investigation found that the Oregon State Police officers had been justified in killing Finicum. Cliven Bundy was arrested just after Ammon and Ryan, when he came to Oregon to help with the occupation. He was apprehended in the Portland airport when he got off the plane from Las Vegas. The four remaining occupiers, Sean and

Sandra Anderson, Jeff Banta, and David Fry, surrendered themselves to the FBI the next day on February 11, 2016, and the takeover came to an end. All three Bundy men spent the next two years in prison.

As I watched the occupation, I tried to understand what it could possibly accomplish; the execution was so poor. But given the high that the Bundy boys felt with their "win" in Nevada, I have to believe they were in some way chasing that feeling of victorious rapture up in Oregon. There is an undeniable exhilaration in confronting a perceived wrongdoing. Staging a public spectacle, engaging the national media, and potentially grabbing the public's attention for five minutes about something you feel is important can be downright heady. I recognized the adrenaline rush. As someone who spent a lot of time protesting, in my case with other environmental activists, I understand the thrill of an action. (I have always been decisively on the opposite side of public land issues from the Bundy family and my experiences have always been peaceful—no one had a weapon, let alone an assault rifle.) Still, the Oregon takeover perplexed me. While Bunkerville could have been a massacre, Malheur seemed, on the face of it, cartoonish.

As I further consider the takeover, I have been haunted by a few unsettling details. After it ended, twenty-two long guns, twelve handguns, 16,636 live rounds, and 1,695 spent casings were collected from the site. One man was dead, and he became a hero to the militia movement. The refuge buildings were left full of garbage. Native land was desecrated and the Bundys were acquitted of all charges in Oregon. Matthew Shea, a non-Mormon Washington state legislator who helped plan and implement the occupation, wrote a manifesto two years after the takeover entitled "Biblical Basis for War." It begins, "1. God is a Warrior. 2. When is it time for war? When God says its [sic] time. 3. Fight to win so you don't have to fight again." Shea has advocated for the implementation of a theocracy in the US and for killing all men who do not abide. His manifesto also states, "Assassination to remove tyrants is just, not murder." The Rampart Group, who authored the report, found that Shea "is likely to plan, direct and engage in additional future conflicts that could carry with them significant bloodshed and loss of life." He is deeply involved in the American militia, specifically with the Bundy family, and although he has been asked to resign by the state legislature, he is refusing to do so. In late December 2019, he posted on his Facebook page, "Like we are seeing with our President [in regards to the impeachment process], this is a sham investigation meant to silence those of us who stand up against attempts to disarm and destroy our great country. I will not back down. I will not give in. I will not resign. Stand strong, fellow Patriots . . . I will continue to defend the Constitution against tyranny and fight to protect our God given rights to life, liberty, property and the ability to defend the same. Blessings to you. Matt." Though the event at Malheur seemed baffling and amateurish, the Rampart report found it was not "a spontaneous act," but rather "the armed takeover was meticulously planned December 2015 by conspirators that included Rep. Shea." The takeover of federal lands in the high desert of Oregon was enacted by a radicalized, fanatical, and flourishing faction of people in the rural West. And these white guys with guns, who feel religiously justified, are getting ever more brazen in their acts over federal lands.

PART 3:

We the People

Indians and Cowboys

This land is soaked in prayer.

—Aaron Lowden, Acoma Pueblo

The year before his arrest at the Portland airport, Cliven Bundy explained his position, laying it out carefully from a large easy chair in his small living room. Cliven's portrait by Jon McNaughton, a Mormon artist who has become famous for depicting Donald Trump in various jejune and weird scenarios, hangs on the wall of this small house, on that day smelling strongly of fried beef. You see, he said in response to a question on how his faith informs his fight, a Mormon settler—say, his hypothetical ancestor—came south with all of his worldly possessions. "Everything he owns on that wagon and he has, you know, his wife and family and maybe a milk cow tied behind." And when this man found a place to settle, he unbuckled his horse, removed its bridle, and led it to water. "When that horse takes the very first sip of the renewable resource, he is beginning to create a beneficial use of that resource. That's how our rights are created."

According to Cliven, land tenure changed when a Mormon man's horse drank from a Paiute river—his rights arrived in the establishment of Zion. "And that's what the range war, the Bundy war, is all about right now—it's really about protecting three things: our life, liberty, and our property." This analysis may in part stem from an interpretation of the 1877 Desert Land Act—a law invoking the concept of *beneficial use*, a legal construct to protect the rights of an individual's use of another's property—but it also reflects an insouciance regarding Native history, rights, and public lands.

Cliven's hypothetical Mormon pioneer, who arrived in Dixie sometime around the 1870s, surely shared convictions with this outlaw rancher, including his disdain for the federal government, devotion to the Mormon faith, and the certainty of his entitlement to the land. Cliven, during my conversation with him, proudly claimed his connection to Nephi Johnson, but he had other ancestors who also homesteaded in the region, such as his maternal great-great-grandfather Dudley Leavitt, Juanita Brooks's father, who founded Bunkerville the same year that the Desert Land Act became law. Leavitt lived for decades in the tiny hamlet (today it has a population of 1,300), which functioned, for a time, as a communal society. For ten years, Cliven's great-great-grandfather and his neighbors worked together, sharing everything, in a carryover from Joseph Smith's utopian ideals that Brigham Young, with mixed success, attempted to instill. It would be forty years after Dudley Leavitt was buried in the Bunkerville cemetery, and twenty-nine years after Nephi Johnson was laid to rest up the road, when David Bundy, Cliven's father, in 1948, purchased the ranch that remains the family's headquarters today. Records indicate that the elder Bundy made lease agreements on adjacent public lands to run cows in 1954. Cliven, however, has claimed, on the right-wing forum *The Blaze*, to hold "adjudicated livestock water rights filed with the state of Nevada" dating back to 1877, "when the first pioneers entered the valley." In addition to the illegitimacy of this legal assertion, Bundy's birthright argument relies on a history beginning with European settlement. So firmly ensconced within the cowboy myth of the West and its narrative of conquest, commodification, and capitalism, Bundy and his family have conveniently dismissed the people who actually have long-time ancestral ties to this place, the Paiute.

The Northern Paiute and Southern Paiute peoples were once mobile societies that spread across the Great Basin, before being subdued and then resettled onto reservations scattered across California, Arizona, Idaho, Utah, Oregon, and Nevada. There are three distinct languages spoken among these bands, all offshoots of a Numic/Uto-Aztecan tongue, and although they are both known as Paiute, the Northern Paiute are more closely related to the Bannock people, while the Southern Paiute are closer to the Ute people.

Although the Southern and Northern Paiute peoples are only loosely connected, Southern Paiute Tribal Chairwoman Tamra Borchardt-Slayton has a deep association with the Northern Paiute people. She's married to one. When the Bundys barged into Malheur, they were trespassing on the site of the very first Northern Paiute reservation. Their occupation and demands traumatized the Burns Paiute Tribe, who today live right next to the Malheur National Wildlife Refuge. During my visit in the fall of 2018 to her office in Cedar City, Utah, Borchardt-Slayton recounted painful conversations her husband had with family and friends during the takeover. Despite the tenuous relationship so many Indigenous people have with the federal government, the Burns Paiute Tribe has maintained a good rapport with the BLM and refuge staff; during the siege, tribal leaders expressed support for the agency managers, whom they said acted in good faith in caring for the historic lands of the Northern Paiute people.

The Bundy militia did not act in good faith. Though the occupiers made overtures to tribal members, their efforts were clumsy and their sincerity questionable. In a video posted online the day before he was shot, LaVoy Finicum is shown going through boxes of Native artifacts that militia members had found stored at the refuge's headquarters. Sporting a cowboy hat and shoulder holster, Finicum makes a plea to the television cameras, asking the tribe to come over and communicate "any claims they have on the land." But the tribe was having none of it—Finicum's plea rang hollow. After all, Ammon Bundy had already said he wanted to give the land back to regional ranchers, miners, and loggers. Read—white people. Burns Tribal Chairwoman Charlotte Roderique conveyed both frustration and disbelief regarding the takeover, explaining, "I don't know what these people are doing . . . if they are doing things to just get a rise or to be a martyr—all they are doing is making enemies out of the people they professed to support." The tribe watched in horror as Finicum pulled sacred items from storage boxes during his online appeal. What the militants saw as an act to repatriate artifacts, the tribe saw as desecrating the dead.

After Finicum died, and everyone else had either abandoned the cause or been arrested, Malheur was left in shambles. Inside the offices, desks sat mounded with bags of half-eaten food. Liquor bottles jammed into couch cushions were presumably left there by the non-Mormon protesters. A wall was punched in. Federal records and Native antiquities were scattered helter-skelter. And the grounds were even worse. The occupiers left garbage strewn about for others to clean up. A pile of abandoned camping equipment sat next to a junked Lincoln Continental. According to journalist Jacqueline Keeler, the Bundy militia bulldozed places near burial grounds and left behind a trench of human feces—acts of shocking defilement to a sacred place. After the occupation, Burns Paiute members offered cleansing prayers to restore the refuge spiritually, but the defilement deeply rattled the tribe.

Of course, the Bundy intrusion is hardly the first time that the Paiute people have seen their land and culture violated. When Ulysses S. Grant established a Northern Paiute reservation in 1872, within its boundaries was Lake Malheur, for "all the roving and straggling bands in eastern and southeastern

Oregon." That reservation failed for a variety of reasons: It wasn't funded, but more significantly, the creation of a permanent settlement for a mobile society did not work. The intransience of agriculture operations was a foreign concept that didn't take root, and ranchers blithely trespassed onto reservation lands, allowing their cattle to destroy wild foods.

One hundred years after they had been unfairly blamed for the Mountain Meadows Massacre, the Southern Paiute people also faced further persecution. Borchardt-Slayton's tribe lost their status, and with it their lands, in 1954 when their homeland was designated a hunting refuge. This came after years of political maneuvering, as Utah Senator Arthur Watkins, in his capacity as Chair of the Senate Interior Committee's Subcommittee on Indian Affairs, shaped and moved through Congress legislation, known as "termination" laws, that revoked Native sovereignty, federal services, exemptions from state taxes, rights to tribal lands, education, health care, and special federal protections for 109 tribes. The first of twelve of Watkins's bills targeted four Southern Paiute bands that had been ravaged for a hundred years. When their status was terminated, there were only twenty-seven Kanosh, twenty-six Koosharem, and ninety-seven Shivwits surviving members. Just twenty-six members of Borchardt-Slayton's band, Indian Peaks, remained.

Although Senator Watkins was a white Mormon farmer, he was in his day heralded as "one of the nation's leading experts in the field of Indian Affairs," though he consulted no tribes. His efforts ultimately forced Borchardt-Slayton's people from their homeland to Cedar City and onto a plot already inhabited by the Cedar City Paiute band, a small compound "donated" by the Mormon Church. Put simply, the Saints handed back a parcel to the band that had been taken from the Paiute people in the first place. On this patch a Mormon church for Paiute members still stands today. "My grandfather helped build it," Borchardt-Slayton told me.

For decades, Borchardt-Slayton's people struggled to eat, to find homes, and to simply survive after their termination, sending this already beleaguered culture into a powerless and desperate situation. Meanwhile, Senator Watkins congratulated himself, comparing his campaign to Lincoln's Emancipation Proclamation. His rationale was that cultural assimilation would be liberating in the long run. And that he was following Mormon prophecy. In 1954, Watkins wrote to the church presidency, David O. McKay and his counselors, that he had become "convinced" that:

> . . . we have made some terrible mistakes in the past. It seems to me that the time has come for us to correct some of these mistakes and help the Indians stand on their own two feet and become a white and delightsome people as the Book of Mormon prophesied they would become. Of course, I realize that the Gospel of Jesus Christ will be the motivating factor, but it is difficult to teach the Gospel when they don't understand the English language and have had no training in caring for themselves. The Gospel should be a great stimulus and I am longing and praying for the time when the Indians will accept it in overwhelming numbers.

The church, like Watkins, was similarly intent on the erasure of Native identities. From 1947 until 2000, Mormon families took in Native children to raise in their homes as part of what was known variously as the Lamanite Placement Program, the Student Placement Program, or the Indian Placement Program. Some forty thousand Native children were placed into this system, fostered through each school year, and taught the Book of Mormon. The rules were that the children must be baptized, practice Mormon Church protocols, and abandon traditional spiritual practices. All this to assimilate to a culture that promised that, in their obedience and piety, they would some-day become white people.

Borchardt-Slayton is a wonder. Just thirty-three years old when I met her, she had already served for a year and a half as head administrator for all of Utah's Paiute bands, following the lead of her mother and her aunt, each of whom had also held this high position. Explaining the impact the termination bill had on her band, Borchardt-Slayton would occasionally pause and show me old pictures that she kept in her purse. The photos—snapshots, mostly of women—were a bit washed-out and well-handled, but still were vivid depictions of family members, smiling from porches and posing on couches. Her mother, her aunts, and great-grandmother, Minnie. Women who had suffered the consequences of the withdrawal of government aid and a further erasure of their identities as a people. "We shouldn't have been terminated," she said. "Older adults were not literate. They signed [their rights away] with Xs and thumbprints." The act of termination, in addition to stripping these people of their lands, services, and benefits, also divested them of their identity. They were the Indian Peaks band that no longer lived in the Indian Peaks. This was done to force their assimilation by a man who believed in a prophecy that foresaw Native people turning white and delightsome. The mind spins, in considering both the folly of Watkins's actions and the wounds he inflicted.

Borchardt-Slayton confided that she and her kin had been lucky. While so many families, including her own, struggled to keep even their immediate kin at home, her great-grandmother had worked as a nanny in the home of a respected Mormon judge who was able to prevent her mother and aunts from being adopted into white households. Her great-grandmother's family even owned their home in Enoch, near the compound in Cedar City. Borchardt-Slayton lives there today with her husband and children.

It turns out, Native peoples had an unlikely ally in President Richard Nixon. The thirty-seventh president, who served from 1969 to 1974, had revered a football coach in high school who was a member of the Jolla band of California's Mission Tribe. Wallace "Chief" Newman inspired Nixon to act on behalf of Native peoples and remind America that we owe them a great debt. During his time in office, he changed the way the United States approached Indian affairs, overturning the position that Watkins and others had brought to Washington and the national stage, with its emphasis on prophecy and the grotesquery of social Darwinism. Nixon gave lands back to disenfranchised tribes and called for better health care, educational opportunities, and self-government programs for Native peoples.

Tamra Borchardt-Slayton's office is inside the labyrinthine building in Cedar City that serves as tribal headquarters for five bands of Paiute: Indian Peaks, Cedar Band, Kanosh, Koosharem, and finally Shivwits, whose lands are just down the interstate. The Shivwits reservation, at 28,153 acres the largest parcel still possessed among Utah's Paiute bands, lies southwest of the tiny bedroom community of Santa Clara. A sleepy historic town not far from St. George, Santa Clara boasts of being the one-time home of Jacob Hamblin, "the Indian Apostle."

Tamra is a Mormon who feels ambivalent about the church. But her uncle, Greg Anderson of Nevada's Moapa Paiute band, who lives on the Shivwits reservation with his wife along the Nevada-Utah border, has a pretty clear opinion. Amid the clatter of plates at a bustling café just off Interstate 15, I met Greg Anderson one autumn morning to learn about his Moapa culture and the surrounding lands upon which his people have lived since—in his words—time immemorial. Anderson, a large man, is great company. But as easy and droll as he is in manner, his principles and convictions are steely. "The Mormons killed our people," he said flatly.

Before the Mormons arrived with their shifting plans to convert and subdue Native populations, the Southern Paiute people lived in what is today Arizona, Nevada, California, and Utah. They moved in bands, ever watchful for the Ute and the Navajo, who made a practice of capturing Southern Paiute hostages and selling them to Mexican slave-traders. Relying on seasonal foods including root vegetables, pine nuts, and wild game, on frigid evenings they'd fill their bellies with scalding stews and huddle together to keep warm. Summer days could reach 125 degrees, but they knew each seep and fold in the sandstone, recesses that offered lifesaving shade and water. Their severe environment was simply part of life's backdrop.

The Paiute origin story, according to Borchardt-Slayton, tells that God blessed her people with homeland when he dropped them from his basket and into a "good place"—those deserts, mountains, rivers, and canyons where the Great Basin, the Colorado Plateau, and the Mojave Desert come together. I'd read about this genesis saga of her people and their fortuitous plunge to this corner of the earth. The deity responsible for bringing the Southern Paiute people into existence is sometimes known as Tabuts, but due to the syncretism of Christianity, and in many cases Mormonism, with Paiute beliefs, often Southern Paiute people refer to their creator as God.

After talking to both Anderson and Borchardt-Slayton, I was struck by their tendencies to emphasize the region's many bounties, descriptions in stark contrast to Mormon accounts that dwell on struggle and scarcity. In their move to Paiute lands, the Mormons, as well as the miners, established settlements around precious water and atop game habitat, bringing paucity to an Indigenous population that once had successfully made its living on the landscape.

Before the arrival of white people, Southern Paiute bands had followed a regular route with the seasons, visiting other bands and harvesting seasonal edibles. They lived well, gathering what they needed, finding nourishment, useful fibers, and natural medicines. They knew the locations of the region's limited water, sources not always easy to find or to access, and they employed irrigation techniques that allowed them to raise small patches of squash. In fact, Greg Anderson told me, his Southern Paiute ancestors taught the Mormons how to survive on the arid land. The Native peoples' generosity in sharing their long-standing resourcefulness and traditions enabled the Yankee and European greenhorns to abide in a place that was disorienting and foreign. The Southern Paiute people helped the Saints raise Zion.

As a kid, Anderson told me, he had herded cattle in the Gold Butte area for Howard Hughes, the eccentric tycoon and germophobe. Gold Butte is sacred for Southern Paiute people; their histories, written in petroglyphs, literally cover the red walls and coral-colored uplifts. On the morning of our breakfast, Anderson wore a bright pendant, beaded by his wife, depicting "the falling man," one of the most famous images from the walls of Gold Butte. The figure is a person plunging backwards, arms outstretched and legs following helplessly behind. It's an eerie image, suggesting helplessness and gravity. It captures a man in the throes of death, reminding the generations of this inevitability.

Having grown up on horseback, chasing cattle across the landscape, Anderson sees nothing wrong with cows in this desert land. But he thinks Cliven Bundy has a lot of nerve, claiming the place as his own personal ranch. "I know him," Anderson said, "and he's a damn good melon farmer." But Gold Butte is not Cliven Bundy's personal property. As the conversation veered further into ownership and proprietary rights, Anderson made it clear the region was Southern Paiute land. Of the time another local livestock producer, not Cliven Bundy, had the gall to declare public land as his very own ranch, which Bundy encourages public leaseholders to do, Anderson told me, "I said to him, doesn't look like England to me!"

On December 28, 2016, President Barack Obama designated both Bears Ears and Gold Butte, lands in the public trust, as national monuments. While Bears Ears, set to be jointly managed by several tribes and the government, received most of the national attention, Gold Butte garnered the most buzz on the Bundy Ranch Facebook page. Totaling 296,937 acres, the Gold Butte National Monument is a glorious desert landscape, with cinnamon sand fins that tower high above lush, slow seeps, nurturing palm trees, and emerald-green vegetation. Desert tortoises, ravens, and mountain lions share the place with Bundy's freeloading cows. Earlier in 2016, Vernon Lee, the former Moapa tribal councilman, spoke about Gold Butte. "As a native, and as the tribe that actually had that land granted by the federal government back in the 1800s, he really doesn't got a right at all," Lee said of Cliven Bundy. "If anybody's got a right it would be the Moapa band of Paiutes." For the Southern Paiute, monument status offered a layer of protection to their lands and habitat for wildlife like the bighorn sheep, the sacred animal whose likenesses are depicted in many of the region's rock drawings. When the Obama administration put their homeland into national monument status, many Southern Paiute people felt relief.

The Bundys, on the other hand, felt that it was just more federal land-grabbing. "A national monument!?!" Supporters on the Bundy Ranch Facebook page spewed venom and conspiracy theories. It was surely a Russian plot. Or a Chinese scheme. No, it amounted to a sinister government design to steal land from "we the people" and allow the feds to corral Americans into urban compounds where they could better be controlled. One commenter suggested that resistors shoot BLM agents if any tried to enforce the monument status. A woman called President Obama "a Muslim in Degise!" and others hurled the nickname "Obummer," a moniker so glib it could have come from Donald

Trump. Most comments demonstrated that the authors either did not understand that the monument was actually public land—not Cliven Bundy's private property—or deliberately chose to ignore that fact, following Bundy's lead.

After the monument's declaration, the family issued a press release that read:

> We, the Bundy Family, would like to say to President Obama that we are saddened, but not surprised, by your decision to make our ranch and home a national monument. If any of this were really about protecting the land, you would come here, work with the local people who love this land, those who have a vested interest in this land, and take the time to learn what this land really needs. This is about control, pure and simple. You don't love this land, you have never visited here, but you love being in control of this land. . . .

The Southern Paiute people, to repeat, had been dispossessed of the same land the Bundys referred to in their letter. According to James Spencer, a federal Indian agent in 1880, the Moapa people were "eking out a precarious existence by working, begging, root digging and insect eating, a life not of their choice." After their land was taken and they were relegated to reservation lands, the Moapa people have subsisted by ranching, farming, and operating a dairy. They dabbled in the sale of manure and, in the 1980s, grew hydroponic tomatoes. They also developed coal plants on the Moapa reservation, but after people got sick, Greg Anderson and others turned to clean energy. Today the reservation is home to a giant solar operation that provides power to eleven thousand homes. "Every Moapa who wants a job on the site has one," Anderson said of this new enterprise. The Moapa people, in spite of devastating circumstances, have continued ongoing resistance to colonialism.

Hearing Anderson's enthusiasm over job opportunities and clean energy, I was reminded of Ryan Bundy's statement, issued at Malheur: "Native Americans had the claim to the land, but they lost that claim. There are things to learn from cultures of the past, but the current culture is the most important." I'm not sure what a modern culture is, as every culture is hamstrung by its own history. The Bundys are certainly not embracing modern standards or laws. They insist that their rights were established over 150 years ago, allowing them, so they claim, to do whatever they want, which means reenacting the same stories as their ancestors. Their sense of history and entitlement begins with the arrival of their own ancestors, and they base their justifications within early church theology. It seems to me that the Paiute people, who have overcome enormous adversity, are the ones acting as the progressive culture and the Bundys are the ones living in the past.

Black Hats, White Hats

I've got a shotgun. It's loaded and I know how to use it. We're ready to do what we have to do, but we'd rather win in the court of public opinion.

—Carol Bundy

I had hoped that, in the story of the Bundys and American public lands, as in any fine old western, the good guys would win, and the bad guys would meet with swift justice. But it's not so simple as good guys versus bad guys in this horse opera, nor has justice really been served. The Bundys skated on all charges in Malheur and in Bunkerville. Cliven continues to graze cattle illegally and completely free of charge. The family incited the militia, organized an armed standoff, took over a wildlife refuge, jeopardized the lives of hundreds of people, and saw one man killed. Lauded as heroes by some, they've left other Americans feeling fleeced, robbed of justice, and very unsettled. And yet it turns out that, although the Bundys most certainly broke laws in Nevada and Oregon, some federal players acted badly as well, both in the field and in the courtroom.

For years, the BLM handled the Bundy case in a very uneven and confusing manner. There had been multiple orders to remove his cows. Here are the highlights. Bundy stopped paying his fees in 1993, claiming the government did not own the land that he leased. In response, the BLM issued a Trespass

Notice and an Order to Leave Notice that same year. A 1998 US District Court of Nevada ruling ordered him to remove his cows, and he appealed. The appeal was denied and the ruling upheld. Bundy continued to run the cows, growing the herd in spite of the fact that he was breaking the law. In 2011, the BLM sent a Cease and Desist Order and Notice of Intent to confiscate his cows. When it seemed like a roundup was going to happen, in 2012 Cliven desperately appealed to the Clark County sheriff, Douglas Gillespie, issuing a "Range War Emergency Notice and Demand for Protection." Evoking posse comitatus, he wanted Gillespie to come to his rescue if the feds came to take his cows. The feds backed down due to safety concerns.

In 2013, the US District Court of Nevada ruled that Cliven Bundy was in violation of the law. He again appealed, and was again denied, the court warning that he had forty-five days to remove his one thousand trespassing cows. The BLM announced their intent to round up the cows in March 2014 and close off the area. The earlier concerns about safety had prompted the FBI to conduct an assessment; it determined that Bundy wasn't a threat. Dan Love, head of BLM law enforcement, paid no heed to the report and took a military stance. And only when Cliven and Carol Bundy reported to their militia networks increasing numbers of armed law enforcement officers in the vicinity of Gold Butte, and acts of surveillance against their family, did the threat actually manifest.

In advance of the roundup, the BLM had been advised to focus on community outreach and education in order to temper feelings and acts of rebellion among Bundy supporters. The public should have understood the intent of the federal steps was to deal with trespassing cattle that had long grazed for free. The government agents were not cattle-rustling, as some had accused them, nor did they intend to deprive anyone of his or her liberties. Cliven Bundy was a non-permitted rancher in violation of the law. This should have been better communicated.

But no such outreach or education effort took place and instead the BLM poured fuel on a fire.

The situation in Gold Butte was a full-on imbroglio, and Special Agent Love made it worse. Widely disliked throughout BLM Region 3 (which covers Nevada and Utah), even among other federal employees, Love was the kind of government official that the Bundys and their supporters imagined all feds to be. Callous, macho, and controlling, he stoked the Bundy confrontation rather than defusing it. The whole operation turned into a cowboy standoff, in part because Dan Love was a cowboy himself.

The days leading up to the Battle of Bunkerville, in April 2014, were tense, as an influx of federal agents came into an ordinarily quiet and remote stretch of the Mojave Desert. Armed personnel drove the back roads in unmarked sedans. Officers stood with leashed police dogs and helicopters buzzed overhead. The BLM set up Free Speech Areas, nicknamed "First Amendment Zones" by some and "Free Speech Cages" by others, little cordoned-off spaces supposedly for protest speechifying, where one protester planted a sign proclaiming, "The First Amendment is not an area." Amid all the militarization, the Bundys seemed to be watching the narrative that they long embraced become reality—that of an evil government intent on stealing their life and liberty. As word spread across the West, then across the country, more and more people arrived to stand with the Bundys and their cows.

In photos and video of the standoff, Dan Love is conspicuous. Tall, wearing a pair of sunglasses he might have borrowed from the Terminator's collection and a black baseball cap turned backwards, he came to a gate, after the confiscation had been aborted, to talk to the Bundys. "We're going to work with you," he said. "But you need to back up." He was offering to open the choke point. The crowd stood resolute, screaming at him, but gave no ground. Love continued his appeals, but Ammon Bundy refused to parley. Finally, Love turned, walked toward the other agents and officers, and signaled it was over. The feds all climbed into their vehicles and drove away. Ammon, wearing a black T-shirt printed with the sentiment "Cows are Good," opened the gate. Cheers ran through the crowd. Ryan Bundy threw his arm up and declared victory.

Four years later it was a matter for the courts. Dan Love should have been a key witness for the prosecution during the Nevada trials. Instead he was one of its biggest liabilities. By the time he testified, he had been fired by the BLM for mishandling an unrelated case and destroying evidence. He had been accused of telling employees to lie for him and intimidating those who countered him. He wasn't really committed to public land resources either, as he was known to hand out protected geological treasures as presents—"moqui marbles," sandstone orbs made by erosion—dispensing them from a confiscated stash sitting in BLM evidence storage. But what Love was really hated for, before his transgressions in Bunkerville, was his treatment of the Redd family, distant relatives of Charlie Redd.

In 2009, Love was part of a raid on Dr. James Redd and his wife, Jeanne Redd, at their home in Blanding, Utah. An informant had told authorities that Jeanne was illegally collecting and selling ancient Native artifacts. In a gripping piece in the *Los Angeles Times*, reporter Joe Mozingo describes agents in flak jackets, with their weapons drawn, arriving at the Redd house to search for illegal antiquities. Among the Mormon community in San Juan County, this was a very unpopular sort of crackdown, though regional tribes were quite supportive in principle of government enforcement. During the raid, Dr. Redd, a physician who practiced there in Blanding, was taken into his garage and subjected to grueling questions for hours, notwithstanding that it was his wife, not he, who was the accused. Just days after the raid, he committed suicide. The informant in the case, a guilt-ridden, struggling alcoholic man named Ted Gardiner, also took his own life; so did a third man, Steven Schrader, who had been indicted for looting Native items as well. The sting went by the lurid and classical code name Operation Cerberus—for the three-headed mythological dog that guards the gates of hell.

It should have been a legitimate operation for protecting regional antiquities, just as the Bundy cattle roundup should have been a legitimate action in the enforcement of a grazing contract and the protection of public land. The ongoing looting of Native artifacts impoverishes the historical record of our public lands, unravels tribal stories, and desecrates sacred areas, including burial sites. But, as with the Bunkerville operation, BLM tactics were not well thought-out. Instead of fixing problems such as looting and illegal grazing, these operations riled the local communities and fueled their anti-government sentiments. But there was some good that came of the Blanding raid. Cooperative efforts between regional tribes and federal parties, in the creation of Bears Ears National Monument, grew out of the attention drawn to ransacking antiquities, some of which was generated by Operation Cerberus.

It wasn't just Dan Love who screwed up the Bundy situation. US attorneys involved in the standoff case were accused by the presiding judge, Gloria Navarro, of "flagrant prosecutorial misconduct." She declared a mistrial, "with prejudice," meaning that the government couldn't retry the case, though at the time of this writing, the feds are attempting to bring it back before a court. Her decision came in response to prosecution withholding exculpatory evidence. There were other issues, ones that didn't influence this determination, but nonetheless made the government look very bad. The FBI sent a bogus documentary film crew from a bogus company, Longbow Productions, to the Bundy ranch to ensnare Ammon, Ryan, or Cliven into admitting a desire to kill federal agents. And then there was the BLM whistleblower, Larry Wooten, whose leaked memo further damaged Dan Love's credibility. "I routinely observed, and the investigation revealed, a widespread pattern of bad judgment, lack of discipline, incredible bias, unprofessionalism and misconduct, as well as likely policy, ethical, and legal violations among senior and supervisory staff at the BLM's Office of Law Enforcement and Security," Wooten wrote. He referred to their bias against Mormonism and their use of slurs aimed at the Bundy family and their supporters, such as "ret*rds, r*dnecks, overweight woman with the big jowls, d*uche bags, tractor face, idiots, inbreeds, etc., etc., etc. . . ." Most disturbingly, Wooten alleged that Dan Love kept a "kill book," a written commemoration of his role in the suicides that resulted from Operation Cerberus. This memo has not been corroborated. All the same, the actions of Special Agent Love, the deceit of the prosecution, and the leaked letter ruined a case that should have been a slam dunk.

On January 8, 2018, Judge Navarro dismissed all sixteen charges against Cliven, Ryan, and Ammon Bundy, as well as those against Ryan Payne. Mel and Dave Bundy also walked free. But not all were so lucky. Gerald "Jerry" DeLemus, a Trump campaign co-chair in New Hampshire and former marine, pleaded guilty to conspiracy and got seven years. Blaine Cooper, an anti-Islam activist from Prescott, Arizona, pleaded guilty and was sentenced to twenty months. Todd Engel, a militia member from Idaho, was sentenced to fourteen years for interstate travel in aid of extortion and obstruction of justice. Greg Burleson, a militia member from Arizona, is serving the longest sentence: eighty-six years for assault, obstruction of justice, extortion, and threats. He was also ordered to pay one-and-a-half million dollars in restitution to the government. Posing as the Longbow documentary filmmakers, agents had recorded him saying, "I was hell-bent on killing federal agents that had turned their back on we the people." Adding, "I literally went there to put them six feet under."

Bunkerville could have been a disaster. It attracted many people who wanted a stage from which to scream their hatred, some of whom itched for violence. Of the people involved during and after the Battle of Bunkerville, both on the family's side and on the federal side, no clear champion emerged. No one to cheer and laud. The Bundy backers became more empowered and the feds appeared both corrupt and inept. There were those on the scene with level heads. Officer Tom Jenkins, of the Las Vegas police, said that the decision to back down that day was made to save lives. "We were dealing with people who could have been set off by anything," he said. "Nobody was going to die over cows that day."

But there had been those willing to do just that. Carol Bundy told me that even her youngest son, Arden, then just sixteen, had been prepared to lay down his life if the standoff became a shootout. Her boy had said before the Battle of Bunkerville, "This is a good day to die," a phrase attributed to Low Dog, an Oglala chief who fought in the Battle of Little Bighorn. She was proud of her son's conviction, and I don't know what struck me more profoundly—the ironic cultural appropriation of Arden's declaration or Carol's satisfaction in a son willing to be shot for his father's transgressions and pile of unpaid bills.

The year before the feds turned away from the standoff, Carol said of the family's fight with the government that "Arden doesn't know life any other way. We've been fighting this war before he was born." In fact, the Bundy war was generations in the making, its layers found in the foundation of Zion. The BLM had no idea what they were up against. The history and religious myths that underpin the family's animus, and their dogmatism—as you have seen here—go back before even Cliven was born.

Enemies of the People

It used to be, everyone was entitled to their own opinion, but not their own facts. But that's not the case anymore. Facts matter not at all. Perception is everything.

—Stephen Colbert

Two weeks after he was freed on January 8, 2018, Cliven Bundy came to speak in Paradise, Montana, before a packed house of (for the most part) backers. He held forth on some of his favorite themes. The Constitution. God. Ranching. And his faith. He grew sentimental with this audience of about four hundred people, a large one for a small town in western Montana. He told the people how much he appreciated the support, especially from those who had come to help his family in Oregon and Nevada. "I don't know how to thank you," he said, "except to tell you, I love you." He talked about forgiveness, gratitude, the importance of children, families, and wives. And he reminded all of us sitting there in the old gymnasium, under the gaze of armed men placed throughout, of how "our Heavenly Father has blessed us so much."

Ryan Bundy spoke earlier in the evening. Dressed in a tight leather vest with his hands jammed into his jeans pockets, he got up to talk about the Heavenly Father as well and to let us know further his grounds for his fight. In the Bible, he told the audience, Genesis gave "man" full sovereignty over the land and authority over every "creeping thing that creepeth upon the earth." When man's counterpart, woman, came around, God decreed that these two should procreate and subdue the earth. Man was given the freedom, Ryan continued, to do whatever he pleased with the birds, fish, plants, and herbs, all placed here for his use and pleasure. Ryan didn't mention *Gopherus agassizii*, the desert tortoise, which was listed as endangered in 1989 and later as threatened in 1991, but I think this was implied.

He cited Genesis 1, which tells of man being made in the image of God and then given dominion. In Genesis 2, man is told to "till and keep" the earth. The Bundys seem to suggest these references as a religiously given carte blanche to do what they want without any regard to the other living things dependent on the fast-dwindling bounty of our shared planet.

A few months after this rally in Paradise, Ammon Bundy headlined another gathering, the Range Rights and Resource Symposium at Modesto Junior College in California. His lecture topped off a two-day conference inside a huge campus agricultural pavilion that also serves, at times, as a venue for livestock shows and tractor pulls. I had been scheduled to interview him the day before, but he hadn't been allowed to fly, presumably stopped by TSA, and therefore was forced to drive to the gathering. In lieu of a face-to-face chat, we spoke briefly by phone. "Can you believe they call *me* a domestic terrorist?" he had asked. Yep.

When he did arrive and take the stage, Ammon told the audience, "I first need you to know that I'm a Christian." From there he parroted his brother Ryan, referencing Genesis, dominion, subduing the earth, and multiplying. He followed his thoughts on the Old Testament with the meat of his speech— that environmentalists and scientists are frauds. In their zeal to protect species and landscapes, they threaten to "destroy the happiness of human life." Conservationists are immoral adversaries, akin to ancient worshipers of Baal, Ammon told us. He blamed researchers for spreading lies about water shortages and overpopulation. There's plenty of land in this world, according to Ammon, and if anyone says differently, they are double-dealing.

He then offered us statistics on land availability, starting with California. This state, he said, could provide every household 12.42 acres of land. In Nevada, every family could have 88 acres. If we apportioned the United States in this same manner, every family would receive 21.3 acres. And if we divvyed up the world, each household could live on their own 42 acres. I won't spend too much time refuting these figures because they are untethered to logic or data.

Ammon announced that environmentalists who care about species do so at the expense of people, with the ultimate goal "to drive humans off the land." Such people do not want "humans to be fed" or "to live in the places they want to live." He even told the Modesto crowd that environmentalists do not want humans "to enjoy life." Further, he continued, this movement is actually an extreme religion, spread globally by the likes of Al Gore and Mikhail Gorbachev. Be forewarned, he cautioned. Gore, Gorbachev, and their pals at the United Nations have deceitfully packaged their beliefs and presented their evidences "as science."

Ammon's talk brought to mind a quote from E. O. Wilson in his 2006 book *The Creation*, which is a hypothetical letter to a Southern Baptist minister. "This is not the time for science fiction but for common sense," Wilson wrote, "and the following prescription: ecosystems and species can be saved only by understanding the unique value of each species in turn, and by persuading the people who have dominion over them to serve as their stewards." In Ammon's presentation, he made the point that ecosystems and species are irrelevant in humanity's plight. He did not accept that the earth has finite resources such as water and food, and he argued that a human population could never exceed carrying capacity. Dominion to Ammon, according to this speech and his other frequent sermons, does not include a stewardship that values species, but rather grants authority to bend the earth to meet all human aspirations, in spite of consequences to other life forms or the current climate crisis.

Denying science is nothing new for the Bundy family. But it is one tendency that actually departs from the early Mormon Church. The Saints, Brigham Young once told his people, "differ very much with Christendom in regard to the sciences of religion. Our religion embraces all truth and every fact in existence, no matter whether in heaven, earth, or hell. A fact is a fact, all truth issues forth from the Fountain of truth, and the sciences are facts as far as men have proved them." All the same, Cliven Bundy has derided scientific findings that call grazing a threat to wildlife habitat as "lynx and spotted owl land grab science." Any data suggesting that impacts of cattle harm wild species, be they owls, cats, tortoises, willow flycatchers, or sage grouse, are examples of a plot by the Fish and Wildlife Service, the Nevada State Department of Wildlife, and the BLM to impound cattle and put public land ranchers out of work, according to Cliven. So also with Ammon at Modesto. Instead of accepting the evidence and conclusions of studies he disagreed with, Ammon offered his own facts and data to support his beliefs.

He went on to raise his family's gripe with the BLM, especially regarding the desert tortoise. To environmentalists, he said, the tortoise is more important than a family living off the land. He claimed that the reptile population fares better when sharing the desert with cows. And besides, it wasn't the ranchers who were killing the tortoise; it was the government. They killed thousands of them during supposed recovery efforts, he told us.

There is some basis to this, but only a little. After being declared an endangered species in 1989, and later downgraded to threatened, the tortoise and its recovery required the establishment of grazing restrictions in the Southern Nevada Grazing District. In addition to canceling permits (and compensating ranchers for those cancellations), the BLM established the

Desert Tortoise Conservation Center. This was a facility outside of Las Vegas, built to help reestablish tortoise numbers in Clark County. Thousands of the reptiles were turned in, for a new life in the facility, by people in the region who had kept them as pets. Then, during later phases of the recovery effort, the government released a total of ten thousand tortoises. Hundreds of tortoises (not thousands, as Ammon suggested) were euthanized at the center after showing signs of a respiratory infection, to prevent further spread of disease to the wild. Yes, the federal program had been problematic. Officials initially feared that bacterial infection could threaten wild tortoises, but later studies showed that there was far less danger than originally assumed. Many animals were killed unnecessarily in the earlier years of the program, before a new policy called for fewer tortoises to be put down. The center, supported by the same Las Vegas development deal that paid the ranchers to stop grazing their cows in rural Clark County, closed after the money dried up following the housing crisis of the 2000s and the subsequent deceleration of development.

As Ammon went on and on in Modesto, refuting many claims environmentalists make in regard to current conditions, he arrived at the idea of water shortages. If water was scarce, he asked the gathering, then what accounts for an 18 percent increase in freshwater being dumped into the ocean last year? Some members of the audience nodded their heads in affirmation of his line of thinking. In fact there had been a major increase in the amount of freshwater flowing into the ocean last year and even more this year. But it wasn't an overabundance of rain, and it wasn't wasteful people simply turning on their faucets and letting water run down the drain. It was ice melt, from rising global temperatures. Here we all sat, in California, the state that has seen six of its most destructive fires (since record-keeping began) within just the last three years, yet Ammon made no mention of dryness, fire cycles, or climate.

In his continued challenge to the notion that our planet is at risk, Ammon concluded his presentation citing a study from 2013, conducted by the University of East Anglia's School of Environmental Sciences in Norwich, England, which reported that earth will remain hospitable for life for another 1.7 billion years. The researchers based their conclusion on observations from seven other planets outside our solar system, which allowed them to calibrate how temperatures and water supplies were affected by a growing sun. (As a sun ages, its core collapses and outer layers expand and burn hotter.) The study estimated that humans have nearly two billion years before we need to worry about lethal temperatures or the evaporation of our water supply. Ammon conceded that the results had included a disclaimer—a nuclear war or an errant asteroid might destroy us sooner. But what Ammon failed to mention was that the East Anglia scientists, by their own admission, had not factored in the impacts of climate change. His perceptions, incongruently hopeful for a person bound by an apocalyptic religion, were unencumbered by an ongoing and dizzying uptick in global temperatures. Ironically, it is the very thing that he omitted which might indeed bring us face-to-face with end-times.

In his wide-ranging and lively book *Fantasyland*, Kurt Andersen takes the reader through the history of Americans believing whatever the heck we want to believe. What started out as the pilgrims' pursuit of religious freedom—a choice to embrace heterodox beliefs—has turned into a downright mulish insistence, Andersen shows, that "truths" can be based on faith or gut feelings rather than on evidence. Andersen refers specifically to Joseph Smith, questioning whether Smith was "a heartfelt believer in his delusions or among the greatest confidence men ever." He touches on Mormonism and details wave after wave of new fads throughout our country's history—from treasure-seeking, to séances, to mesmerism, to guns and anti-science. Andersen introduces us to Clark Stanley, the man who invented snake oil, a product that did absolutely nothing and hence became the archetypal metaphor for products that do absolutely nothing. Ours is a culture that upholds people's right to have their own "truths." It's their freedom! But this has created a complete mess.

There is value in such a laissez-faire attitude; it allows for tolerance and the building of relationships among people who practice different faiths, hold different priorities, or embrace weird idiosyncrasies. And what's the problem if Mrs. Peters down the street thinks it's good luck to dangle a rabbit's foot from her rearview mirror? (To the rabbit, it's a problem.) What's the big deal if your dentist holds his breath when he rides his bike past graveyards? But there is a flashpoint, Andersen argues, where an absence of consensual beliefs, even on the empirical level, drops us into a fact-free melee where people may disregard any evidence challenging their personal version of reality. When the subjective overrules the objective, the result is a society of people who believe and behave as if "feelings were as true as facts." When Ammon Bundy tells his audience that science is actually the religion of heretics, we not only see his own disbelief in objective data—one crucial part of the work of science—we also witness his campaign to further denigrate fact and reality. By conflating science and religion, we are free to cheerily pick and choose among scientific statistics, and to look for "data" in scripture.

Cleon Skousen, the Mormon thinker so influential to the Bundys (and their militia supporters), spent a good chunk of his career analyzing prophecy—from the Bible, the Book of Mormon, the Doctrine and Covenants, and other Mormon sacred texts. He mined these in order to understand "truths" about the future of mankind. To some Mormons, including the Bundys, prophecy throughout the last few thousand years is germane and persuasive, certainly more so than the predictions of climatology, population biology, and range science. When considering the state of the land, by this view, there is more merit in words of revelation from favored prophets than in methodical data collection. Data are of no interest to Ammon Bundy, insofar as they challenge his faith and worldview.

Skousen compiled revelations from the visions of Mormon and Christian prophets in his book *Prophecy and Modern Times*. He wrote that one day "the earth will bring forth its strength" as oceans drain and mountains level. The environment will become more accommodating and pleasant for humans and agriculture. Valleys will flatten and "nature's hostile barriers" will be transformed into a "graceful contour of broad meadows and rich plains, broken only by shallow vales or gentle slopes." Though he concedes that this might be hard to imagine, considering that "only 28% of the earth's surface is above sea level," Skousen wrote, "this will be changed." Skousen declares that we are getting ready for the planet to be a continuous expanse of perfect farmland. People will have plenty of tillable acreage to grow food and run cattle. Though today they may sit at the bottom of the ocean, in the latter times, Skousen assures his followers, these soon-to-be-dry lands will be accessible to humans.

On July 15, 2018, just before Todd Engel was sentenced to fourteen years for his role at the Battle of Bunkerville, some friends and supporters held a rally for the militia member in Las Vegas. On that blazing-hot day, people assembled in the air-conditioned back room of the Boulevard Bar and Grill, a twenty-four-hour-a-day casino a few miles from the Strip. Cowboy poet Kenny Hall, from Heber City, Utah, gave a reading of "The Old Cow Man," by Charles Badger Clark, an old-time cowpuncher and the poet laureate of South Dakota, born six years before Charlie Redd. The poem is a sad lament for bygone cowboy days and the once wide-open American plains. Hall, in a flat-brimmed hat, with a carefully waxed mustache, recited it for us that day. A few select bits:

I rode across a valley range
I hadn't seen for years.
The trail was all so spoilt and strange
It nearly fetched the tears.

T'was good to live when all the sod,
Without no fence or fuss,
Belonged in partnership to God,
The Gover'ment and us.

When my old soul hunts range and rest
Beyond the last divide,
Just plant me in some stretch of West
That's sunny, lone and wide.

Let cattle rub my tombstone down
And coyotes mourn their kin,
Let hawses paw and tromp the moun'
But don't you fence it in!

The verses despair of a lost time when the Lord and the feds had worked together to keep the plains open to the cowboy. But alas, no more. As the poem winds toward its conclusions, the Old Cow Man imagines his own death along with that of the cowboy dream. Laid to rest out on the prairie, he remains defiant, yet haunted by days long gone.

After the poetry, lunch was served, along with a program focused on liberty, freedom, and the moral code of "no man left behind." This was a war, after all, and their comrade had been found guilty of "obstruction of justice and interstate travel in aid of extortion," so here they were to support him as he awaited sentencing. When Engel had arrived in Bunkerville four years earlier, according to his verdict, he did so with "the intent to commit a crime of violence against federal law enforcement officers who were executing a federal court order." He had been one of the men wearing a tactical vest and holding an AR-15 who was photographed lying in wait behind a concrete barrier, his rifle aimed at law enforcement officers such as Tom Jenkins.

At the rally, Ryan Bundy, whose contorted face reflected the old trauma of having been run over by a truck at the age of seven, replaced Roger Stone as the keynote. Stone, Donald Trump's advisor, who'd been stumping on behalf of the Battle of Bunkerville militia and the Hammonds, was a no-show—occupied with other matters, namely Robert Mueller's investigation in Washington, DC. Ryan, microphone in hand, talked about his Nevada gubernatorial candidacy as well as a dream he'd had while staying at the Malheur National Wildlife Refuge. "God speaks to men in many ways," he said, and in this case, he spoke in Ryan's sleep. In the dream, Ryan stepped through a corridor. There in front of him was a lion on a pedestal. A bucket of meat lay on the ground nearby. Ryan fed the beast and, he told us, this "satisfied him." Then many lions showed up, all running toward Ryan, wanting to be fed as well. The meat from the bucket was, according to Ryan, "good steak." Suddenly, one feline got a bone stuck in his throat. The gagging animal woke Ryan out of the dream. He was left to wonder, "Did he eat it or did he choke?" Months later, when he sat in a courtroom in Portland, Oregon, looking at the presiding judge, the dream made sense to him. "I realized that meat was the truth. In the end, the jury delivered the bone and the judge choked on it." In this, Ryan saw his dream come true.

In Oregon, Ammon, Ryan, and five others including Shawna Cox had pleaded not guilty to a list of charges stemming from Malheur, which ranged from property damage, firearms violations, and "forced intimidation and threats," to acts to "conspire against and impede government officials." In spite of overwhelming evidence and numerous eyewitness accounts,

Cox, Jeff Banta, Kenneth Medenbach, and David Lee Fry were released. So was Neil Wampler, an occupier and self-described "old hippie," who had been convicted of killing his own father in 1977. Part of the reason these occupiers walked was the prosecution's overconfidence in pinning its case to a very hard-to-prove conspiracy charge. The defendants had faced other charges, ranging from "depredation of government property" to "possession of a firearm and a deadly weapon in a federal facility," but these allegations were contingent on proving a conspiracy to keep federal employees from their jobs. Marcus R. Mumford, Ammon's attorney, focused on presenting the government assertions of conspiracy as unprovable. The jury agreed and issued not-guilty decisions for each of these seven defendants.

During a later go-around, in 2017, federal prosecutors were much more successful. This time, they hired a consultant to help the Oregon jury better understand the charges, such as what "conspiracy" actually means. In exchange for plea deals, Brian Cavalier, Jake Ryan, Darryl Thorn, Jason Patrick, and Duane Ehmer pleaded guilty. Ryan Payne, a leader in the Malheur occupation and a logistics coordinator at Bunkerville, had expressed remorse at his sentencing hearing, but the judge found him to be disingenuous. Judge Anna J. Brown was made aware that, during his presentence release a couple of months earlier, Payne posted on Facebook pictures of himself posing with Ammon near the Bundy ranch. That, the judge told Payne, demonstrated that he "once again thumbed your nose, I'll say politely, to the rule of law and to the Constitution. The grin on your face at the Bundy ranch. The big smiles . . . convey something different from a disavowal of your associations." Payne paid a price for his preening, receiving thirty-seven months in jail and an order to pay ten thousand dollars restitution to Friends of Malheur, the nonprofit organization whose mission is to "promote conservation and appreciation of natural and cultural resources."

Most Malheur occupants who pleaded guilty were given time served. Cavalier served nine months. Duane Ehmer, one of the most photographed figures at Malheur, riding his horse Hellboy, served a year and a day for degrading government property around a Native burial site. Jake Ryan also served a year and a day, in his case for digging the trenches, and he and Ehmer were ordered to pay restitution to the Burns Paiute Tribe. Jason Patrick and Darryl Thorn were guilty of conspiracy charges, the former serving twenty-one months and the latter eighteen months. Both got time served. Patrick was further guilty of tampering with government vehicles, destruction of federal property, and trespassing, all misdemeanors. Blaine Cooper was the last to be sentenced in 2018, with two years time served.

In spite of Ammon Bundy's insistence that environmentalists are liars, there is a small but vexing piece of the Oregon case that shows Ammon's own relationship with veracity. During the Oregon proceedings, Ammon fought for the right to wear his cowboy hat and cowboy boots in the courtroom. His lawyer, Marcus R. Mumford, told the judge that this rancher persona was essential in order for the jury to be assured of Ammon's "authenticity and credibility." Ammon wanted to present himself as a cowboy. His request was denied when the judge cited "safety issues."

By then, in 2017, the Bundy Ranch Facebook page had over two hundred thousand people following the family's carefully curated cowboy mythology. Romanticized though this image may be, it remains, to many Americans, a touchstone in a rapidly changing world. There is a wistfulness in its stubborn embrace. According to BEEF, a media outlet for cattle ranchers and agribusiness, the cowboy is an icon for "good old-fashioned values." A career in livestock production, claims the BEEF website, Beefmagazine.com, is one of wholesome toil while riding life's dusty trails side by side with the Lord. The cowboy represents traditions for future generations so that children "will one day find their way back home to the ranch and faith that there is a future in agriculture for them." But this ideal is at odds with an industry rapidly adjusting to globalization, shifting consumer interests, and a dire warning that globally beef production is a huge contributor to methane release. As new generations of ranching families face those realities, conventions and expectations passed down from mothers and fathers aren't guaranteed fulfillment.

This happened with both Ammon and Ryan. Neither are cowboys themselves. They are not ranchers. Unlike their father, they do not labor in the livestock production industry. Opportunities in that line of work are few and far between. The brothers have created other career paths. Ryan has most recently been on the campaign trail for Nevada's governorship (he lost), and Ammon, besides tending to his truck repair business, is making appearances around the West and spreading muddles of inaccuracies. Their dad, Cliven, is also making the rounds. With each rally, county fair, and town hall meeting they attend, the Bundys' voices reach more ears, their worldview infects more minds. At a time when we, as a nation, a society, and world community, face very real and very grave political, environmental, and cultural crises, the Bundys are obscuring fact with fabrication. Truth is one casualty. America's public land is the other.

Spellbound

Any critical question—the kind that a scientist would wel-
come—was not acceptable . . . anything that questions belief
means something evil, bad or Satan. It's wrong to listen, it's
wrong to even play with ideas that are different. This is how
unthinkable things can happen.

—Diane Benscoter, cult expert and author of
Shoes of a Servant: My Unconditional Devotion to a Lie

Like the Bundys, the Trump administration doesn't much care for science. It's very industry/business-friendly, as reflected in its emphasis on extraction rather than conservation. There has been a focus on deregulation, in the Interior Department and elsewhere, much like during the Reagan administration and its Interior Department under the leadership of James Watt. Donald Trump's first interior secretary Ryan Zinke and later Acting Secretary David Bernhardt have worked toward undoing laws and regulations protecting public lands, species, and resources, rather than bolstering those protections or upholding them. These efforts range from lowering standards on methane emissions and allowing dirty coal operations for projects on public lands, to shrinking the sizes of Bears Ears and Grand Staircase-Escalante Monuments. It's therefore surprising that the controversial Gold Butte National Monument has thus far remained intact.

Gold Butte is an utterly breathtaking place, a landscape marked by the lives, struggles, and industries of the peoples who have called it home for thousands of years. To get to the new monument, head north on Interstate 15 from Las Vegas and take exit 112, the site of the Battle of Bunkerville. You'll see tattered flags—American, Nevada state, and Clark County—attached to dual poles painted white, bearing Cliven's favorite phrase, broken, with unintended symbolism, into two halves—"we the" here, and "people" fifteen feet away. Turn down Gold Butte Road and pass the Bundy ranch, or maybe stop in and buy some melons. This route heads south toward the monument on blacktop that was first paved, according to local lore, by Howard Hughes. If you head southeast, you cruise past the old ranch of Keith Nay, Bundy's pal who wrote *The Nay Book*, a work of Mormon prophecy and constitutional sophistry. The place is now a vacation getaway, catering to tourists, boy scouts, and yoga retreaters. A sign tells travelers, "NO DIRECT ACCESS TO GRAND CANYON NATIONAL PARK," though the road actually does stretch to the North Rim. That false warning was posted after BLM agents, and the people who bought the Nay spread from Keith's widow, grew weary of rescuing tourists who high-centered their rental cars on a road best handled in a four-by-four with very good clearance.

On a 2018 trip to Gold Butte along this route, at first I saw no trace of Bundy's illicit cows, but then I glanced great bare patches and a proliferation of noxious weeds indicating substantial impacts. I felt at first as though I were passing through a vast expanse of no-man's-land. But as I've mentioned, Gold Butte, like the entire West, has been a hive of human activity over the centuries and millennia. There are no untrodden or empty spaces. The walls of Gold Butte carry the tales of the Southern Paiute people, and the desert floor shows signs of American miners who flocked here at the turn of the twentieth century to make their fortunes, hundreds of years after Spanish explorers searched the area for gold. A longtime resident of the Gold Butte area, Eddie Bounsall, wrote of his search for Spanish mines in his colorful self-published memoir, *Crazy Ed's Sagas and Secrets of Desert Gold*. Bounsall was a prospector in the region who used a dowsing rod (also known as a divining rod) in treasure-seeking, 150 years after Joseph Smith employed the same technique in upstate New York. He never found the mother lode while working his mining lease for 22 years and died of cancer in 1994 at the age of sixty-four. The last mine in Gold Butte was shut down in 2006, when its owner, John Lear, whose father developed the Lear jet, forgot to file an annual thirty-dollar permit fee. Lear is said to have harbored no ill will after he lost the claim, though he'd sunk six hundred thousand dollars into his investment.

Steve Dudrow, a jovial retiree and volunteer for Friends of Gold Butte, an organization dedicated to protecting the monument, hosted me and a small group of others during this trip to the monument. We camped at a place called Little Finland, named for its red, wind-carved fins. It's an arresting scape of Joshua trees, creosote bushes, and towering sandstone, where palm trees pop from sands wet with slow seeps—little trickles sustaining brilliant patches of jade among desert and dusty rock uplifts. Gold Butte is not the destination for ill-prepared travelers or vehicles with weak axles, as days of driving over jarring roads made abundantly clear.

En route to our campsite, we passed a sign to the settlement of Gold Butte, a ghost town twenty miles from where we'd spend the night. This area has old silver, copper, lead, and gold mines scattered throughout; in the 1890s, some two thousand people called it home. The last folks to live in the town of Gold Butte were a pair named Bill Garrett and Art Coleman, who together shared a cabin and made their meager living by ranching, prospecting, and distilling moonshine. Art died in 1958 and Bill in 1961. The men were laid to rest together at the old town site. And they rested in peace there—until the Battle of Bunkerville.

Then, when the BLM closed the area to capture Bundy's cattle, some person or persons dug up Art Coleman's grave, presumably looking for valuables. The perpetrators left behind a hole but took most of Art Coleman's remains. Amid the danger that existed at the time—federal officers faced with so many militia members—the BLM did not investigate the grave robbery.

Many in the area believe that this desecration was carried out by ne'er-do-wells at the Bundys' standoff who used the chaos as a distraction. In any case, it was deeply upsetting to locals. Two years passed before what was left of Coleman's remains were reinterred. A big ceremony was held on the occasion, with lots of reminiscing by people who had heard stories about the pair but had never met them personally. No one was charged for the offense, adding just one more crime left unpunished among so many committed during the Battle of Bunkerville.

It wasn't just grave robbing. In addition to their own acts, the Bundys inspired several odious crimes. Greg Burleson, the Battle of Bunkerville participant who made violent threats both on his Facebook page and to an undercover FBI agent, became "mesmerized" by Cliven Bundy, according to his lawyer. This raises a question or two: Who else did the Bundys leave spellbound? And how have those captivated by their cowboy stories acted while under the influence? During the Oregon takeover, the sheriff of Harney County, Oregon, Dave Ward, received death threats, as did his wife and his elderly parents. During the Nevada standoff, workers employed by hotels in Mesquite, Nevada, just up the road from Bunkerville, were also menaced by an anonymous caller who told one hotel receptionist to expect to get shot in the parking lot or killed with a bomb for hosting federal agents. An estimated one hundred thousand dollars was lost in Mesquite during the period of heavy militia presence, due to threats of violence and precautions taken, while the robbers of Art Coleman's grave were at work.

Among those entangled with the Bundys were two young people, a married couple, who joined in at Bunkerville hoping to finally bring the government to its knees. Jerad and Amanda Miller arrived at the Bundy compound in April of 2014, ready for something big, titillated by insurgency and armed militancy. They had come from Lafayette, Indiana, to Las Vegas, and from there to the frontlines of the revolution. The woman, Goth-pale and blond, was twenty-two years old and full of hate toward the government; her husband Jerad was nine years her senior.

From the first, something about this pair didn't sit right, not even with their fellow militants. Finally they were asked to leave the Bundy place, according to Jerry DeLemus. He told a reporter, "I felt bad about running them off, but if someone was there potentially breaking the law, that was something we couldn't have there." (Seriously, he said that.) He continued to express regret that there was no system in place to vet the folks who'd shown up, some system to sort the good from the bad. After the Millers were kicked out, they took their anti-authority bile with them back to Las Vegas. Two months after their time in Bunkerville, they shot and killed two police officers and a civilian at a Walmart. According to witnesses, before they fired, they had shouted, "This is the start of a revolution." Perhaps they were angry about their ejection from Bunkerville. Or perhaps they had simply taken inspiration from the gathering, fed off its excitement, and crafted their own rebellion.

Since the Bunkerville confrontation, the BLM has stopped regularly monitoring Gold Butte. That means not only that Cliven Bundy continues to graze his cows for free, but also that no one is keeping any record of the condition of the desert ecosystem or the number of cows on public land. In 2015, three surveyors for the Great Basin Institute, a nonprofit partner with the BLM, the Forest Service, and the Fish and Wildlife Service, made camp in Gold Butte, as part of a study of cattle impacts on water sources. On their first night in the field, someone fired shots near their campsite, causing them to abandon the research and seek safety. Afterward, the BLM ordered all its personnel and contractors out of the area, and although recently there has been some BLM presence, that presence is tentative and minimal.

Truth be told, it's not as if the BLM had been vigilant in monitoring public resources before the Bundy showdown. The tortoise recovery plan places Gold Butte off-limits to cows, so it doesn't fall under any official grazing management plan. However, range managers in the region have a history of slacking on their assessments, according to one retired BLM agent, and of chummy relationships with ranchers. This has resulted in a tendency to let violations slide.

From 2002 to 2017, Richard Spotts was the planning and environmental coordinator of the BLM out of St. George, Utah. He oversaw environmental compliance under the National Environmental Policy Act (NEPA) for the Arizona Strip District and Grand Canyon-Parashant National Monument. He considers himself an atypical BLM guy, having come at it after a career as a lawyer and a conservation advocate. Most BLM staff are from rural backgrounds and are conservative, Spotts told me, but he was quick to add, "Not that that's bad." We were sitting in his home in St. George. His wife, he said, was "crafting" in another room. The house smelled of pumpkin spice and brimmed with knick-knacks, baskets, and pillows, one of which was inscribed with the word "Gratitude." This sentiment does not extend to Spotts's experience with the BLM, one marked by exasperation and tension. "I really pissed off the range team," he said. Unlike his colleagues, he advocated protection for threatened species and was vocal about incidents of overgrazing. "Whenever I saw an area that was hammered," he told me, he would call it out—in response to which, both the ranchers and the BLM agents made excuses. They wouldn't take steps to restore the damage or make future corrections or adjustments. They didn't want the feedback from Spotts. "They stopped inviting me," he said of the trips into the field.

When he took the job with the BLM, he learned that trespass grazing, the act of letting cows go into areas where they were not authorized, was not at all uncommon. It wasn't only the Bundys. Just off the Arizona Strip, in the bajada below the Virgin Mountains and Pakoon Springs, about twenty miles south of Gold Butte, someone else's cows had been moving illegally into critical tortoise habitat. These areas were open to grazing only between October and March, during which time the cold-blooded tortoise sought refuge underground in a period of brumation, or as Spotts called it, "Chilling. . . . Mammals hibernate, reptiles brumate." But cattle were allowed to remain in the area, or enter it, also during months when the tortoises were active, in spite of the rules. Ranchers were taking illegal liberties. Mike Small, a tortoise biologist for the BLM, kept records on such transgressions for years and, when he retired, handed over these data to Spotts. Until then, no matter how many people Small had approached, pressured, or pleaded with, no one did anything. His supervisors didn't appreciate Small's years detailing violations—paper trails were a big no-no because they could be requested by environmental lawyers through the Freedom of Information Act. As reflected in the BLM's decades of reluctance to file a complaint against Bundy, rules were more conveniently ignored than enforced. Other incidents of grazing trespass, involving other cows and other ranchers, were likewise met only with annoyance and inertia.

"The media focuses a lot on Cliven Bundy and those scofflaws and people that are kinda lawless and maybe arrogant about land rights," explained Spotts. But other ranchers likewise ignore the regulations and get away with it. In Spotts's opinion, the BLM bears a healthy half share of blame for incidents of grazing trespass on public lands in Nevada, Arizona, and Utah.

"The culpability for that history of well over twenty years rests with federal agencies," he said. "BLM, but also Fish and Wildlife Service, National Park Service at Lake Mead, and the Justice Department." In other words, if the agencies responsible for taking care of our public lands were doing their jobs, Bundy and others might be obeying the law.

It's not just the fact that the cows are grazing and trampling tortoise habitat. It's a more basic question of appropriate use and decent treatment of animals—all animals. The life of a western cow isn't easy, and conditions at Gold Butte are especially hard. "How would you like to be a cow in the Mojave Desert?" Spotts asked. A question we all might well ponder. The temperatures can exceed 120 degrees for stretches in the summer. Not only are cattle ecologically unsuited for these fragile lands, but it can also be argued that grazing cows in the desert, year round, is inhumane. Gold Butte is just not a good place for them. Unlike the desert tortoise, these mammals can't brumate. And they face other travails besides the withering heat; for instance, they could easily get stuck in the mudflats of Lake Mead, looking for water. And die. But who knows? No one is keeping a record of cows in Gold Butte.

Mary O'Brien's house sits in the middle of one of the most striking places in the state of Utah: Castle Valley. This is the woman who, decades ago, in her teaching days, introduced me to strange-sounding federal acronyms such as FLPMA, NEPA, and ESA—the Federal Land Policy and Management Act, the National Environmental Policy Act, and the Endangered Species Act—laws that protect the public lands and endangered species on behalf of "we the people." After leaving the faculty at University of Montana, O'Brien joined the Grand Canyon Trust and is now the Utah Forests Program director. There is no one in the world with a laugh more infectious than Mary's. She's a tall, wiry woman whose hair has gone gray since I was her student in Missoula. She is striking, and she's also smart as hell.

Despite having spent decades as an advocate for wild places and being an inspiration to many students, at the end of her career O'Brien confesses to feeling rather hopeless. Like Spotts, she is seeing public lands left unmonitored and overgrazed. Standards laid out under NEPA are meant to keep native plant and wildlife communities intact, but those standards are largely being ignored. Annual plans are supposed to establish the amount of grass cows and sheep can eat—requirements set in order for plants to bounce back after each season of grazing—but the amount is regularly set too high. And even these unsustainable limits written into grazing plans are regularly exceeded. It is the job of managers to hold permittees accountable for not letting their livestock mow down grasses, trample stream banks, or pollute water sources, but they aren't upholding their duties. In many places, especially in southern and central Utah, according to O'Brien, rules are being flouted. So ranchers and their livestock can do whatever they want on public lands, because US laws aren't being enforced by those being paid to administer them.

In her research on the impacts of grazing on public lands in southern Utah, Mary has watched places that she monitors "just getting nuked. Utter destruction. There are no flowers or pollinators, no insects." She told me that recovery isn't happening, and that the damage is just getting worse. As climate change dries the land and alters its fecundity, and pollinator populations plummet, oversight is more important than ever. The current administration has a cozy relationship with the livestock industry, and, frankly, the public trust is not being managed in the way our laws dictate. Some BLM and Forest Service personnel want to do their jobs, but whether their supervisors have encouraged them to stop citing violations, or whether the Bundys have so incited ranchers as to make management impossible, public lands aren't getting looked after or safeguarded as they should be in Nevada and Utah.

So those lands are really in trouble right now. And they matter more than ever in the face of a wildly changing climate. They are precious to the human spirit, but they're also essential ecological reserves for other species and act as vital carbon sequestration sites. According to *Smithsonian Magazine*, the original Grand Staircase-Escalante National Monument, for instance, is home to an astounding 660 bee species. Eighty-four of those species now exist only in populations living outside the new boundaries, as recently redrawn by the Trump administration, making the monument smaller. His administration has also shut down a federal honeybee study collecting data on fragile populations of pollinators and buried federal climate studies that warned, potentially, of a dire future. O'Brien told me that, after all her years of environmental advocacy, she now feels that she has not made any lasting contributions to the protection of public lands. This is a shocking register of despair. "There is just no standing up for facts or limits," she said. It's a trend throughout Trump's EPA and Department of the Interior—studies on bee populations have been cut, the impacts of climate change aren't being assessed, and in Utah and Nevada, grazing impacts are not being scrutinized, nor are lawbreakers being held accountable.

Doing the Right Thing

Almost any sect, cult, or religion will legislate its creed into law if it acquires the political power to do so.

—Robert A. Heinlein

Riding a horse is pure joy. It just is. And being on horseback offers a heady insight into why the cowboy life has such a powerful pull. Horseback riding is life-affirming and freeing. Maybe it's just the mythos that goes along with the whole deal, but it's so damn fun. I've already told you a little bit about Kelton Hafen, his son Lyman, and the day I met them over lunch in St. George for a conversation centered on silver mining. They also invited me to their ranch, where I got to play cowboy. Casper, a big white quarter horse, both sturdy and sweet, carried me around the family spread and I was in heaven.

The Hafen ranch is a tidy collection of corrals, farmhouses, and pastures tucked into a swale where today Kelton, Lyman, and other family members spend part of their time, shuttling back and forth between here and St. George. A schoolhouse, spruce and whitewashed, where Kelton's grandmother once practiced her letters, remains to this day. And old Gunlock Hamblin, long dead from poisoned coffee, lies buried in a small, well-tended graveyard on the property. This is in Clover Valley, Nevada, geographically central to Dixie's history and the events that undergird the Bundy story, sitting below Bunker Mountain, so named for the cofounder of Bunkerville, Edward Bunker. Beside the ranch is the Shivwits Paiute reservation, home to Greg Anderson, as well as Kelton's old grazing allotment, long ago bought out by the Vegas developers and now empty of cows. The route to and from St. George on Highway 18 is straight through the Mountain Meadows Massacre site and its many monuments to the dead.

Kelton still runs cows on his own land, which contrasts jarringly with the arid public lands of the region: the pea-green of irrigated grass surrounded by creosote and Joshua trees. Kelton, a little wobbly from age and hard work, explained to me that, as a Saint from a long line of Mormon ranchers, he had a special knowledge of how best to utilize desert land and raise cows on next to nothing. When he did graze the scrubby, unirrigated public lands adjacent to his own property, it was a feat that often mystified other ranchers. Out-of-state visitors, like me, who came to visit the place, often marveled that anyone could raise cattle on such marginal range. "Most cattlemen, say from Montana, Wyoming, come down here and take a look at this and they can't see a thing that a cow can live on." On one occasion, folks from Wyoming gazed out on the land and asked Kelton, "How can those cattle look so good and there's not a damn thing here for them to eat?" He told me that outsiders don't understand the environment down here. Cows eat what's called "blackbrush," which provides marginal feed in the winter, he explained. "We don't expect to get a cow fat on the winter range." Rather, ranchers out here hope that blackbrush will get the cattle through winter and that then, throughout the fullness of the year, there will be enough other forage and enough rain so that each cow can have a healthy calf.

Many Mormon ranchers in this region pride themselves similarly—on doing what other ranchers cannot do, maintaining herds on the most meager of rangeland. They know how to wring the desert of everything it has to raise cows. Regional ranchers view this ability as a testament to Mormon fortitude—and a certain know-how passed from generation to generation. These are the people whom Lyman Hafen depicted in one of his books, *Roping the Wind*, as "leather-faced, chappy-lipped, gravel-voiced old boys, all of them grandsons of Mormon pioneers, all of them living the only lives they have ever known—extensions of the lives of their fathers." As romantic as it sounds, though, the sons of Mormon cowboys can't all be public land ranchers.

In addition to the fragile ecology of this landscape, the productivity of the land, even for people with a passion for ranching, is rather puny. In the ranking of cattle production among the fifty US states, Utah comes in thirty-sixth and Nevada thirty-seventh. Added together, these states match only 9.7 percent of the cattle production of the top-ranked state, Texas. Livestock producers may be able to run cattle operations in arid climates, but there are ecological limits to these desert lands. It is not easy to raise cows in places so scant, which begs the question, should cows even be here?

Though the Hafens gave up their public land lease, Lyman and Kelton have supported the Bundy fight. Both feel that ranchers have gotten a bad rap from conservationists, who have created a culture of government restrictions that leads to the disappearance of the family ranches. Although both men concede that making an alliance with the right-wing militias was taking things too far, they maintain nonetheless that there was merit in Cliven Bundy's stance, in spite of the fact that he broke the law and stopped paying his fees. Kelton said that the Bundys, though reckless, truly believe that they "are doing the right thing."

And what is the right thing? Since the time of Brigham Young there has been a tendency—or call it a point of honor—among the people of Dixie to flout government mandates and regulations in favor of "a higher law." The law that God communicates directly, by this view, is "the right thing." Especially when the federal law of the land, contrary to God's, constrains traditional use. In Zion, the land of the Mormon people, rightness lies in doing things as they've always been done.

Back in Paradise, Montana, on that winter day in 2018, I watched as Cliven Bundy, dressed in a gray jacket and a dun-colored cowboy hat, explained to the audience that he had spent seven hundred days in jail, and asked them, "Who would you say that I should hold accountable?" The spectators, some also in cowboy hats, others in baseball caps, and a few with colonial-style tricorns, the style of chapeau favored by pirates and Paul Revere, shouted back, "Obama!" "The sheriff!" "Harry Reid!" And of course, the obligatory name, yelled so often at such assemblies, "Hillary Clinton!" But instead of whipping his spectators into more screamy anger, Bundy gentled the crowd. Sticking to oft-made points such as the-government-can't-own-land and the-Constitution-is-divine, he also explained that anyone who holds rights to public lands has acquired them "preemptively through beneficial use . . . created through our pioneer fathers." He continued, saying that these are "property rights, not privileges, not allotments." In fact, he said, "They *are* your ranch!" He told of an old neighbor who'd lived near the Bundy place and who had advised him never to call public land "an allotment." No, at the end of the day, those that leased federal lands, according to Bundy and his long-deceased neighbor, should call the land something altogether different. He told the ranchers in the crowd to go ahead and just "call it your ranch."

Bundy's dismissal of environmental laws, his misinterpretation of the Constitution, and his take on entitlement are all very popular in some western, libertarian circles. It's not hate that attracts most of Bundy's followers, it's the sense of power that these ideas give those who feel themselves powerless. Part of this need for a sense of empowerment goes back to the economic anxieties common in white rural American communities.

According to J. J. MacNab, who writes about the American militia movement, "To Bundy and his supporters, the fight isn't just about money; it's about a deep-seated belief that they are right, and the rest of the nation is just too brainwashed or stupid to understand."

Additionally, a lot of support for the Bundys bubbles up from umbrage livestock producers feel over land regulations that did not exist when they were growing up. It's a common theme in America right now, to glorify the old days. And Bundy is telling people that their government is lying to them, constitutionally speaking, about the very right of owning land—a right allowed to individuals, he maintains, not to the US government. Federal land is "your ranch." Still, most public land ranchers are not at all like the Bundys and most pay their grazing fees. Not to say that there aren't many western ranchers irate over federal regulations. But most obey the law. Like Kelton Hafen. Although he understands why the Bundys got angry, and he even believes in their rectitude, Hafen never stopped paying federal fees when he ran cattle on public lands. Nor did he rally the militia, threaten innocent people, or consider pushing others to the brink of a violent confrontation that would have caused a national horror. He wasn't happy about the desert tortoise plan, nor had he wanted to give up his allotment, but he followed the law of the land.

Senator Ron Wyden of Oregon, a tall man, aged seventy, said during the Malheur occupation that it seemed as though a "virus was spreading." Wyden, as the son of Jewish parents who fled Nazi Germany, knows a thing or two about the viral aspect of hate and incitation. He worried publicly, after Malheur, that by not forcibly putting a stop to the takeover, the government had encouraged more people to show up on public lands and do whatever they please. He demanded that there be accountability and appropriate consequences for the actions of the Bundy family. But there haven't been any. So now, Cliven is free to spread his beliefs, which are being passed from one rural community to another.

Todd MacFarlane, the lawyer who helped Mary Bulloch in the 2000s when she was waging her fight with federal land managers, is a loyal Bundy supporter who participated in both the Oregon and Nevada campaigns. His great-grandfather was none other than Isaac Haight, the man so committed to Zion that he was among those responsible for the murder of 120 innocents at Mountain Meadows. Haight lived eighty miles north of Kanosh, Utah, where MacFarlane owns a ranch. This lawyer has become very vocal about the war over public lands and responded to Wyden's warning in a blog post, wondering what the senator meant by "virus." Of the refuge takeover, he wrote, "Some say it was extremism. Others say it was the truth. Yet others say it was the so-called militia." What must be most worrying to the Oregon senator, MacFarlane opines, was the fact that the Bundys are sharing their perspectives and encouraging others to take similar positions. The Bundys, MacFarlane says, are preaching "what I have come to refer to as a Gospel—the Good News—of Property Rights."

Gospel? Virus? The answer, I suppose, lies within what you've come to value. As the Bundys, with a victory in hand, continue to spread their points of view, they do so at the peril of public lands and civil order. But they think they are doing the right thing, and no one, not the state of Nevada, not the federal government, not law enforcement of any sort, is stopping them.

The Bundys have taken a position that many Mormon politicians want to advance—the further opening up of public lands. Utah and Nevada led this charge for decades, starting with pushing for land transfers to states in the 1970s, and continue today. Ken Ivory, currently a Utah state representative, and US Senator Mike Lee have been among many Mormon politicians very eager to get land transferred back to western states. Lee has even been among those considered for a Supreme Court position, which would really be dangerous for the future of public lands. Neither man believes the federal government should control or even own any such lands. Ivory was declared legislator of the year in 2014 by the American Legislative Exchange Council (ALEC), a nonprofit organization funded by David (now deceased) and Charles Koch, the wealthy right-wing libertarians. This federalist organization creates model legislation for states to customize, then pass and implement—templates promoting land privatization schemes and the weakening of federal conservation laws. ALEC also works to make federal lands seem wasteful and unnecessary, so that the public does not value them. Although the organization has not directly supported the actions of the Bundy family, ALEC advances the same legal arguments and rationales that the Bundys preach, as a way of undermining federal holding of public lands.

At a conference in 2014, a week after the BLM stood down at Bunkerville, Becky Lockhart, a member of ALEC and the speaker of the Utah State House of Representatives, spoke of the Bundy standoff. She told participants at a conference called the Legislative Summit on the Transfer of Public Lands that "what's happened in Nevada is really just a symptom of a much larger problem." Meaning, there would be no armed takeovers if public lands were managed by states. Or sold off to the highest bidder. The problem in Nevada was not a bunch of rogue militia, to Lockhart, or the fact that Cliven Bundy had broken multiple laws. It was that the federal government owns land in western states, American public land.

Mormon leadership denounced the 2016 Oregon takeover, issuing a statement that read, "Church leaders strongly condemn the armed seizure of the facility and are deeply troubled by the reports that those who have seized the facility suggest that they are doing so based on scriptural principles. This armed occupation can in no way be justified on a scriptural basis." All the same, there has evidently been a degree of church support over the years as well as among Mormon politicians.

Once so humble that bills were left unpaid in Kirtland, over the years the church has become very wealthy, with a diverse investment portfolio. According to various estimates, the church now holds billions of dollars in assets, though the organization has not disclosed financials since 1959. In the fall of 2019, whistleblower David A. Nielsen, himself a financial advisor to the Mormon Church, sent a complaint to the Internal Revenue Service. He reported that the church diverted donations—tithes for educational and charitable purposes—into business investments that now total somewhere in the ballpark of one hundred billion dollars. This figure doesn't include other accounts or assets that Nielsen's firm does not manage. (The Mormon Church owns millions of acres of land as well as commercial properties across the United States.) Nielsen, according to *The Washington Post*, the newspaper that broke the story, is a forty-one-year-old Latter-day Saint who had been a senior portfolio manager for a nonprofit affiliate of the Mormon Church. His complaint also states his firm's leadership justified this outrageous buildup of funds by explaining that, in the event of Armageddon and Christ's return to earth, the church must have a whole lot of ready cash.

Even before this bombshell, the church's hidden wealth has given some members pause, in considering both the church's aggrandizement and the impacts these investments have on culture and on land. In their book *Decolonizing Mormonism*, scholars and Latter-day Saints Gina Colvin and Joanna Brooks point out that the church is focused on increasing membership and its bottom line. "With an expanding financial base through ever-growing numbers of shell companies and property portfolios," Colvin and Brooks write, the church's lack of transparency, and its disregard of other cultures and the environment, "leads us to wonder if the yearning for Zion hasn't been abandoned in the face of a praxis that urges the institutional church towards pursuit and safeguarding of capital as an end in and of itself." One truly distinctive characteristic of Mormon worldview, different from views of life-versus-hereafter among other Christian denominations, is that Zion exists right now on earth. It's the physical instantiation of the idealized promise that Joseph Smith made—that of a sacred Mormon homeland. First it had been localized in Missouri, then in Nauvoo, Illinois, and then, as we've seen, Brigham Young carried it westward to Utah and Nevada. Zion arose as Latter-day Saints farmed and ranched across land that Native peoples too believed was sacred. And still today these lands remain contested, cherished, and coveted.

American Zion is a place as well as an idea. But if the idea itself has been degraded and undermined by church culture in its increasingly materialistic "praxis," then what is left for Mormons who truly love land? For Native peoples and other Americans? For wildlife? Or even for zealots such as the Bundys? Doesn't the destruction of an idealized Zion, along with the exquisite cultural and biological diversity of its geographical reality, represent the abandonment of exactly those key moral principles, central to at-its-best Mormonism, that encourage true safeguarding of a sacred space—not with guns and screams of entitlements, but with stewardship and collective management? Whereas Cleon Skousen looks to end-times to bring forth vicissitudes that would empty the planet of life, and thereby allow for its replenishment, Colvin and Brooks propose that the church, here and now, curb materialistic practices that desecrate what Mormons know as Zion and others know as Native and public lands.

Anti-environmental Mormon politicians such as Senator Mike Lee, former senator Orrin Hatch, former representative Jason Chaffetz, US Representative Rob Bishop, and Utah state reps Mike Noel and Phil Lyman all want to open up public lands for plunder. In fact, in a 2017 report from the Center for

Biological Diversity titled "Public Land Enemies: Fifteen Lawmakers Plotting to Seize, Destroy and Privatize Public Lands," eight of the fifteen senators and representatives called out as the worst offenders are LDS. Of course, Mormon politicians like Harry Reid and even Reed Smoot have been champions of public land in the past. But the overall pattern does raise the question: If land-use wars are dangerous to people, land, and the idea of Zion itself, why hasn't the church come out and countered policies being pushed by Mormon politicians?

There are other Latter-day Saints who are very devoted to public lands protection. Terry Tempest Williams, raised Mormon, is one of the most powerful voices in the American conservation movement. In her 2016 book, *The Hour of Land: A Personal Topography of America's National Parks*, she recounts with fierce affection her days spent in Utah's Zion National Park, Canyonlands, and Capitol Reef. These are places she cherishes, as a Mormon woman and a lover of wild landscape. Williams writes, "To this day, my spiritual life is found inside the heart of the wild. . . . When I am away, I anticipate my return to touch stone, rock, the trunks of trees, the sway of grasses, the barbs of a feather, the fur left behind by a shedding bison."

George B. Handley, professor of humanities at Brigham Young University, wrote in his book *Home Waters*, "I am not like the Mormon pioneers of the nineteenth century," describing himself instead as "a twenty-first-century Utah Mormon." He continues, "In our heady embrace of the recompenses of an engineered world, we rejected the recompenses of its wilderness, failing to see that the desert blossoms with its own brilliant colors." Williams, Handley, Brooks, and Colvin have all come to a spiritual understanding that singular emphasis on the extraction of resources impoverishes the earth and contradicts their own understanding of faith. Though early notions of Zion were of a place developed, many Latter-day Saints are revisiting the idea of Zion and seeing in it a strong call for conservation.

There is an "Environmental Stewardship and Conservation" position statement issued by the Mormon Church, accessible on one of its webpages. It states, "All are stewards—not owners—over this earth and its bounty and will be accountable before God for what they do with His creations." It contradicts the Bundy family's argument, in that ownership of public lands is the very thing they want to secure. In addition to their constitutional notions, they assert their dominion, and with it, a complete free rein to do with the land as they want. If one were to believe Ammon Bundy, one might suspect that any such "Environmental Stewardship and Conservation" policy might well have been written by subversive Mormons—because, according to him, the church contains its own deep state that meddles with true Mormon ideology.

At yet another rally that Ammon headlined in 2019, this one in Smithfield, Utah, he told the audience that the Church of Jesus Christ of Latter-day Saints has been compromised by environmentalists, globalists, and socialists. He said that lower- and middle-level church leadership has been "infiltrated by these same people, but not on the higher levels." Ammon assured attendees that he knew the top-tier church leaders to be "honest, good, righteous men who follow the Lord's guidance and inspiration, and I believe they will guide us through these rough times." Based on this comment, among other indications, it seems that high-level church leaders have somehow insulated themselves from Bundy criticism, as well as ignored the Bundys' armed actions and their ongoing agitation among rural western communities.

The lack of a strong position by church leaders is especially curious in light of the fate of historian D. Michael Quinn, who was excommunicated from the Mormon Church in 1993 for charges of conduct unbecoming to a member of the Church and apostasy. I am not a Mormon, so I admit to not fully understanding why Quinn's wrongdoings were seen by the hierarchy as more threatening than armed actions performed, to large extent, under the banner of the Mormon faith. Quinn had been a highly respected historian at Brigham Young University, at one time groomed to become the central church historian. Deeply devout, he was also resolute in tackling knotty issues such as early church cover-ups, polygamy, its hierarchy, and magic world-views. His enthusiasm was due, in part, to Church President Spencer W. Kimball's encouragement "not to work for the office or try 'to curry favor' with church leaders," but rather to pursue a truth "the Lord desired for me," Quinn told an audience after his ouster. (Kimball was the leader who ordered that Cleon Skousen's constitutional agenda not be taught in Mormon temples.) Quinn's own faith was not shaken in the face of the church's historical imperfections, but Mormon leaders felt his research undermined their image and credibility. He and four other academics, who had also challenged church narrative and image, were expelled. Quinn has since struggled to find a community and secure gainful employment. The reaction of the church to Quinn in comparison to the response to Cliven Bundy seems uneven, irresponsible, and enabling.

It's hard to know how the church may change. It is governed by the Quorum of the Twelve, a group of men who range in age from their sixties into their nineties. The current church president and prophet, Russell M. Nelson, is ninety-four. In *Decolonizing Mormonism*, Colvin and Brooks describe the current Mormon power structure as a "white, American, Utahn, colonial patriarchy," a small group of elders who largely control Mormon messaging and direction. Cliven Bundy might easily fit in a photograph with these men, if he ditched his cowboy duds for a suit and tie. So how will this culture shift under the leadership of appointed conservative "male insiders," famous for their secretiveness? Colvin and Brooks' proposal seems both far-fetched and crucial: current church leaders should look to the idea of Zion and call on church leadership "to govern our spiritual instincts instead of the rigid financial, institutional, and legal mechanisms that protect the capital of the Corporation of the President." During a presentation in Utah, Colvin recently challenged her audience, "They call it [Utah] Zion, but does it meet the conditions of Zion?" Their plea to LDS leadership and its members is to change their relationship to Zion, our shared world, and to cease a "conversion of the Earth into land title for sale, and the extraction of its bounties for cash." In other words, practice the church's very own policy on environment and stewardship. Again, that is: "All are stewards—not owners—over this earth and its bounty and will be accountable before God for what they do with His creations." But will the church ever confront the Bundys over their insurrections and ecological abuses?

New West

The world is moving on in its heedless way, and many western people feel they are being tricked out of their natural heritage. They feel humiliated by their economic powerlessness; some have come to fear and hate strangers. Many would like to close the gate, lock down the West, and call it their own forever.

—William Kittredge

Twenty-one years after the creation of Grand Staircase-Escalante National Monument, the place where Mary Bulloch once chased her feral cows, the Trump administration's Department of the Interior announced they were chopping it to 46 percent of its original size. The reduction was celebrated by many residents of Kane, Garfield, and Wayne Counties, who imagined a sudden rush of mining jobs, devoted to digging up coal, uranium, cobalt, and tar sands. Nationally, by contrast, there has been a huge outcry against shrinking the borders, as well as objection by some dissenting locals.

Boulder, Utah, is a tiny hamlet on the northern flank of the monument, where two women who own a very popular restaurant are actively fighting the monument decision. They live in the same place where the founders of the Southern Utah Wilderness Alliance were once hung in effigy. It's quite remote—four hours to the closest airport. To get there, head south on Utah's Scenic Byway 12 from Capitol Reef National Park. Drive along a two-lane highway that winds through rocks, variously contoured, into a geography that unfolds in extravagant color. Maroon and rose. Winter mint and ecru. Cinnamon and cocoa. Mauve, blush, and champagne. Hues that both disorient and delight. This is a place like none other.

As Wayne County gives way to Garfield, the land changes, rising onto the Aquarius Plateau, part of the Dixie National Forest. Pines and aspens replace sage and sandstone. Cross over Boulder Mountain and signs announce the town for miles before you reach it, when finally a cluster of homes and businesses under enormous cottonwoods herald your arrival. North of town lies the Box-Death Hollow Wilderness, named for the cows that have fallen to their deaths there. The Grand Staircase-Escalante National Monument spreads out east and south. Boulder is a little place, containing a resident population of about 250 people and one extraordinary restaurant—Hell's Backbone Grill, headquarters for the fight over Escalante.

When I visited in the spring of 2019, the Grill was filled with travelers. How do they find this gastronomic hideaway? Why do they come? They read *The New Yorker*, Blake Spalding told me, over the din. The year before, in 2018, Pulitzer Prize-winning journalist Kathryn Schultz featured Spalding and her business partner, Jen Castle, in the magazine, describing their farm-to-table operation and the women's fight to save the monument. Hell's Backbone Grill, named after a nearby geological feature, is the largest single employer in Garfield County. It's also one of the highest rated eateries in the state of Utah, according to Zagat, and has twice been a semi-finalist for a James Beard award. Spalding, as she greeted her guests that evening, heard from most of them the same thing: they had been lured there by Schultz's piece. That and the glorious Grand Staircase-Escalante National Monument.

Spalding is small and blond. She's as convivial as she is determined, a woman who handily oversees the commotion of a restaurant at full capacity while shrugging off the derision she's encountered for her tough pro-monument stance. Earlier that afternoon, as the staff scrambled to close windows against the heavy wind and intermittent rains, we talked about her public-land battle as well as her history in the area.

When she first came to Boulder, four years after Bill Clinton designated Grand Staircase-Escalante, Spalding faced the enormous task of building relationships in an isolated Mormon community with a distrust of newcomers. Her 1999 arrival coincided with the influx of what she describes as "preppers," folks who came to rural Utah to prepare for Y2K and the end of the world. "It's their lifestyle," she said. "They have guns and ammo and things like that." Somewhat bemusedly, she told me that it's actually the newer preppers, more than the original Mormon population, who have been vexed by the publicity the restaurant has garnered. Nearly twenty years after the predicted collapse of society at the Y2K millennium, preppers still want to keep Boulder off the map. The recent recognition of Hell's Backbone Grill spurred one to photocopy the first page of *The New Yorker* article and plaster it all over town, accusing Spalding and Castle of destroying the community.

In spite of the preppers' indignation, she counts many locals as dear friends, even those opposed to the monument, such as former Garfield County commissioner and LDS ward bishop Dell LeFevre. LeFevre, who has ranched in the region for decades, at first called the monument designation "a chicken-shit trick, as underhanded as you can get." But time has eased resentment in Boulder, and Spalding says that many residents have gravitated toward the tourism industry. Even LeFevre, she told me. "My beloved Dell is currently building a thirteen-bedroom B and B." He also bought a local convenience store/gas station. "All over Escalante are businesses that were built for tourism, owned by anti-monument people," said Spalding. In 2003, LeFevre accepted a buyout of his eighteen-thousand-acre grazing allotment along the Escalante River, swapping it for another with less tourist traffic and impact on the watershed. However, in 2019, the Trump administration announced it wanted to open the Escalante River to cows, after it has run clean and unpolluted for sixteen years. Taking the former allotment out of retirement, a riparian corridor that today offers habitat to healthy otter, beaver, and fish populations, as well as staggering scenery to visitors, feels baffling, deleterious, and even snide.

When former secretary of the interior Ryan Zinke visited Garfield County in May 2017 to hear local opinions about plans to shrink the monument, he refused to meet with Spalding or Castle, and gave his time to anti-monument activists. His snub might sound odd or gratuitous, but Zinke was on a selective-listening tour. These women have brought lots of money and good jobs to Garfield, but they've also been agents of change. Two rarae aves who espouse environmental sustainability and Buddhist principles, core tenets upon which their restaurant has been built, the women represent a culture repugnant to other, more conservative county residents. Boulderites, with their tourist-pandering ways, have become very unpopular in Garfield County. "We're ISIS. We have a Democratic mayor," said Spalding. To the right-wing Republican population of Panguitch, the county seat, these neighbors, a mix of ranchers, artists, outfitters, federal employees, and the Hell's Backbone workforce, are radicals that challenge long-held Mormon and rural traditions as well as county politics.

As the evening wore on, dinner guests walking past our table stopped to compliment Spalding and her staff. "Don't forget to tell your congress members about the monument," she implored of an older woman wearing hiking boots and shorts. Spalding and Castle have written two cookbooks, the second of which, *This Immeasurable Place*, was released the same week that the Trump administration announced that the monument would be shrunk by a new executive order. Now Hell's Backbone Grill is part of a lawsuit filed by Grand Staircase-Escalante Partners, along with other plaintiffs, trying to reverse that action. Fond as she is of her friends and neighbors, Spalding's greatest passion is the monument. Absent its preservation, unroaded and intact, she fears she'll lose her business. With this, her fifty-plus employees would lose their high-paying jobs—an aspect of her business that she makes a priority, having herself grown up in poverty with somewhat irresponsible hippie parents. The restaurant was just named one of the best-to-work-for restaurants in America (among the top nineteen), by *Food and Wine* magazine. The downside is that, though tourist-industry jobs might be good ones, they are seasonal. Spalding's younger employees appreciate the time off for skiing or travel, but employees with families have a harder time taking the winter months off. And even as people who live around the monument have found ways to profit from increased visitation, many regional Mormons still favor extractive industries, in spite of the erratic nature of those businesses.

During their lifetimes, Ryan Bundy, born in 1972, and Ammon, born in 1975, have watched their region change. There aren't as many ranchers as there used to be. This is due to a variety of reasons: market consolidation, family ranches competing with corporate beef production, years of drought and years of debt. Although the Bundys view their world as one of increasing deprivation, over the decades the West has actually moved far toward industrial diversification and economic prosperity. The Bundy boys, though not ranchers themselves, have focused on the disappearing opportunities for mom-and-pop cattle operations. But, according to Headwaters Economics, an independent nonprofit organization based in Bozeman, Montana, which has tracked economic trends since 1970, the western economy has grown tremendously in that time. Nearly six million new jobs have been created in intermountain states, with over 90 percent of this growth emerging from tourism and other service industries, as well as health care, real estate, and professional, scientific, and technical services. These fields are replacing extractive jobs, susceptible to the boom-and-bust cycles of non-renewable resources—endeavors such as logging, mining, and agriculture, that have left parts of the West marred by clear cuts, open pit mines, and the erosion, invasive weeds, and habitat destruction that come with too many cows grazing in places unsuited for them.

The Bundys are part of a culture resistant to transition. They are not unlike many western farmers and ranchers, so focused on seasonal demands and annual bottom lines that the idea of adopting new methods—methods that might prove more lucrative, efficient, environmentally responsible, and in compliance with federal standards—is just too daunting. It's true that insisting on doing things the way they've always been done is in itself a means of honoring tradition. All the same, the Bundy family, in their refusal to find a business model that complies with the law, is pursuing a path that's not only dangerous and destructive but also delusional in its failure to accept that some practices and vocations need to adapt or fade into history.

And yet, although the West is moving toward a more diverse economy, the traditional jobs—jobs worked by ranching fathers and farming grandfathers—continue to hold more prestige, at least in some circles, than those in the service industry. But those old-style jobs bring in only a small percentage of the revenue earned in Dixie's counties. There is more money to be made in sustainable industries than there is in the extraction of resources.

The region has also seen a big shift in demographics. In Utah, Mormon homeland now includes the retirees (and their golf courses) of Washington County, and the Best Friends Animal Sanctuary, the largest non-kill animal shelter in the United States and one of the biggest employers in Kane County. In Nevada, the Las Vegas Strip and high-stakes gamblers now define Clark County. Utah's Garfield and Wayne Counties haven't fared as well economically as their neighbors, but are holding steady nonetheless. Garfield is rich in tourist destinations and encompasses parts of Bryce, Canyonlands, and Capitol Reef National Parks, plus Dixie and Fishlake National Forests, Glen Canyon National Recreation Area, and Grand Staircase-Escalante National Monument. Visitors flock here year after year to visit public lands, reminding aggrieved locals that much of their own backyard belongs as much to outsiders as it belongs to them. The 1996 designation of the Grand Staircase-Escalante National Monument stirred a great deal of ill will, though, of course, regional hostility toward an interloping federal government was around long before the monument. In 1999, Lenza Wilson, then mayor of the town of Escalante, said that any new residents lured by the monument "need a better grip on Escalante's background, customs, and culture." He added, "The jury (of local opinion) has returned a very strong verdict, and they are not welcome here."

Economic data indicate that rural communities remain robust when nearby public lands stay protected. Data also show that communities dependent on resource extraction are dying in the West. But this doesn't fit the cultural narrative. County commissioners in Utah and Nevada, congressional representatives, and senators want to drill, log, and graze. They want control over what they perceive as their land. Zion. Homeland. The monument had remained open for grazing after its 1996 designation, but Trump, in reducing the boundaries, has opened new areas to large-scale mining. If this happens, the roar of massive trucks on additional roads, and the yawning open pits of surface mines, will take the Escalante region off the list of America's most lovely destinations. Scenic values will disappear, and there will be impacts on wildlife, including the hundreds of species of bees. Tourism-based jobs will vanish. That is why the women of Hell's Backbone Grill are so invested in the campaign to save the monument. When the Department of the Interior proposed shrinking the monument boundaries of Bears Ears and Grand Staircase-Escalante, 2.8 million comments came in, an unprecedented amount of feedback over this type of federal measure. Americans clearly value these public lands and want them to remain protected, but Mormon politicians and the mining industry have their own agendas.

In response to their vocal opposition to the shrinkage, Spalding and Castle have encountered ugliness, vandalism, and nasty online reviews from people who think the women are robbing them of jobs. Mining in Escalante might bring some short-term employment at the boom end of the cycle, but there will certainly be a bust. When the resources dry up, folks will be out of jobs, leaving a place once noted for its beauty pocked by gaping holes and papered with pink slips.

Mormonism, as I've mentioned, is a culture historically skeptical of mining. Brigham Young disapproved of the vices the prospectors brought with them to Park City, Utah, and hoped that God would hide the gold from the Mormon people. But traditional western jobs, such as the mining and logging industries offer, are regarded as "real jobs," according to economist Ray Rasker. Rasker, the executive director of Headwaters Economics, which has analyzed economic data from every county in the United States, believes that in the Escalante region the tourist industry is considered degrading and not particularly lucrative. Rasker recalled hearing about a comment from a Garfield County representative sharing her impressions of tourists: "They come here with dirty shorts and a twenty-dollar bill and don't change either." No doubt there are indeed many such thrifty dirtbags who come to Utah's and Nevada's public lands, staying in tents or trucks, eating freeze-dried food and drinking beer from their own coolers. But other tourists visit as well, presumably doing laundry and spending money in places like Hell's Backbone.

Tourism is lucrative. Protecting regional destinations that attract sightseers and recreationists puts money in the bank. According to a 2017 article in *The Salt Lake Tribune*, "Outdoor recreation provides 76 times as many jobs in Utah as coal—122,000 versus 1,600—and 27 times as much in salary and wages—$3.6 billion versus $132.8 million." But old-timers don't buy it. Chris Mehl, currently mayor-elect of Bozeman, Montana, formerly with Headwaters Economics, told me that when he met with Garfield County commissioners a few years back, their response to his data regarding the economic values of public land protection was something along the lines of, "You seem like a nice young man, but we don't believe you." He added, "I was forty-eight at the time."

Both of these men, Mehl and Rasker, are very sympathetic to rural community struggles. But they also see the merits of our public lands. It is a fact that in communities like those in Garfield County, resource extraction is one way of creating jobs. True also that there is deep resentment toward tying up lands that might offer jobs. When the Grand Staircase-Escalante National Monument was declared, Kane and Garfield County residents felt blindsided and bitter. Prior to its designation, many residents who lived around the monument, such as Shawna Cox, were hoping for a huge coal-mining operation on the Kaiparowits Plateau—one similar to the abandoned 1970s plan that earned Robert Redford a burning in effigy. But then Bill Clinton prevented the coal mine from going forward, with an executive order. And people were so angry that nothing, including hard data, could convince them of the benefits of this action. Before the monument was declared, Escalante had been a land frequented by cowboys and a few off-the-beaten-path backpackers. In 2014, it saw 878,000 visitors, before President Trump hacked it in half.

There are legitimate reasons why locals do not like tourists. Visitors who venture into the vast backcountry of Escalante don't generally embrace the traditions and etiquette of the local population, who depend on these lands for their livelihoods. When I told Marti Hulet, Mary Bulloch's daughter, about my love of hiking in Escalante, she did not get it. Any appeal of backpacking through this wild country, where she grew up riding with her mother, was lost on her. The monument, in Hulet's estimation, was a place built for longhorn cattle and the family's feisty Catahoula hounds that she'd adored growing up. It's pasture, not playground.

Hulet told me a story about Boyd, her stepdad, coming back to his cabin, built on his allotment, and finding a backpacker soaking his dirty, trail-weary feet in the family's well. She laughed at the memory, recalling how angry Boyd had been. Not only was this man impolite, he was gross. Boyd ended up chasing him out of their family's water supply. The episode left the drinking water fouled and Boyd with a bad taste in his mouth about interlopers. It's one of a million examples of colliding priorities, protocols, and perspectives that happen on American public land. Public land ranchers face frequent inconsiderateness from ill-mannered tourists. Backpackers often neglect to close cattle gates behind them and leave garbage behind and excrement unburied.

This culture clash, in addition to many other issues, is what drives the people of Garfield County and others in rural corners of the West to demand that they be allowed to make land-use decisions themselves. Ray Rasker understands. Imagine it, he said to me. We are in Bozeman. We have our public lands and our skiing and our wildlife; we've worked out a way to take care of all of the things that we care about. Then suddenly someone from outside comes in and puts a strip mine in our mountains. And there is nothing we can do about it. No, Rasker does not want to see Escalante developed, but he gets the reason locals feel so dragooned.

Fallout

It is simply delusional to maintain that all public land within the boundaries of Nevada belongs to the State of Nevada.

> —Judge Jim Crockett of the
> 8th Judicial District Court in Las Vegas

Oregon ranchers Dwight and Steven Hammond were pardoned by Donald Trump on July 10, 2018, and released from prison. This act was facilitated by an Indiana billionaire, Forrest Lucas, founder/underwriter of Protect the Harvest, the organization that sponsored the Modesto range rights conference where Ammon keynoted, and pal of Mike Pence. According to an excellent article on Lucas by Buzzfeed's Anne Helen Petersen, Salvador Hernandez, and Ken Bensinger, Protect the Harvest spokesman Dave Duquette said that the Bundys' actions at Malheur had actually prolonged the Hammonds' time in jail.

Several months after their release (and their private jet ride back to Oregon, again courtesy of Forrest Lucas), the Hammonds received their grazing permit back, after Ryan Zinke, in one of his last acts before leaving his scandal-marred tenure as Secretary of the Interior, restored it. It had been revoked after the father and son were found guilty of arson, but is now in place until 2024. At the time of writing, three conservation groups have sued to suspend the Hammonds' grazing permits in order to protect redband trout and sage grouse habitat. For years the

Hammonds obstructed federal operations, cut fence, grazed cattle illegally, and threatened violence against federal workers. It remains to be seen how the family will handle their relationships with refuge staff, especially with the current restrictions imposed on them.

But conservationists aren't the only ones pursuing legal recourse. In the aftermath of Malheur and Bunkerville, Ryan Bundy filed a lawsuit against former attorneys general Jeff Sessions, Eric Holder, and Loretta Lynch, former FBI director James Comey, and former head of the BLM Neil Kornze, accusing them of violating his constitutional rights and discriminating against his religion. Additionally, Ryan's filing claims that "under the guise of collecting grazing fees, an alleged and unverified debt," the feds had "invaded the Bundy ranch . . . assaulted and extorted Ryan and his family members and killed his family's cattle." Also in the filing, he asserts that "plaintiff Ryan Bundy is a natural man, who at all times was and is a Nevada State nations, who lives upon the land known as Nevada." This is typical language of an anti-government agitator who is trying to describe himself outside the identity of American.

Cliven filed a third suit of his own against the government in January 2018. Both he and Ryan continue to challenge the idea that the government can own public lands, and unsurprisingly, in April 2019, Nevada Judicial District Court Judge Jim Crockett threw the elder Bundy's case out, issuing a statement that the case was based on the "fundamentally flawed notion advanced by Bundy since 1998 regarding ownership of federal public lands in Nevada. For two decades, Bundy has made the same claims that federal public lands within Nevada belong not to the United States, but instead to the State of Nevada." The judge continues, "Three federal court decisions—Bundy I, Bundy II, and Bundy III—have now considered and rejected Bundy's repeated arguments." Although thus far the courts have made it clear that the federal government can indeed own land, the Trump administration is changing the character of our federal court system and it remains to be seen what the future holds for constitutional reinterpretations in regard to public lands.

Ryan's suit, still pending, makes an odd reference to a joke that President Barack Obama told during the White House Correspondents' Dinner in 2014. This was shortly after Cliven, newly famed for the Battle of Bunkerville, had gone on record telling a *New York Times* reporter in April 2014 that there was "something I know about the Negro. They didn't have nothing to do. They didn't have nothing for their kids to do. They didn't have nothing for their young girls to do. And because they were basically on government subsidy, so now what do they do? They abort their young children, they put their young men in jail, because they never learned how to pick cotton. And I've often wondered, are they better off as slaves, picking cotton and having a family life and doing things, or are they better off under government subsidy?" During the press dinner, the president referred to these comments and Bundy's plunge from right-wing media darling to racist pariah. Then, in reference to an aerial stunt by Olympic gold medalist Jamie Anderson, a spectacular female snowboarder, the president quipped, "I haven't seen anybody pull a one-eighty that fast since Rand Paul disinvited that Nevada rancher to this dinner." In his suit, Ryan alleges that the joke was a threat against his father.

Bundy may have put off his celebrity admirers, like Sean Hannity and Glenn Beck, with those offensive observations, but not his avid base of supporters. On the Bundy Ranch Facebook page, supporters posted comments excusing Cliven's remarks about "the negro" as having been taken out of context. Some argued that the old livestock operator was making a metaphor; others, more disturbingly, felt that Bundy was simply calling it as he saw it. Racism did not drive the Bundy base away.

But more recently, the family has met with some angry pushback—on one issue, anyway—from many of their former supporters. This came, ironically, in response to Ammon Bundy expressing sympathy for migrants seeking asylum on American soil. In 2018, assorted militia from groups across the country had already heeded Trump's "call to arms," packing up supplies and guns, heading for the southern border to help thwart what the president was calling an invasion. Ammon instead posited that people coming toward the border were not terrorists invading the nation; rather, they were families who needed help. He criticized Donald Trump, renouncing the proposed wall and the hate-filled rhetoric about the people seeking asylum, telling folks on social media that such talk "is all fear based, you know, and it's frankly based on selfishness." He continued, "Fear is the opposite of faith." Wearing his ever-present cowboy hat, he speaks softly on a posted video on YouTube in 2018, telling listeners to focus on facts, not on fearmongering. He admonishes his base, explaining that vilifying migrants is "completely opposite of who we are as a Christian nation." Ammon's call to help migrants caused some of his supporters to pivot—their rage, threats, and hatred had found a new target, shifting from government and liberals to, of all people, Ammon Bundy.

The Facebook page of the Three Percenters (one militia group that had been at the Bunkerville standoff) was crammed with statements of disbelief and outcries of betrayal and odium. Some called Ammon a "sheeple," a derogatory term that conflates sheep and people. They accused him of the great sin of watching CNN and labeled him "a FAKtriot!" One post wondered if Ammon had been given money by George Soros to express his support for the Honduran families stuck in Mexico. Others contended that Ammon's position was being issued by a bot or an imitator. The Ammon they knew couldn't possibly like immigrants. There was an uglier backlash as well. In a video posted shortly after his pro-immigration position went public, Ammon tells his audience he was hearing from people "out there who wish me dead." Things had changed. Back when God asked Ammon to gather militia to Oregon, his supporters could understand, though most chose not to join him. Likewise all had been acceptable when the Heavenly Father directed Cliven to summon patriots for a standoff in Nevada. But when Ammon told the militia community that "we've been asked by God to help. To be welcoming, to assist strangers, to not vex them, and I think that as we do this, the Lord is going to bless us . . ."—well, that was just crazy talk.

Our Myths

The great enemy of the truth is very often not the lie, deliberate, contrived and dishonest, but the myth, persistent, persuasive and unrealistic.

—John F. Kennedy

In 2015, I went to Bunkerville to visit the Bundys because I wanted to understand why they were breaking the laws governing public lands. And they welcomed me, seeming to appreciate the chance to tell their story. Booda, then serving as Cliven's bodyguard, came into the living room after I'd been there a couple of hours. When I asked why he hadn't checked things out earlier, he said a woman driving a Prius with two sleeping dogs in the back was not going to put him on high alert. "I knew you weren't much of a threat," he told me. As I left, Ryan walked me to my car. I headed down their driveway with some understanding of the family's justifications for their rebelliousness, but I've since wondered if they themselves ever considered the cost to others that came with their war. They have helped to undermine the rule of law; scatter falsehoods on the Constitution throughout the rural West; empower armed militia groups from Oregon to New Hampshire; and encourage abuse (and perhaps privatization) of our American common ground—public lands.

The West can be explained through a series of myths, from the myth of the cowboy to the myth of Zion. The Bundys embrace both of these as well as constitutional, prophetic, and conspiracy myths. Edward Abbey perpetuated the myth of wilderness as solitary—a land without humans. But lands are in fact filled with people and have been long before European colonization. There is also a myth that longstanding convention is better than change. This idea is embodied in such slogans as "make America great again," demanding that the practices of yesteryear continue unabated no matter the political, ecological, cultural, or economic consequences. With this last myth, I'm reminded of a quote from Ralph Waldo Emerson, the man who has, at times, affronted Mormon sensibilities. He famously asserted that "a foolish consistency is the hobgoblin of little minds, adored by little statesmen and philosophers and divines." Public lands have fallen victim to the playing out of untenable and outmoded myths—and it's these foolish consistencies, these hobgoblins of concocted scripture, that are robbing the American people of one of our greatest assets, one of our most serious responsibilities: American landscapes for all, not just for those who dream of American Zion.

So . . . what aren't myths? For starters, the need for large-landscape conservation. In the face of the climate crisis, vast areas such as the 640 million acres of public lands are essential reserves to mitigate increasingly violent weather. Second, public lands hold our watersheds and provide crucial habitat for species at a time when wildlife populations all over our planet face extinction. Third, only 1.9 percent of the cattle raised in this country set foot on public lands, but in order to keep the livestock protected, Wildlife Services, a government program formerly known as Animal Damage Control, reported in 2018 that agents culled nearly 1.5 million native animals on public land, including black bears, wolves, foxes, bobcats, mountain lions, coyotes, beavers, river otters, herons, eagles, hawks, and owls. They also killed livestock and family pets. Fourth, according to the Outdoor Industry Association, tourism on public lands generates

887 billion dollars annually in consumer spending and provides 7.6 million jobs. Protected lands mean incomes. Ranching adds only 0.1 percent of the total revenue to western rural economies. Fifth, according to polls, most of us value lands and species and want them kept healthy.

A year after my trip to Bunkerville, Ammon and Ryan took over the Malheur National Wildlife Refuge. Peter Walker, a professor at the University of Oregon, studies the impacts of the Bundy occupation on the community of Burns in his fascinating book, *Sagebrush Collaboration*. Ten years before the occupation, a collaborative management program among various parties had worked with federal personnel in decision-making. According to the High Desert Partnership, the organization overseeing those cooperative efforts, a great divide between differing priorities dogged the region for decades, resulting in a situation that left the refuge in serious ecological decline. But over the years, High Desert Partnership sat folks down and successfully brokered agreements that have led to the restoration of aquatic resources and wildlife habitat. Collaboration is hard and it doesn't work in most cases due to bad players and bad plans, but it worked, to some extent, in Harney County.

Malheur had a good story before the takeover that the Bundy boys tried to rip up. The decade before the Bundy militia stormed Harney County, ranchers, conservationists, and the Burns Paiute Tribe realized that business as usual wouldn't protect their shared resources. So they decided to do things differently and worked toward collaboration. Contrary to Ammon's claim, Malheur is a place where ranchers do ranch. In fact, thirteen different ranches hold grazing leases within the refuge. Its wetlands provide habitat to over three hundred bird species, fifty-eight kinds of mammals, and a few reptiles and amphibians, as well as moths, butterflies, and other insects. The refuge brings the county roughly fifteen million dollars annually, mostly through tourist dollars, not grazing fees.

During the Malheur occupation, most Harney County residents wanted the Bundys out of their backyard. But journalist Tay Wiles, in one of her many great articles for *High Country News*, notes that the takeover could have gone another way in another place. Take, for example, the town of John Day, Oregon, just down the road, where a constitutional sheriff and Bundy sympathizer, Glenn Palmer, has gained a reputation for his anti-government stance. He, like the Bundys, thinks that a sheriff's position holds more authority than that of any federal officer. It was en route to John Day to meet with Palmer that the Bundys and their supporters were arrested and LaVoy Finicum shot.

There is a man named Stanton Gleave, to whom people point as perhaps the next Cliven Bundy. He was a participant in the Battle of Bunkerville, and has been butting heads with federal agents for years over his own grazing practices. He fits the scofflaw model. A Skousen-annotated Constitution is ever jammed into Gleave's shirt pocket, and he boasts of Mormon ancestry that goes back to the 1880s. Right now he's flouting livestock rules, grazing public lands in a place called Monroe Mountain, Utah, because, by his reasoning, if the government can't own land, they can't tell him what to do on it. Except that the government does own it—it's public.

In 2013, the Forest Service reduced the number of animals Gleave could run on his allotment by half, in order to restore an aspen grove damaged by heavy browsing. He simply ignored the instructions and continued grazing as many animals as ever. As with Bundy until April 2014, no one has stopped him. Gleave's second cousin, Marty Gleave, who happens to be the Piute County sheriff and a constitutional sheriff, has vowed to protect his relative if the feds try to enforce their reduction order. To date, the sixty-nine-year-old livestock operator runs one thousand head of cattle and three thousand sheep on public land, animals that graze illegally beyond the permitted season. The aspen grove at issue, which has suffered damage not just from

Gleave's cattle but also from elk (reintroduced, in overabundance, by the state of Utah), remains imperiled due to unlawful livestock presence, broken agreements, and lack of enforcement.

Enforcement has become a big problem, especially in counties like Piute. Zoe Nemerever is a PhD candidate at the University of California, San Diego, researching state political parties and legislative institutions. She notes that "counties that elect constitutionalist sheriffs have higher rates of violence against employees of the federal Bureau of Land Management compared to other western counties that do not elect constitutionalist sheriffs." As a result, she explains, "BLM employees will often choose to allow illegal grazing rather than engage in armed conflict with citizens. By this logic, ranchers who are denied grazing permits should prefer using violence to access federal grazing lands, instead of enduring the slow and costly legislative process." A survey conducted by a watchdog organization, PEER (Public Employees for Environmental Responsibility), found that "70% of BLM respondents feel the Bundy episodes have made their jobs 'more dangerous' with large percentages citing 'threats to our safety due to resource management issues.'" This is a federal agency that puts personnel in positions where they are either scared or unwilling to do their jobs, instead of helping them enforce the law. It's easy to imagine that if these weren't white ranchers breaking the law and threatening violence, enforcement strategies would be very different.

In April 2019, Craig Hoover, a twenty-one-year veteran with the BLM, was fired from his position in Nevada. Now challenging his termination under the Whistleblower Protection Act, he asserts that he was pushed out when he notified agency managers of multiple public land grazing violations, including trespassing livestock and over-stocking beyond permit limits. Agency leaders don't want to hear about abuses because they don't care or they don't want to stir up a hornets' nest of ranchers and constitutional sheriffs.

Gleave is currently in violation of his lease, but with the protection of his cousin the sheriff, and no federal oversight, he is left to do whatever he wishes on public lands. In an article by Todd MacFarlane, first published in *Range Magazine* in 2018, and later on MacFarlane's blog, Gleave is portrayed as a man facing "governments [sic] which seem to be bent on his destruction." For years, by MacFarlane's account, Gleave had been gainfully employed in various jobs, including a position at Kaibab Forest Products (now closed) and a stint as a truck driver, while struggling to put food on his family's table and run a ranch. He told MacFarlane that he had seen the grave impacts of regulations and conservation efforts. He watched what Grand Staircase-Escalante National Monument brought to the region, and its impacts on surrounding counties. "The harder the federal government worked to push people out of business and off the land," MacFarlane wrote of Gleave, "the more determined he became to hang-on and survive." MacFarlane's article offers the same spin that other rural westerners have adopted—that government overreach and extreme environmentalism, not shifting economies, tapped-out resources, and habitat destruction, are diminishing opportunities in the West. In truth, those factors are changing opportunities, yes. But not diminishing them.

In places like Gleave's Piute County in rural south-central Utah, halfway between Salt Lake and Kanab along a two-lane highway, a person does have fewer job options than in counties with airports. Because of constrained access, isolated communities are less likely to attract vibrant companies that hire large workforces. Utah's Washington, Kane, and Iron Counties, all close to the regional airport in St. George, have grown rapidly in recent years. (So has Clark County, just over the state line in Nevada, not surprisingly because Clark contains Las Vegas.) In addition to the convenience of travel, one of the biggest attractions for businesses, job seekers, and retirees—along with their savings and their transfer payments—to southern Utah is indisputably the landscape. It's the huge draw. Without the beauty of Cedar Breaks and Grand Staircase-Escalante National Monuments, Grand Canyon, Zion, Capitol Reef, and Bryce Canyon National Parks, the many surrounding communities would not be prospering.

Bundy and Gleave, stuck in their obdurate rut, cannot represent the future of this region, though right now they are holding it hostage. Both are subsidized heavily in their livelihoods. Bundy still owes over a million dollars to US taxpayers and Gleave, according to USDA subsidy information, received $512,187 from 1995 to 2017. In the *Range Magazine* piece, Gleave is quoted as bragging that, "I've just been too stubborn and bull-headed to give-up." The old man, now using a cane for balance and to prod his sheep into their pens, must have felt this boast would earn him admiration among his supporters, and maybe it does; but to other readers it demonstrates a hoary, short-sighted, and dangerous consistency.

When I began my research, first for a PhD in environmental history from Montana State University (later deepened for this book), on the subject of how Mormonism has influenced public-land feuds, the notion of "end-times" seemed preposterous. Now it doesn't. We are in the middle of a climate crisis, which could very well end life as we know and cherish it. This makes it even more imperative to keep large landscapes intact. In addition to all that public lands offer, they are among our world's carbon sequestration sites. Extraction on public lands, such as logging old-growth forests, oil and gas drilling, and beef production, leads to the release of more carbon and puts us ever closer to an irreparable tipping point.

The Trump administration's newly appointed director of the BLM, William Perry Pendley, has been advocating throughout his career the end of public land ownership. He is but one component of the current political age that has been a disaster for our air, climate, water, wildlife, and lands. This administration has been hard at work shrinking boundaries of national monuments; reducing emission standards; deregulating insecticide use; gutting the Endangered Species Act to make it easier to pull imperiled species off the list, allowing industry to cry foul if protections are too expensive. With Pendley, there is now the threat to sell public lands for further resource extraction. Currently one-quarter of US carbon emissions result from the burning of fossil fuels that are pulled from federal lands. Now, with Pendley's appointment, a leader in the administration wants to liquidate our public lands entirely, so that the private sector can further drill, with fewer restrictions, putting us ever closer to what could really seem like latter days.

We are at an impasse right now regarding these public lands, where core values, priorities, and various interpretations of appropriate use have tangled and matted. As Americans, we hold divergent views on economics, scientific findings, legalities, constitutionality, and religion. We cherish different truths—or "truths." Ken Rait, formerly executive director of the Southern Utah Wilderness Alliance, now with the Pew Charitable Trusts, expressed deep dismay over the reduction of the Grand Staircase-Escalante National Monument. After twenty years, the regional anger it once provoked had abated, he told me during a phone call. That's true to an extent. But among some, convictions and vengefulness run deep, especially in Dixie. Utah politicians have been looking for their chance to undo the protected status of the monument ever since it was decreed. These people are no less hell-bent than conservationists, who are pursuing reinstatement of the full monument boundaries and reestablishment of regulations and enforcement. But the conservationists are following legal strategies.

They aren't making land anymore, as Mark Twain said. No god or creator is manufacturing new earthly geography. Not Tabuts, the deity who bestowed upon the Southern Paiute people the choicest place to live in the Southwest, nor the Heavenly

Father, who gave the Mormons their Zion. And although Cleon Skousen promised fertile lands at the bottom of the sea, there will be no farmland under the oceans made suddenly available. Our public lands are finite and precious. Our mountains, deserts, prairies, meadows, lakes, rivers, beaches, and forests are the grand mosaic of the American landscape, and as Americans, we share them—these 640 million acres. They amount to one-quarter of this entire country. Public lands, home to grizzly bears and bison and condors and desert tortoises. In totality, that's more land than the states of Nevada, Alaska, California, and Montana combined. Aldo Leopold once wrote that an ecological ethic, in the sense of one human individual's behavior among other creatures, means limiting "freedom of action in the struggle for existence." A philosophical ethic, he continued, derives from the "differentiation of social from anti-social conduct." He saw these as two definitions of one thing. "The Golden Rule tries to integrate the individual to society; democracy to integrate social organization to the individual." We need to live in ways that allow others to live securely. But, he added, "There is as yet no ethic dealing with man's relation to land and to the animals and plants which grow upon it." This was published in 1949, in Leopold's essay "The Land Ethic," the finale of *A Sand County Almanac*. Thanks to him and others, nowadays we do recognize—some of us recognize—that lands and their inhabitants, apart from their utility to humanity, must be appreciated and safeguarded. Because even in this, we are sustained.

The Bundys disagree. They have defied and rejected these principles—Golden Rule, land ethic, stewardship, or conservation—in their fight to possess and use American public land. They have insisted upon being anarchic atop fragile landscapes harboring vulnerable species, and they have done it in a most anti-social way. They have bullied the public and federal agents, broken laws, and brought guns to their fight. And they have browbeat those who haven't fully embraced their level of lawlessness. When the Hammonds were released from jail, those men got their grazing permits returned to them by then Secretary of the Interior Ryan Zinke. At a June 2019 gathering in Nephi, Utah, Cliven told a small audience of his disgust—"The Bundys thought that was the worst thing, the terriblest thing, that could happen for the Hammonds"—that they had accepted again a contract with the government regulating their cows. The Bundys want no regulation on lands they believe, in spite of everything, that they reign over.

During my phone conversation with Ken Rait, a year after Ryan Zinke's announcement about shrinking the boundaries of Bears Ears and Grand Staircase-Escalante, Rait told me he was heartbroken. To remedy that feeling, he said, he was planning a trip to Utah's backcountry, the place where he feels most solace, even though it is currently under siege. He has long since left Utah, because of death threats and a concern over raising his children in a community where they might feel isolated or targeted. But he longs for the red curve of rock in the deep canyons, and it's there he will take his heartache and disappointment. Rait's plan, his remedy, is a good reminder of something fundamental: in addition to the species that depend on the public lands of Escalante country, humans have habitat needs too, spiritually as well as physically. The canyon country of Utah and Nevada is a palliative to the human soul.

I've talked with many people who work, or have worked, in the field of public lands, both in federal positions and in nonprofit organizations. There is fear, frustration, and pessimism. And for good reason. Things are grim, in the ways I've described. Yet, there remains one large piece of very good news: right now, as I write, we Americans collectively share some of earth's most exquisite geography. In fact, our public lands are among the best things about being an American. And they are worth fighting for—with zeal and with grit. Against the Bundys, right-wing politicians, the fossil fuel industry, climate deniers, those that want to privatize, and the militia. Our land has never faced so many threats, and we need to battle together more than ever to save it.

In Gold Butte National Monument, there is a certain place, off the trail a bit, a narrow crevasse, sheltered from the wind and the unforgiving sun. It holds a petroglyph of a bee. It's quite old, of course, but very vivid in its outline, cream-colored lines scratched across the pale rock wall. Obviously, the image was meaningful to the person who created it, perhaps drawn in celebration of a creature that dances among flowers. Someone left this sketch behind—one that continues to prompt interpretation—for those of us lucky enough to see it. To a visiting apiologist, this image might raise thoughts about the evolution of an extraordinary social insect. To a naturalist, it might evoke an animal fixed to the desert rains and the seasonal plants. An orchardist might smile at the idea of six pollen-dusted legs and the promise of fruit. A Mormon cowboy might see the image and think of Brigham Young's empire of Deseret, long ago inspired by this creature. A conservationist might furrow her brow and worry over the many perils that bees and other pollinators face, including the introduction of European honeybees by white settlers. Here within a lonely crevasse in Gold Butte, a glyph hides on a wall in a region known by various cultures as Dixie, Zion, Tabuts's best place, and American public land. We are all free to go find it, this little image, and dream of its meaning. Because right now, it's on land shared by all of us.

Acknowledgments

I'd like to first thank David Quammen for reading nearly every draft of this book and giving me incredible feedback. Marta Tarbell, my dear friend and former editor at the *Telluride Times-Journal*, you gutted the hell out of an early draft and offered so much careful criticism and direction. Kirsten Allen, thank you for seeking me out and having faith in my story and ability. Thank you, Dr. Michael Reidy, for providing brilliant, dogged, and steadying counsel alongside lots of laughter and goodwill during my dissertation process. Gratitude to Gene Gaines, Katie, David, Lily, and Mae Madison, Patti Gaines, Nancy Holland, and Catherine Gaines for your love, encouragement, and patience. Thank you, Lynda Sexson, for your support and enthusiasm throughout the entire process—you were the one who started me on this entire path. So grateful to the amazing and supportive Anne Terashima and Rachel Davis! Drs. Robert Rydell, Brett Walker, William Wyckoff, and Jared Farmer provided great direction in my work and encouraged me to turn my dissertation into this book. I so appreciate Nathan Waite and Dr. Jedediah Rogers, both wonderful historians and terrifically helpful to me in this process. Thank you, Tay Wiles, for your feedback and your crackerjack reporting. Hal Herring, thank you for your take on Malheur—it was so good! Warm regards to wonderful Lyman and Kelton Hafen who spent hours and hours with me explaining their Dixie history and showing me around their incredible place. Marti Hulet, I so enjoyed getting to know you—thank you for bringing your mother to life. Robert Redd, it was a true pleasure to speak with you and hear about your father.

Carol, Cliven, and Ryan Bundy, and Shawna Cox, thank you for your hospitality, time, and candid perspectives. My appreciation to Joel Skousen and his family for opening up your home to me. Thank you, Terry Tempest Williams, for supporting me early on in this process. I'm grateful for your advocacy and your gift of putting words together in exquisite and provocative ways. Thank you, Jon Krakauer, for your inspiration and kind encouragement after I first began to pursue my connection between Mormonism and the militia movement. Thank you, Tamara Bouchard-Slayton and Greg Anderson, for sharing beautiful stories and intricate histories. Thank you to Claire Sands Baker, Sue Higgins, Rebecca Watters, Ixtla Vaughn, Gigi Aelbers, Scott Swanson, Ian Kellett, Faye Nelson, Lynn Donaldson, Sally Uhlmann, Chris Zinda, Anne Helen Petersen, Roger Lang, Sean Beckett, Danielle Girard, Suzanne Truman, Sabina Lee, Ann Down, Judi Brawer, Greg Carr, Pat Shae, Anna Patterson, Laura Hoehn, Betsy Buffington, Jacqueline Keeler, Dan Duggan, Moe Carrick, Chris Thomas, Doug and Andrea Peacock, Sarah Davies Tilt, Robin Chopus, and Chimgee Luvandash for years of listening to this story and bearing with me during the process. Thank you, Mary O'Brien, for lighting a fire in me. Thank you to Brigham Young University's Charles Redd Center for Western Studies, Dr. Brian Cannon, and Brenden Rensink for your fellowship and guidance. Special thanks to the Southern Utah University's Paula Mitchell, and to her predecessor Janet Seegmiller—you were both so brilliant, fun, and helpful. Zion National Park archivist Miriam Watson graciously sat with me in the archives when she was pregnant. Thank you! Much appreciation to Ray Rasker, Richard Spotts, Chris Mehl, Ken Rait, Erik Molvar, and Lisa Rutherford for your insights, direction, and time. Thank you, Beth Ann Kennedy, Kietra Nelson, Maclaren Latta, Ryan Lenz, and Richard Francaviglia, for helping me tell this story. Thank you, Steve Dudrow, for taking me into the thick of things and showing me the beauty of Gold Butte. Thank you, Blake

Spalding, for sharing your truth and some pretty awesome food. Ted McDermott, you were a gem to send me a copy of your amazing article. And my forever love to Nick, Stella, Harry, Steve, and Manny who have been with me for various points, and years, throughout this entire process. BDE.

Finally, I've written this book because I want to protect public lands. Please, please support these nonprofit organizations: Torrey House Press, Utah Diné Bikéyah, WildEarth Guardians, Center for Biological Diversity, Western Watersheds Project, Southern Utah Wilderness Alliance, Grand Staircase Escalante Partners, Friends of Gold Butte, Grand Canyon Land Trust, Earthtone Outside, Montana Racial Equity Project, and the *Mountain Journal*.

Endnotes

PART 1: THE COWBOY AND THE PROPHET

THE BATTLE OF BUNKERVILLE

We didn't show any fear, CBS News Las Vegas Channel 8, "LVMPD vs Brand Thornton on Bundy Ranch," YouTube, Richard Henry, April 14, 2014, https://www.youtube.com/watch?v=_bEs8vNbJQc.

The West has now been won, InfoWars, "Historic! Feds Forced to Surrender to American Citizens," YouTube video, April 13, 2014, https://www.youtube.com/watch?v=bD61YFxUga4.

If the standoff with the Bundys, Kevin Jenkins, "Bundy with Feds, a Spiritual Battle," *The Spectrum*, August 12, 2014, http://www.thespectrum.com/story/news/local/2014/08/02/bundy-showdown-feds-spiritual-battle/13536097/.

THE SEEKER

The Nay Book, Keith Allen Nay, *The Nay Book*, a scrapbook of quotes and prophecy, introduced with a letter from Cliven Bundy, dated 1999. Copy of pages in author's own collection.

Isaac Bullard, Fawn M. Brodie, *No Man Knows My History: The Life of Joseph Smith* (New York, New York: Vintage Books, 1995), 12

Disorderly person and imposter, "Introduction to People v. JS," The Joseph Smith Papers, https://www.josephsmithpapers.org/paper-summary/introduction-to-people-v-js/1.

Come up to Zion the next season, "Letter from Martha Campbell, 19 December 1843," The Joseph Smith Papers, https://www.josephsmithpapers.org/paper-summary/letter-from-martha-campbell-19-december-1843/1.

Exquisite whiteness, "The Testimony of the Prophet Joseph Smith," The Church of Jesus Christ of Latter-day Saints, https://www.churchofjesuschrist.org/study/scriptures/bofm/js?lang=eng.

Pretentious affair, Mark Twain, *Roughing It* (London, United Kingdom: Signet Classics, Penguin, 2008), 68.

Glimpsed or "hefted" them, Richard Lyman Bushman, *Joseph Smith: Rough Stone Rolling* (New York, New York: Vintage Books, 2007), 62–63.

EARLY DAYS

No one shall be appointed, Doctrine and Covenants (D&C), 28:2.

The promise of gifts and visions, Bushman, 151–52.

Follow the Spirit of truth, ibid.

Today the Mormon Church cites the story of Hiram Page, "Lesson 34: Doctrines and Covenants 28," The Church of Jesus Christ of Latter-day Saints, https://www.churchofjesuschrist.org/study/manual /doctrine-and-covenants-and-church-history-seminary-teacher -manual-2014/section-01/lesson-34?lang=eng.

In the beginning, Jon Krakauer, *Under the Banner of Heaven: A Story of Violent Faith* (New York, New York: Anchor Books, 2003), 78.

The genie was already out of the bottle, ibid., 79.

Bring forth their shining city, A statement made by Albert Gallatin Riddle in 1831; Leonard Arrington, *Great Basin Kingdom: An Economic History of the Latter-day Saints, 1830–1900* (Urbana, Illinois: University of Illinois Press, 2004), 12.

I command thee that thou, D&C, 19:26.

The hands of enemies, This is part of the following revelation: "If ye are faithful, ye shall assemble yourselves together to rejoice upon the land of Missouri, which is the land of your inheritance, which is now the land of your enemies," D&C, 52:42.

Concerning your brethren, D&C, 101:1.

There were jarrings, D&C, 101:6.

My bowels are filled, D&C, 101: 9.

All the land, D&C, 101:71.

Eagles and turkey buzzards, "History, 1838–1856, volume A-1 [23 December 1805–30 August 1834]," The Joseph Smith Papers, 494, https://www.josephsmithpapers.org/paper-summary/history-1838 -1856-volume-a-1-23-december-1805-30-august-1834/500; Matthew C. Godfrey, "We Believe the Hand of the Lord Is in It: Memories of Divine Intervention in Zion's Camp," *BYU Studies* 56, no. 4 (2017): 124–25.

A MILITIA THEOLOGY

Beheld the temple was filled with angels, B. H. Roberts, *A Comprehensive History of the Church of Jesus Christ of Latter-day Saints*, Volume 2 (Salt Lake City, Utah: Deseret News, 1930), 428.

If the salt have lost its savor, Sidney Rigdon, July 4, 1838, Far West, Caldwell County, Missouri. No complete text of the speech remains; F. Mark McKiernan, "Sidney Rigdon's Missouri Speeches," *BYU Studies* 11, no. 1 (Autumn 1970): 1.

I, the Lord, D&C, 98:37.

Arise and thresh, Michael D. Quinn, *The Mormon Hierarchy: Origins of Power* (Salt Lake City, Utah: Signature Books, 1994), 93.

Unlike other American religious denominations, Quinn, "National Culture, Personality and Theocracy in the Early Mormon Culture of Violence," *The John Whitmer Historical Journal,* Nauvoo Conference special edition (2002): 167.

Go scout on the border settlements, Roberts, *A Comprehensive History,* Volume 3, 180; Leland Gentry, "The Danite Band of 1838," *BYU Studies* 14, no. 4 (1974): 428, https://contentdm.lib.byu.edu /digital/collection/byustudies/id/460.

The most sacred obligations, John D. Lee, *Mormonism Unveiled or Life and Confession of John D. Lee* (Albuquerque, New Mexico: Fierra Blanco Publications, 2001), 57.

Like Samson, Lee 62–63.

The unconscious [Samuel], Quinn, "National Culture, Personality and Theocracy," 185–86; Andrew Jenson, The Historical Record (Salt Lake City, Utah: privately published, 1886–90), 688, https://archive. org/details/historicalrecord01jens/page/n4.

Nits will make lice, Jenson, 682.

Nauvoo

The great emporium of the West, "How Large Was the Population of Nauvoo?"*Nauvoo Neighbor,* October 1843; Susan Easton Black, "How Large Was the Population of Nauvoo?" *BYU Studies* 35, no. 2, art. 7 (1995): 91, https://scholarsarchive.byu.edu/byusq/vol35/iss2/7.

Bullet or blade, Etta H. Spendlove, *Memories and Experiences of James Jepson, Jr.* (Salt Lake City, UT: Utah State Historical Society, ms. no. A-31, 1934), 9–10.

Eulogy for his friend King Follett, Joseph Smith, "Classics in Mormon Thought: The King Follett Sermon" The Church of Jesus Christ of Latter-day Saints, https://www.churchofjesuschrist.org/ study/ensign/1971/04/the-king-follett-sermon?lang=eng.

Nauvoo Expositor, "Prospectus of the Nauvoo Expositor," *Nauvoo Expositor,* June 7, 1844, https://archive.org/details /NauvooExpositor1844.

A set of unprincipled, lawless, debauchees, This is from a letter written by Joseph Smith to Governor Thomas Ford on June 14, 1844; George Cannon ed., *Millennial Star* (London, England: Latter-day Saints Depot, 1862), 75.

Maid of Iowa come down, Joseph Smith's journal entry, June 15, 1844. https://www.josephsmithpapers.org/transcript/journal-december-1842-june-1844-book-4-1-march-22-june-1844.

Law of the land which is constitutional, D&C, 98:5–6

This nation [America], Joseph Smith, discourse, ca. 19 July 19, 1840, as reported by Martha Jane Knowlton Coray [ca. 1850s], Martha Jane Coray notebook, MS 1998, Joseph Smith Papers, Church History Library, 12–13.

All ye lovers of liberty, Roberts, *A Comprehensive History,* Volume 6, 499, https://byustudies.byu.edu/content/volume-6-chapter-24.

For never, since the son of God, Eliza R. Snow, "The Assassination," June, 27, 1844, https://erslexicon.wordpress.com/poems-25-30 /#eighteen.

Brigham Young's Deseret

The Saints would continue to suffer, Jenson, 497

Do you want the church properly organized? Brigham Young's speech in "Special Public Meeting of the Church," August 8, 1844, 234, text available via BYU Studies, https://byustudies.byu.edu/content /volume-7-chapter-19.

We would esteem a territorial government, Letter of the Council Signed by Brigham Young to President Polk, August 9, 1846; Roberts, 3:89–90.

I am he who led, D&C, 136:22

This is the place! Although oft repeated in Mormon lore, there is no record of this being said by Brigham Young.

Received nothing but one continued, Orson Pratt, "The Kingdom of God," *A Series of Pamphlets* (Liverpool, England: R. James, 1851), 18; Richard V. Francaviglia, "Mapping Deseret: Vernacular Mormon Mapmaking and the Spiritual Geography of the American West," *Believing in Place: A Spiritual Geography of the Great Basin* (Reno, Nevada: University of Nevada Press, 2003), 112–13.

A wide expanse of chaotic material, Parley P. Pratt, ed. William B. Smart and Donna T. Smart, "Report to the Legislative Council of Deseret, 5 Feb. 1850," *Over the Rim: The Parley P. Pratt Exploring*

Expedition to Southern Utah, 1849–50 (Logan: Utah State University Press, 1999), 181.

There is not a day passes over my head, Jacob Hamblin, "Journal of Jacob Hamblin, 1854-1859," March 8, 1855, typescript, MSA, 567-1, Utah State Archive.

Scatter them evenly around the earth, Utah American Western Center, University of Utah, *Paiute History,* http://www.utahindians. org/archives/paiutes/history.html.

Utah War

Supersede the Negro Mania, Excerpt from a letter written by Robert Tyler, April 27, 1857, a Pennsylvania democrat and son of the former president John Tyler; John Turner, B*righam Young: Pioneer Prophet* (Cambridge, England: Belknap Press, 2012), 268.

God has commenced, Brigham Young, *Journal of Discourses by Brigham Young, His Counselors, Twelve Apostles and Others* (Liverpool, England: F.D. and S.W. Richards, 1854–86), 5:75, 78.

All practical purposes, there was no law, Will Bagley, Blood of the Prophets: Brigham Young and the Mountain Meadows Massacre (Norman, Oklahoma: University of Oklahoma Press, 2002), 190.

The deserts of Utah, From a letter written by Brigham Young to Jeter Clinton, September 12, 1857; Bagley, 89.

Mormoni and *Mericats,* Martha Knack, *Between the Boundaries: The Southern Paiutes, 1775–1995* (Lincoln, Nebraska: University of Nebraska Press, 2001), 75.

The United States will kill us both, Letter from Brigham Young to Jacob Hambin dated August 4, 1857, appears in "Church Letter Book No. 3," 737–38 and is copied in its entirety in Juanita Brooks, *The Mountain Meadows Massacre,* 3rd ed. (Norman: University of Oklahoma Press, 1991), 34–35.

I have been driven from my home, A statement by Isaac Haight recorded in a Cedar City ward meeting on September 6, 1857; Brooks, *The Mountain Meadows Massacre,* 52; Bagley, 120.

This is Uncle Sam's grass, This story was told to Will Lund second-hand, but indicates the dialogue around the strained relationships between the Baker-Fancher party and the Mormon settlers; Mountain Meadows file, Church Library Archives; Bagley, 102.

Dead from grief, Lee, 222.

A company of men with shovels, 1908 statement by Nephi Johnson to Washington County officials; Brooks, *The Mountain Meadows Massacre*, 224.

Considered the generally peaceful Paiutes, Todd M. Compton, *A Frontier Life: Joseph Hamblin, Explorer and Indian Missionary* (Salt Lake City, Utah: University of Utah Press, 2013), 101.

Human skeletons, 1859 observations by James Lynch, Bagley, 219.

It should be vengeance is mine, Wilford Woodruff journal, May 25, 1861, https://archive.org/stream/WoodruffWilfordJournalSelections /Woodruff_Wilford_Journal_Selections_djvu.txt.

He didn't give an order, This statement came from a story passed down through the Brooks and Leavitt families. Dudley Leavitt's granddaughter, Juanita Brooks, recalled having heard it repeated; Brooks, *The Mountain Meadows Massacre*, 183.

Anything to do with the killing of emigrants, Letter from Nephi Johnson to Anthon H. Lund, March 1910; Bagley, 130.

My eyes have witnessed things, David Bitton and Maureen Ursenbach. "Riding Herd: A Conversation with Juanita Brooks." *Dialogue: A Journal of Mormon Thought* 9, no. 1 (1974): 9, 26, https:// www.dialoguejournal.com/wp- content/uploads/sbi/articles /Dialogue_V09N01_13.pdf.

Blood, blood, blood, Brooks, *The Mountain Meadows Massacre*, vii.

Branded me an apostate, Bitton and Ursenbach, 29.

Although Juanita, Levi S. Peterson, "In Memoriam: Juanita Brooks," *Sunstone Magazine* (October 1989), https://www.sunstonemagazine .com/pdf/073-06-08.pdf.

Oath for blood atonement, Levi S. Peterson, *Juanita Brooks: The Life Story of a Courageous Historian of the Mountain Meadows Massacre* (Salt Lake City, Utah: University of Utah Press, 1988), 44.

PART 2: AMERICAN ZION

SILVER

There shall be no private ownership, Arrington, *Great Basin Kingdom*, 201; Sara Dant questions the accuracy of this quote in her essay "The Lion of the Lord and the Land," *The Earth Will Appear as the Garden of Eden: Essays on Mormon Environmental History*, ed. Jedediah Smart Rogers and Matthew C. Godfrey (Salt Lake City, Utah: University of Utah Press, 2019), 29–46.

Utah will become, E. H. Tullidge, "The Reformation in Utah," *Harper's New Monthly Magazine* 43, no. 256 (September 1871): 602.

Instead of hunting gold, Arrington, Great *Basin Kingdom*, 203.

About one-half of the community are thieves, Kathleen Lillywhite, "Mining Town Day; Pioche, the Roughest Town in the Wild West," *St. George News*, September 11, 2016, https://www.stgeorgeutah.com/news/archive/2016/09/11/kli-mining-town-day-pioche-the-roughest-town-in-the-wild-west/.

Two Gods

In the south there is a grandeur, "The Silver Mountains of Utah," *Harper's New Monthly Magazine* 52, no. 317 (October 1876): 641–42.

As pioneers the Mormons, Frederick S. Dellenbaugh, *A Canyon Voyage: The Narrative of the Second Powell Expedition Down the Green-Colorado River From Wyoming, and the Explorations On Land, in the Years 1871 and 1872* (Tucson, Arizona: University of Arizona Press, 1984), 175.

Thousands of tired, nerve-shaken, John Muir, *Our National Parks* (Layton, Utah: Gibbs Smith, 2018), 1.

Nothing exceeds the wondrous, Clarence Dutton, "The Physical Geography of the Grand Canyon District." *Second Annual Report of the United States Geological Survey to the Secretary of the Interior 1880–1881* (Washington DC: Government Printing Office, 1882), 88.

God was on the mountaintop, William Cronon ed., "The Trouble with Wilderness or Getting Back to the Wrong Nature," *Uncommon Ground: Rethinking the Human Place in Nature* (New York, New York: W.W. Norton, 1996), 73.

I knew immediately what it was, Interview with Lulu Jones Waite by Fielding Harris, May 28, 1969, Voices of Remembrance Foundation, Oral History Collection, Dixie State College of Utah, 6.

We did not call them miracles, Interview with Glenn Waite by Fielding Harris, transcript, May 28, 1969, Voices of Remembrance Foundation, Oral History Collection, Dixie State College of Utah, 15.

Welcome to Utah

Cool springs, green meadows, John Wesley Powell, *The Exploration of the Colorado River and Its Canyons* (Simon and Brown, 2003), 293.

Mr. Chairman, Kathleen Flake, *The Politics of Religious Identity: The Seating of Senator Reed Smoot, Mormon Apostle* (Chapel Hill, North Carolina, University of North Carolina Press, 2004), 65.

There are accounts that Nephi Johnson, There is a letter from Nephi Johnson's father, Joel, dated April 20, 1877, urging him to go to

Mexico. "Joel Hills Johnson letter, Bellevue, Utah to Nephi Johnson," MS 23834, Church History Library; Robert Briggs, "Nephi Johnson," 1857 Iron County Militia Project, http://www.1857ironcountymilitia .com/index.php?title=Nephi_Johnson.

Mr. Smoot, you are a good, Michael Harold Paulos, "Under the Gun at the Smoot Hearings: Joseph F. Smith's Testimony," *Journal of Mormon History* 34, no. 4 (Fall 2008), 186.

Wednesday April 10, 1912, Reed Smoot Journal, April 10, 1912, typescript, Reed Smoot Papers, Book 11, MSS1187, Tom Perry Special Collections, Harold B. Lee Library, Brigham Young University, 5.

With a reporter from The Salt Lake Tribune, O. J. Grimes. "More of the Beauties of the 'Dixie' Land in Utah," *The Salt Lake Tribune,* June 11, 1916, https://newspapers.lib.utah.edu/ark:/87278/s6r797j7 /14703105; also see O. J. Grimes, "More Beauties of the Dixie Land [part 2]," *The Salt Lake Tribune,* June 25, 1916, https://newspapers.lib .utah.edu/ark:/87278/s6m33p0j/14664900.

Was in fair shape, Reed Smoot Journal, June 23, 1923, typescript, Reed Smoot Papers, Book 33, Vol. 8, Box 4, MSS1187, Tom Perry Special Collections, Harold B. Lee Library, Brigham Young University, 73.

Use of the people of the United States, B. L. Flanagan, "Zion-Mt. Carmel Road Opens," *Salt Lake Telegram,* July 4, 1930, https:// newspapers.lib.utah.edu/ark:/87278/s66q357z/16126673.

Would take a picture of scenery, Interview with JL Crawford by Dena Markoff, transcript, January 18, 1982, Zion 12352, Box 5, National Park Service, Zion National Park Collection, 2.

Bless the water and elements, Janice F. DeMille. "Generations, William Louis Crawford," *Color Country Spectrum Outlook,* May 7, 1978, MS57 B6F7, JL Crawford Collection, Special Collections, Gerald R. Sherratt Library, Southern Utah University, 10.

I was trying every way I could, Eviend T. Scoyen, "Eviend T. Scoyen: An Interview About His Experiences as the First Superintendent of Zion National Park, 1927–1931," interview by Lucy C. Schiefer, transcript, January 28, 1971, Zion 12352, Box 5, National Park Service, Zion National Park Collection, 19; Wayne K. Hinton, "Getting Along: The Significance of Cooperation in the Development of Zion National Park," *Utah Historical Quarterly* 68, no. 4 (Fall 2000): 313–31.

A Collision of Convictions

Published by God Almighty, Jack Lait, "An Appreciation of Zion National Monument," *United States Railroad Administration*, 1917, PAM 599, Utah State Archive, 3.

A man could ride for miles, Layton J. Ott, "Life Sketch of Joseph Wallace Thompson," transcript, January 3, 1939, Federal Writers Project, Special Collections, Merrill Cazier Library, Utah State University, 5.

The time when there was not, Carl H. Dopp, "Statement of Independence Taylor, Concerning Early Range Conditions in the Vicinity of New Harmony, Utah, and Subsequent Changes," Special Range Report, October 15, 1935, MSS 009, F5, Special Collections, Merrill Cazier Library, Utah State University, 1–2.

Don't let your animals stop and drink, G. Lynn Bower, Zion on the Muddy (Springhill, Utah: Art City Publishing, 2004). I went to the Church History Library to read Israel Bennion's journal. He makes reference to quicksand and the dangers to a "horse and mule outfit." There is even a passage of his own near demise, "having forgotten previous warnings, paddled in the sand and water at the river's edge . . . The result was such a struggle that I shudder to think of it now." Part of his journal was restricted and I did not get to see the quotes referenced in the Bower book. "Israel Bennion Reminiscences, Undated," MS 11324 and MS 11684, Church History Library, n.p.

The most notable feature of conservation, Karl Jacoby, *Crimes Against Nature: Squatters, Poachers, Thieves and the Hidden History of American Conservation* (Berkeley, California: University of California Press, 2003), 2.

I think people were better off, Interview with Dan Winder and Marion Winder by Rosslyn Stewart, Zion Reunion, transcript, August 26, 1978, Zion 12352, Box 5, National Park Service, Zion National Park Collection, 4, 7.

You might just as well, "Meeting Held at Price, Utah, June 26, 1936, for the Purpose of Discussing the Proposed Escalante National Monument," Escalante File, Series 22028, Box 11, Folder 11, Utah State Historical Society, 24 .

Several years of drought, Nethelia King Griffin, *Life in Boulder,* unpublished manuscript, 1940, MSSA562, Utah State Historical

Society, 8, 10–11. Mormon co-op cattle was livestock tithed to the Mormon Church.

Is not very promising, "Meeting Held at Price, Utah," 12–13.

Spasms and near convulsions, Arrington, *Utah's Audacious Stockman: Charlie Redd* (Logan, Utah: Utah State University Press, 1995), 16.

For a specified term, "Meeting Held at Price, Utah," 3–4.

As it was when Brigham Young, ibid., 24.

There are a great many people, ibid., 8.

Cows in the Wilderness

This is true, but do they eat enough? Edward Abbey, *Desert Solitaire* (New York, New York: McGraw-Hill, 1968), 35.

There are enough cathedrals and temples, Abbey, 200.

Drums of War

FLPMA, "Federal Land Policy and Management Act of 1976;" Sec. 101, https://www.blm.gov/or/regulations/files/FLPMA.pdf.

This is the time and day, "Redford Burned in Effigy for Opposing Power Plant," *The New York Times,* April 19, 1976, https://www.nytimes.com/1976/04/19/archives/redford-burned-in-effigy-for-opposing-power-plant.html.

There are many malicious rumors, "B.L.M. Official Comments on Criticism of Portions of Organic Rules," *Times Independent,* March 24, 1977, https://newspapers.lib.utah.edu/ark:/87278/s62v3t8d/20431510.

I'm a sagebrush rebel, Jedediah S. Rogers, "The Volatile Sagebrush Rebellion," *Utah in the Twentieth Century,* edited by Brian Q. Cannon and Jessie L. Embry (Louisville, Colorado: University Press of Colorado, 2009), 78.

The Sagebrush Rebellion's true intent, Margot Hornblower, "The Sagebrush Revolution," *The Washington Post,* November 11, 1979, https://www.washingtonpost.com/archive/opinions/1979/11/11/the-sagebrush-revolution/7ebf91e7-cbed-4bae-80c9-9a0cce5fe5d7/.

We've had enough of you guys, Moab District Staff Report, April 11–12, 1979, Reel 1, Series, 19269, Governor Matheson County Records, Utah State Archives and Record Service; Rogers, 72.

Most abused by the federal government, John Herbers, "West Taking South's Place as Most Alienated Area," *The New York Times,* March 18, 1979, http://www.nytimes.com/1979/03/18/archives/west-taking-souths-place-as-most-alienated-area-replacing-the-south.html.

I hear rumors, Buckley Jensen, "Remarkable Life from Humble

Start, Giants of San Juan," *San Juan Record*, October 1, 2008, http://www.sjrnews.com/view/full_story/6746237/article-Cal-Black.

One of the least inhabited, Betsy Marston, "Wilderness Fight leads to Symbolic Hanging," *High Country News*, June 11, 1984: 5, http://s3.amazonaws.com/hcn-media/archive-pdf/1984_06_11_rfs.pdf.

If you want wilderness, ibid.

Stop Destructive Welfare Ranching, Dirk Johnson, "A Range War of Words on Grazing in the West," *The New York Times*, August 5, 1991, https://www.nytimes.com/1991/08/05/us/a-range-war-of-words-on-grazing-in-the-west.html.

User conflict, "Lymans Forego Grazing Rights on Escalante River Allotment," *Garfield County News*, June 11, 1992, https://newspapers.lib.utah.edu/ark:/87278/s6w103dj/3435990.

It makes no difference, Dirk Johnson, "A Range War of Words on Grazing in the West," *The New York Times*, August 5, 1991, https://www.nytimes.com/1991/08/05/us/a-range-war-of-words-on-grazing-in-the-west.html.

Showcase of multiple uses, "Legislation Introduced for Escalante Conservation Area," *Garfield County News*, June 25, 1992, https://newspapers.lib.utah.edu/ark:/87278/s6029p1b/3432719.

In a park, ibid.

Would do nothing more, Lee Davidson and Joseph Bauman, "Hansen Pushes for Creation of a Conservation Area in Escalante Canyons," *Deseret News*, June 18, 1992, https://www.deseret.com/1992/6/18/18989996/hansen-pushes-creation-of-a-conservation-area-in-escalante-canyons.

GOD AND GUNS

He sent a telegram, A telegram addressed to Dean Rhodes, serving on the Subcommittee on Mines and Mining Oversight Hearing, November 20, 1980; William Perry Pendley, *Sagebrush Rebel: Reagan's Battle with Environmental Extremists and Why It Matters Today* (Washington, DC: Regency Publishing, 2013), 38.

Most environmental groups, Patrick Dawson, "Armed, Crazy and Lost in the Wild West," *High Country News*, May 15, 1995, http://www.hcn.org/issues/35/1043.

Boy, you guys really screwed that one up, Cori Brosnahan, "Ruby Ridge, Part Three: Fear & Faith," American Experience, PBS, February 14, 2017, https://medium.com/americanexperiencepbs/ruby-ridge-part-three-fear-faith-f2f045f6806d.

Head for the hills bags, Tara Westover, *Educated: A Memoir* (New York, New York: Random House, 2018), 9

No authority to own, William Chaloupka, "The County Supremacy and Militia Movements: Federalism as an Issue on the Radical Right." *Publius: The Journal of Federalism* 26, no. 3 (Summer 1996): 163.

End apartheid, Gary Andrew Poole, "Hold It! This Land Is My Land!: Led by Commissioner Dick Carver, Nevada's Nye County Is Now Ground Zero in the West's War Against the US Government," *LA Times,* December 3, 1995, *https://www.latimes.com/archives/la-xpm-1995-12-03-tm-9835-story.html.*

All it would have taken, Jon Christensen, "County Commissioner Courts Bloodshed," *High Country News*, April 3, 1995, http://www.hcn.org/issues/32/919.

The finest energy field, James Brooke, "New Reserve Stirs Animosities in Utah," *The New York Times*, October 13, 1996, https://www.nytimes.com/1996/10/13/us/new-reserve-stirs-animosities-in-utah.html.

I feel like I'm back in the 1850s, ibid.

A COWBOY NAMED MARY

Federalism, constitutionalism, Chaloupka, 161.

A county (or parish), "United States Christian Posse Association," *Identity* 6 (1972): 2–3; Michael Barkun, *Religion and the Racist Right: The Origins of the Christian Identity Movement* (Chapel Hill, North Carolina: University of North Carolina Press, 1996), 69.

In Utah, 28 of 30, Ross D. Franklin, "The Troubling Sheriffs' Movement That Joe Arpaio Supports," *Politico*, September 1, 2017, https://www.politico.com/magazine/story/2017/09/01/joe-arpaio-pardon-sheriffs-movement-215566.

Spent 20 years, Shawna Cox, *Last Rancher Standing: The Cliven Bundy Story, a Close-up View* (New York, New York: Legends Library, 2016), 5.

It's the job of the BLM, Electa Draper, "Rancher Draws Line in Grazing Fight," *Denver Post*, November 26, 2000, https://extras.denverpost.com/news/news1126b.htm.

Choked over 20 heads, Mary Bulloch, "An Open Letter from Mary Bullock," *Garfield County News*, October 26, 2000, https://newspapers.lib.utah.edu/ark:/87278/s6bz73ks/3469662.

I knew a confrontation, "Bulloch's Cows Released after Salina Auction Is Called Off," *Garfield County News,* November 9, 2000, https://newspapers.lib.utah.edu/ark:/87278/s68g9h7k/3466434.

Waco situation, Brent Israelson and Thomas Burr, "Sherriffs Defy Feds, Take Back Seized Cattle," *The Salt Lake Tribune,* November 9, 2000.

Pretty western, ibid.

Have been beaten down, ibid.

Direct result of Kate Cannon's, Draper, "Rancher Draws Line in Grazing Fight."

With luck I'll see, Curly Musgrave, "The Ol' Fifty Mile," *The Heritage,* recorded 2003, http://tidido.com/a35184374391338 /al55f185bba5f3907573943ca8/t55f185bca5f3907573943d1b.

Fighting to Keep America Strong, Turner, 137.

Prophecy and End-Times

I welcome the opportunity, Excerpted from a letter written on April 12, 1962, from J. Edgar Hoover to Sister Mary Shaun, Notre Dame Convent in Trenton, New Jersey. I requested Cleon Skousen's FBI file via the Freedom of Information Act, but was never sent any information. However, Ernie Lazar, a researcher for the Berkeley Center for Right Wing Studies, researched Cleon Skousen and has FOIAed and received much of his FBI file. He posted the documents, revised December 16, 2019, on https://sites.google.com/site /ernie124102/home.

Were usually a cheerful lot, Cleon Skousen, *The Making of America: The Substance and Meaning of the Constitution* (Washington, DC: The National Center for Constitutional Studies, 1985), 131.

When the Constitution, Journal of Discourses 2:32.

Is the form of the Government, Journal of Discourses 8:321.

The day is not far distant, Journal of Discourses, 21:8.

I believe that it is the destiny, Melvin J. Ballard, Conference Report, April 1933, 127.

Satan is anxious, Ezra Taft Benson, "Our Immediate Responsibility," speech, Brigham Young University, October 25, 1966, https://speeches .byu.edu/talks/ezra-taft-benson/immediate-responsibility/.

The man is also a master of half-truths, From a letter from J. Bracken Lee to Mrs. Elizabeth Laine on August 8, 1960.

The biggest factor, Alexander Zaitchik, *Common Nonsense: Glen Beck and the Triumph of Ignorance* (Hoboken, New Jersey: Wiley and Sons, 2010), 213.

I fear that the United States, Krissah Thompson, "Conservative Class on Founding Fathers' Answers to Current Woes Gains

Popularity," *The Washington Post*, June 5, 2010, http://www
.washingtonpost.com/wp-dyn/content/article/2010/06/04
/AR2010060404918.html.

They just didn't want to leave, ibid.

Postmillennial religion, Morris Dees and James Corcoran, *Gathering Storm: America's Militia Threat* (New York, New York: Harper Perennial, 1996), 24.

Some ranchers, Marina Abalakina-Papp et al., "Beliefs in Conspiracies," *Political Psychology* 1, no. 3 (1999): 639.

All Stake Presidents, "Letter from the Office of the First Presidency, Spencer W. Kimball, N. Eldon Tanner, Marion G. Romney," The Church of Jesus Christ of Latter-day Saints, February 15, 1979; Alexander Zaitchik, "Meet the Man Who Changed Glenn Beck's Life," Salon, September 16, 2009, https://www.salon.com/2009/09/16 /beck_skousen/.

Close, warm, and cordial, This was from December 12, 2010, Paul Skousen's comment in response to a December 11, 2010, post by *By Common Consent* blogger John C. who was critical of his father, "God Does Not Particularly Care about Your Civil Liberties," https:// bycommonconsent.com/2010/12/11/god-does-not-particularly-care -about-your-civil-liberties/.

RANGE WAR

Dear friends, Leah Sottie, "Cliven Bundy's Fight Against the Feds Has Roots in Interpretation of Mormon Scripture," *The Washington Post*, December 7, 2017, https://www.washingtonpost.com/national /cliven-bundys-fight-against-the-feds-has-roots-in-interpretation -of-mormon-scripture/2017/12/07/0ef8fea6-d93b-11e7-a841 -2066faf731ef_story.html.

Margaret Bodel Jensen Bundy, Obituary of Margaret Bodel Jensen Bundy, Find a Grave, https://www.findagrave.com/memorial /16177597/margaret-bodel-bundy.

The environmental movement, Lyman Hafen, *Roping the Wind: A Personal History of Cowboys and the Land* (Logan, Utah: Utah State University Press, 1995), 4.

When the US government, Mike Blake, "Before Cliven Bundy Stand- Off, a Collision between Ranchers and Tortoises," *Reuters*, May 30, 2014, https://www.reuters.com/article/us-usa-ranchers-nevada -tortoises-insight/before-nevada-stand-off-a-collision-between -ranchers-and-tortoises-idUSKBN0EA1I420140530.

Direct conflict, "Courthouse Meet Draws Angry Ranchers, Sheriff, Commissioners on BLM Cattle Sale and Utah Ag Department Deal with Feds," *Garfield County News*, February 8, 2001, https://newspapers.lib.utah.edu/ark:/87278/s6vx1d4q/3469468.

A big chunk was coming, ibid.

Now they are claiming, "BLM After More Cows in Nevada Counties; Sheriff Stands for Due Process," *Garfield County News*, March 28, 2002, https://newspapers.lib.utah.edu/ark:/87278/s63b6wqb/3471223.

It looks to me, Sean Whaley, "Nevada Ranching Family Loses Federal Lands Court Case," *Las Vegas Review*, January 18, 2016, http://www.reviewjournal.com/news/nevada/nevada-ranching -family- loses-federal-lands-court-case.

Bundy shall remove his livestock, United States v. Bundy, ruling by US District Judge Lloyd D. George, June 9, 2013, Casemine, https://www.casemine.com/judgement/us/5914f013add7b0493497193a.

The Bureau of Land Management, "Son of Rancher in Public Land Dispute Arrested by BLM," NBC, News 3 Las Vegas, April 6, 2014, https://news3lv.com/archive/son-of-rancher-in-public-land-dispute -arrested-by-blm.

Militia Sighn In, Jamie Fuller, "The Long Fight between the Bundys and the Federal Government, from 1989 to Today," *The Washington Post*, January 4, 2016, https://www.washingtonpost.com/news/the-fix /wp/2014/04/15/everything-you-need-to-know-about-the-long-fight -between-cliven-bundy-and-the-federal-government/.

We need Oath Keepers, This was part of a plea that was also shared with another militia organization, the Three Percenters, "Oath Keepers to Help with Bundy Protest," Sipsey Street Irregulars, Blogspot, http://sipseystreetirregulars.blogspot.com/2014/04/oath-keepers -to-help-with-bundy-protest.html; James Scaminaci, "Chapter 23: The Battle of Bunkerville and Fourth Generation Warfare." Academia.edu, https://www.academia.edu/11658509/chapter_23_the_battle_of _bunkerville_and_fourth_generation_warfare.

Seems very strange, "Oath Keepers to Help with Bundy Protest."

We locked them, From a draft of "The Domestic Terrorist," a 2014 article by Ted McDermott in the new defunct *Missoula Independent*, in author's possession.

We were actually strategizing, Fuller, "The Long Fight between the Bundys and the Federal Government."

I would have put my own wife, Interview with Ben Swann, April 13, 2014. No longer available online, but Mack's been widely quoted from this interview; Dylan Scott, "Why Bundy Ranch Thinks America's Sheriffs Can Disarm The Feds," Talking Points Memo, April 15, 2014, https://talkingpointsmemo.com/muckraker/bundy-ranch -constitutional-sheriffs-oath-keepers.

State police and highway patrol, Marlena Chertock et al., "'No' Sheriff in Town: Some Lawmen Refuse to Enforce Federal Gun Laws," *NBC News*, https://www.nbcnews.com/news/investigations /no-sheriff-town-some-lawmen-refuse-enforce-federal-gun-laws -n185426.

This one was converted, Ryan Lenz, "Former Arizona Sheriff Richard Mack Seeks 'Army' of Sheriffs to Resist Federal Authority," *Southern Law Poverty Center Intelligence Report* 23 (November 11, 2012), https://www.splcenter.org/fighting-hate/intelligence-report /2012/former-arizona-sheriff-richard-mack-seeks-'army'-sheriffs -resist-federal-authority.

THE BIRD REFUGE

We want those arms, Ryan Lenz, "War in the West: The Bundy Ranch Standoff and the American Radical Right," July 10, 2014, Southern Law Poverty Center, https://www.splcenter.org/20140709 /war-west-bundy-ranch-standoff-and-american-radical-right.

If the standoff with the Bundys, Kevin Jenkins, "Bundy: Showdown with Feds 'Spiritual,'" *The Spectrum*, August 2, 2014, http://www .thespectrum.com/story/news/local/2014/08/02/bundy-showdown -feds-spiritual- battle/13536097/.

We the people will have to face, Associated Press, "Cliven Bundy: God Was on Our Side," *Politico*, August 3, 2014, https://www.politico .com/story/2014/08/cliven-bundy-109681.

Maliciously damaging, "Eastern Oregon Ranchers Convicted of Arson Resentenced to Five Years in Prison," US Department of Justice press release, October 7, 2015, https://www.justice.gov/usao-or/pr /eastern-oregon-ranchers-convicted-arson-resentenced-five-years -prison.

I begin to understand how the Lord, Ammon Bundy, "Dear Friends," YouTube video, January 1, 2016, https://www.youtube.com/watch?v =M7M0mG6HUyk.

You start off by raising, Scott Carrier, "Absolutely, God Told Us to Do This," *Home of the Brave*, podcast audio, January 13, 2016, http:// homebrave.com/home-of-the-brave//absolutely-god-told-us-to-do-this.

All the counties across the United States, Robert Anglen, "What

Made Ammon Bundy Go from Arizona Businessman to Leader of the Oregon Standoff?" *Arizona Central*, USA Today, January 27, 2016, https://www.azcentral.com/story/news/local/arizona/2016/01/09/what-made-ammon-bundy-go-arizona-lead-oregon-standoff-federal-government/78420744/.

Native Americans had the claim, A. B. Wilkinson, "A Right to the Land: Native Americans and Militias in Oregon and Nevada," *Huffington Post*, January 25, 2016, http://www.huffingtonpost.com/a-b- wilkinson/gold-butte_b_9044222.html.

We're planning on staying, Les Zaitz, "Militia Takes Over Malheur National Wildlife Refuge Headquarters," *The Oregonian*/OregonLive, January 2, 2016, http://www.oregonlive.com/pacific-northwest-news/index.ssf/2016/01/drama_in_burns_ends_with_quiet.html.

Neither Ammon Bundy, Liam Stack, "Wildlife Refuge Occupied in Protest of Oregon Ranchers' Prison Terms," *The New York Times*, January 2, 2016, https://www.nytimes.com/2016/01/03/us/oregon-ranchers-will-return-to-prison-angering-far-right-activists.html.

It doesn't have to stop, "Armed Militia Occupy Forest Reserve HQ in Oregon, Call 'US Patriots' to Arms, Bundy Bros Join Protest," Signs of the Times, January 3, 2016, https://www.sott.net/article/309698-Armed-militia-occupy-forest-reserve-HQ-in-Oregon-call-US-patriots-to-arms-Bundy-bros-join-protest.

I believe you know that I respect you, Stewart Rhodes, "Recommended Honorable Exit Strategy for Ammon Bundy," Oath Keepers, January 6, 2016, https://www.oathkeepers.org/a-recommended-honorable-exit-strategy-for-ammon-bundy/.

It is my belief, LaVoy Finicum, *Only by Blood and Suffering: Regaining Lost Freedom* (Rochester, New York: Legends Publishing, Inc., 2015), 3.

You want a bloodbath, "Oregon Occupier's Footage Prior to Fatal Shooting Released: 'You Want a Bloodbath?,'" KATU, video clip, April 5, 2016, https://komonews.com/news/nation-world/oregon-occupiers-footage-prior-to-fatal-shooting-released-you-want-a-bloodbath.

If he believed, Matthew Piper, "Cops Who Shot Finicum Had Seen Him Talking about Resisting Arrest," *The Salt Lake Tribune*, March 11, 2016, https://archive.sltrib.com/article.php?id=3649325&itype=CMSID.

1. God is a Warrior, Matt Shea, "The Biblical Basis for War," in author's possession, 1.

Assassination to remove tyrants, ibid., 3.

Is likely to plan, Kathy Loedler and Paul Loedler, "Rampart Group: Report of Investigation Regarding Representative Matt Shea Washington State House of Representatives," December 1, 2019, in author's possession, 81.

Like we are seeing with our President, Matt Shea's Facebook page, December 19, 2019, https://www.facebook.com/mattsheawa.

A spontaneous act, Loedler and Loedler, 18.

PART 3: WE THE PEOPLE

INDIANS AND COWBOYS

Adjudicated livestock water rights, "Now That the Feds Have Backed Off, Where Does This Leave the Nevada Rancher in His Battle with the Gov't?" The Blaze, April 17, 2014, https://www.theblaze.com /news/2014/04/17/now-that-the-feds-have-backed-off-where-does -this-leave-the-nevada-rancher-in-his-battle-with-the-govt.

Any claims they have on the land, "LaVoy Finicum Trying to Save Native American Artifacts," Youtube video, January 27, 2016, https:// www.youtube.com/watch?v=6is6NJhnORE.

I don't know what these people, Jacqueline Keeler, "Oregon Militia Nuts Hold Paiute History, Artifacts Hostage," *Indian Country Today*, January 19, 2016, https://newsmaven.io/indiancountrytoday/archive /oregon-militia-nuts-hold-paiute-history-artifacts-hostage -ldK5a15QqEGWS98aUNSIgw/.

All the roving and straggling bands, 1872 executive order by President Ulysses S. Grant, "Malheur Indian Reservation," Oregon History Project, https://oregonhistoryproject.org/articles/historical -records/malheur-indian-reservation/#.XeKzxy2ZP_8.

One of the nation's leading experts, Carolyn Grattan-Aiello, "Senator Arthur V. Watkins and the Termination of Utah's Southern Paiute Indians," *Utah Historical Quarterly* 63, no. 3 (1995): 281.

We have made some terrible mistakes, ibid.

As a native, Kirk Siegler, "In Nevada, Tribes Push to Protect Land at the Heart of Bundy Ranch Standoff," National Public Radio, August 18, 2016, https://www.npr.org/sections/codeswitch/2016/08/18 /490498442/in-nevada-tribes-push-to-protect-land-at-the-heart-of -bundy-ranch-standoff.

A national monument!?! Bundy Ranch Facebook page, December 28, 2016, through January 2017, https://www.facebook.com/pg /bundyranch/posts.

Eking out a precarious existence, Letter from James Spencer to the commissioner of Indian Affairs, August 30, 1880; William Logan Hebner, *Southern Paiute: A Portrait* (Logan, Utah: Utah State University Press, 2010), 124.

BLACK HATS, WHITE HATS

The First Amendment is not an area, Henry Brean and Ben Botkin, "Rancher's Son Describes Arrest in Protest of Federal Cattle Roundup," *Las Vegas Review-Journal*, April 7, 2014, https://www .reviewjournal.com/news/bundy-blm/ranchers-son-describes-arrest -in-protest-of-federal-cattle-roundup/.

We're going to work with you, "The Standoff at Bunkerville," Frary Brand, YouTube video, April 14, 2014, *https://www.youtube.com /watch?v=_lq1sFkQXyc*.

Flagrant prosecutorial misconduct, Marvin Clemons, "Bundy Trial Dismissed Due to 'Flagrant Prosecutorial Misconduct,'" NBC, News 3 Las Vegas, January 7, 2018, https://news3lv.com/news/local/feds -bungled-effort-to-prosecute-bundys-supporters-may-end-Monday.

I routinely observed, Memo from Special Agent Larry Wooten to Andrew D. Goldsmith, Associate Deputy Director, National Criminal Discovery Coordinator, undated, *http://www.thiswestisourwest.com /index.cfm/draining-the-swamp/whitleblower-larry-wooten-letter/*.

I was hell-bent on killing, James Pogue, "The Government Is Botching Another Bundy Trial," *Outside*, December 18, 2017, https:// www.outsideonline.com/2269531/why-government-keeps-losing -bundy-cases.

We were dealing with people, Ana Ley, "Sergeant Who Patrolled Bunkerville Says Experience Changed How Officers Work," *Las Vegas Sun*, June 1, 2015, https://lasvegassun.com/news/2015/jun/01 /sergeant-who-patrolled-bunkerville-says-experience/.

Arden doesn't know life, "Lone Rancher Is Prepared to Fight Feds for Land," John M. Glionna, *Los Angeles Times*, Septemeber 23, 2013, https://lasvegassun.com/news/2013/sep/23/lone-rancher-prepared -fight-feds-land/.

Enemies of the People

This is not the time for science fiction, E. O. Wilson, *Creation: An Appeal to Save Life on Earth* (New York, New York: W. W. Norton, 2017), 92.

Differ very much with Christendom, Thomas G. Alexander, *Brigham Young and the Expansion of the Mormon Faith* (Norman, Oklahoma: University of Oklahoma Press, 2019), 221.

A heartfelt believer, Kurt Andersen, *Fantasyland: How America Went Haywire* (New York, New York: Random House, 2017), 72.

The earth will bring forth, Cleon Skousen, *Prophecy and Modern Times: Finding Hope and Encouragement in the Last Days* (Salt Lake City, Utah: Izzard Ink Publishing, 2017), 112.

The Old Cow Man, Charles Badger Clark, "The Old Cow Man," 1906, Cowboy Poetry, April 14, 2017, https://blog.cowboypoetry.com /category/classic-poems/the-old-cow-man-by-charles-badger-clark -jr-1883-1957/.

Obstruction of justice, "Idaho Man Sentenced To 14 Years In Prison For Threat And Assault Of Federal Law Enforcement During 2014 Armed Standoff In Bunkerville", US Department of Justice, US Attorney's Office, District of Nevada press release, July 19, 2018, https://www.justice.gov/usao-nv/pr/idaho-man-sentenced-14-years -prison-threat-and-assault-federal-law-enforcement-during.

Once again thumbed, Maxine Bernstein, "Judge Sentences Oregon Refuge Occupier Ryan Payne to Over 3 Years in Prison," *The Oregonian*/OregonLive, February 27, 2018, https://www.oregonlive .com/oregon-standoff/2018/02/federal_judge_sentences_oregon.html.

Authenticity and credibility, Maxine Bernstein, "Ammon Bundy's Lawyer Argues for His Client's Right to Wear Cowboy Boots at Trial," *The Oregonian*/OregonLive, September 7, 2016, http://www .oregonlive.com/oregon-standoff/2016/09/ammon_bundys_lawyer _argues_for.html.

Safety issues, Debra Cassens Weiss, "Ammon and Ryan Bundy Won't Be Allowed to Wear Their Preferred Cowboy Attire at Trial," *ABA Journal*, September 8, 2016, http://www.abajournal.com/news /article/ammon_bundy_wont_be_allowed_to_wear_his_preferred _cowboy_attire_at_trial.

Good old-fashioned values, Amanda Radke, "The Cowboy Way Is Backed With Morals, Values," *Beef Magazine*, January 14, 2013, https://www.beefmagazine.com/blog/cowboy-way-backed-morals -values.

Spellbound

Mesmerized, Tay Wiles, "Bundy Supporter Gets 68 Years," *High Country News,* July 26, 2017, https://www.hcn.org/articles/public -lands-bunkerville-defendant-sentenced-to-68-years-in-prison.

I felt bad about running them off, Brett Logiurato, "Bundy Supporter: I Remember the Alleged Las Vegas Cop Killers, and They Seemed 'Sketchy,'" *Business Insider,* June 10, 2014 https://www .businessinsider.in/Bundy-Supporter-I-Remember-The-Alleged-Las -Vegas-Cop-Killers-And-They-Seemed-Sketchy/articleshow /36318779.cms.

This is the start of a revolution, Mike Hayes, "Everything We Know About Jerad and Amanda Miller, the Las Vegas Couple Who Went on a Shooting Rampage," BuzzFeedNews, June 11, 2014, https://www .buzzfeednews.com/article/mikehayes/everything-we-know-about -jerad-and-amanda-miller-the-suicida.

Doing the Right Thing

Leather-faced, Hafen, 15.

To Bundy and his supporters, J. J. MacNab, "Context Matters: The Cliven Bundy Standoff—Part 1," *Forbes,* April 30, 2014, https://www .forbes.com/sites/jjmacnab/2014/04/30/context-matters-the-cliven -bundy-standoff-part-1/.

Virus was spreading, Brent Weisberg, "Militia at Malheur: 'Virus Was Spreading,'" CBS, KOIN 6 News, January 29, 2016, https://www .koin.com/news/militia-at-malheur-virus-was-spreading/960335710.

Some say it is extremism, Todd MacFarlane, "A Realistic Assessment of Utah's Role in the Current Public Lands Debate," RANGEfire!, January 20, 2017, http://rangefire.us/2017/01/20/a-realistic -assessment-of-utahs-role-in-the-current-public-lands-debate-by -todd-macfarlane/.

What's happened in Nevada, Kristen Moulton, "Western Lawmakers Gather in Utah to Talk Federal Land Takeover," *The Salt Lake Tribune,* April 19, 2014, https://archive.sltrib.com/article.php?id=57836973 &itype=cmsid.

Church leaders strongly condemn, Ted Walch, "LDS Church Condemns Seizure of Oregon Federal Facilities by Militia Citing Mormon Beliefs," *Deseret News,* January 4, 2016, https://www .deseretnews.com/article/865644791/LDS-Church-condemns-seizure -of-Oregon-federal-facilities-by-militia-citing-Mormon-beliefs.html.

With an expanding financial base, Gina Colvin and Joanna Brooks eds., *Decolonizing Mormonism: Approaching a Postcolonial Zion* (Salt Lake City, Utah: University of Utah Press, 2018), 4.

To this day, my spiritual life, Terry Tempest Williams, *The Hour of the Land: A Personal Topography of America's National Parks* (New York, New York: Farrar, Strauss and Giroux, 2016), 10.

I am not like the Mormon pioneers, George B. Handley, *Home Waters: A Year of Recompenses on the Provo River* (Salt Lake City, Utah: University of Utah Press, 2010), xi.

All are stewards, "Environmental Stewardship and Conservation Statement," Mormon Newsroom, July 1, 2014, https://newsroom .churchofjesuschrist.org/2014yearinreview/july-environmental -stewardship-and-conservation/index.html.

Infiltrated by these same people, Sean Dolan, "Ammon Bundy Claims LDS Church Infiltrated by Socialists," *Idaho State Journal*, July 22, 2018, https://www.idahostatejournal.com/news/local/ammon -bundy-claims-lds-church-infiltrated-by-socialists/article_af3435a3 -2893-5dc4-95a5-590aa695652f.html.

Not to work for the office, Peggy Fletcher Stack, "Noted Historian Still Believes in Mormonism, but Now as an Outsider," *The Salt Lake Tribune*, October 1, 2013, https://archive.sltrib.com/article.php ?id=56899817&itype=cmsid.

White, American, Utahn, Colvin and Brooks, 5.

To govern our spiritual instincts, ibid., 4.

Conversion of the Earth, ibid., 4.

They call it [Utah] Zion, ibid., 16.

NEW WEST

Chickenshit trick, Michelle Nijhuis, "Change Comes Slowly to Escalante Country," *High Country News*, April 14, 2003, https://www .hcn.org/issues/248/13869.

Need a better grip, Brent Israelsen, "Greens Not Welcome in Escalante," *High Country News,* May 24, 1999, https://www.hcn.org /issues/155/5016.

Outdoor recreation provides 76 times, Brian Mafly, "Report: Utah's Coal Industry Fading While More Eco-friendly Outdoor Recreation Surges," *The Salt Lake Tribune*, July 25, 2017, https://archive.sltrib .com/article.php?id=5549913&itype=CMSID.

FALLOUT

Under the guise of collecting grazing fees, Bundy v. Sessions, Civil

Action No. 2018-2520 (D.D.C. 2019), June 10, 2019, Court Listener, https://www.courtlistener.com/opinion/4627986/bundy-v-sessions/.

Fundamentally flawed notion, David Ferrara, "Judge Tosses Cliven Bundy's Claim that State Owns All Public Lands," *Las Vegas Review-Journal,* April 9, 2019, https://www.reviewjournal.com/local/local -nevada/judge-tosses-cliven-bundys-claim-that-state-owns-all -public-lands-1637278/.

Something I know about the Negro, Adam Nagourney, "A Defiant Rancher Savors the Audience That Rallied to His Side," *The New York Times,* April 24, 2014, https://www.nytimes.com/2014/04/24/us /politics/rancher-proudly-breaks-the-law-becoming-a-hero-in-the -west.html.

I haven't seen anybody pull, Anna Brand, "Obama Mocks Bundy, Republicans at Correspondents' Dinner," MSNBC, May, 4, 2014, http://www.msnbc.com/msnbc/president-obama-mocks-bundy -republicans-white-house-correspondents-dinner; the complaint filed by Ryan Bundy on October 31, 2018, is available online via *The Oregonian*/OregonLive, http://media.oregonlive.com/oregon -standoff/other/2018/10/31/ryanbundyDCsuit.pdf.

Is all fear based, The video was posted on Facebook on November 27, 2018, before Ammon Bundy went off of social media. I was able to watch it before he took it down in November 2018. The video is embedded in the following article by Kyle Swenson, "Ammon Bundy Breaks with Trump on Anti-migrant Rhetoric: 'It's All Fear-based,'" *The Salt Lake Tribune,* November 28, 2018, https://www.sltrib .com/news/nation-world/2018/11/28/ammon-bundy-breaks-with/.

A FAKtriot! I found abundant negative comments about their former hero, Ammon Bundy, on The Three Percenters Facebook page, posts dating from November 27, 2018, into January 2019. https:// www.facebook.com/theIIIpercenter/.

We've been asked by God to help, Ammon Bundy's video posted to Facebook November 27, 2018, Kyle Swenson, "Ammon Bundy Breaks with Trump on Anti-migrant Rhetoric: 'It's All Fear-based.'"

OUR MYTHS

A foolish consistency, Ralph Waldo Emerson, "Self-Reliance," (N.p.: CreateSpace, 2017): 19.

Animal Damage Control, Testimony of Erik Molvar to the Congressional Federal Lands Subcommittee, July 9, 2018, record in author's possession.

Outdoor Industry Association, "Outdoor Recreation a Large and Growing Percentage of the U.S. Economy," Outdoor Industry Association press release, September 20m 2018, https://outdoorindustry.org/press-release/outdoor-recreation-large-growing-percentage-u-s-economy/.

Counties that elect, Zoe Nemerever, "Federal Managers Who Try to Protect Public Lands Face Threats and Violence, Here's What Makes That Much Worse," *The Washington Post*, June 13, 2019, https://www.washingtonpost.com/politics/2019/06/13/federal-managers-who-try-protect-public-lands-face-threats-violence-heres-what-makes-that-much-worse/.

Governments [sic] which seem, Todd MacFarland, "Stanton Gleave and the Piute Posse," *Range Magazine*, October 24, 2018, http://rangefire.us/2018/10/24/stanton-gleave-and-the-piute-posse-by-todd-macfarlane/.

Freedom of action in the struggle for existence, Aldo Leopold, *A Sand County Almanac: Outdoor Essays and Reflections* (New York, New York: Ballantine Books, 1986), 202–04.

The Bundys thought that was the worst thing, Erin Alberty, "Cliven Bundy: Oregon Ranchers at Center of Armed Occupation 'Failed' Supporters in Flagging States' Rights Movement," *The Salt Lake Tribune*, June 9, 2019, https://www.sltrib.com/news/2019/06/09/cliven-bundy-oregon/.

Selected Bibliography

Abalakina-Papp, Marina, Walter G. Stephan, Ted Craig, and W. Larry Gregory. "Beliefs in Conspiracies." *Political Psychology* 1, no. 3 (1999): 637–47.

Abbey, Edward. *Desert Solitaire.* New York, New York: McGraw-Hill, 1968.

Alder, Douglas D., and Karl F. Brooks. *A History of Washington County: From Isolation to Destination.* Springdale, Utah: Zion National History Association, 2000.

Alexander, Thomas G. *Brigham Young and the Expansion of the Mormon Faith*, Norman, Okalahoma: University of Oklahoma Press, 2019.

———. "Red Rock and Gray Stone: Senator Reed Smoot, the Establishment of Zion and Bryce Canyon National Parks, and the Rebuilding of Downtown Washington, DC." *Pacific Historical Review* 72, no. 1 (2003): 1–38.

———. "Senator Reed Smoot and a Western Land Policy, 1905–1920." *Arizona and the West* 13, no. 1 (Autumn 1971): 245–64.

Allaman, John Lee. "Policing in Mormon Nauvoo." *Illinois Historical Journal* 89, no. 2 (Summer 1996): 85–98.

Andersen, Kurt. *Fantasyland: How America Went Haywire.* New York, New York: Random House, 2017.

Arrington, Leonard. *Brigham Young: American Moses.* Urbana, Illinois: University of Illinois Press, 1985.

———. *Great Basin Kingdom: An Economic History of the Latter-day Saints, 1830–1900*, Urbana, Illinois: University of Illinois Press, 2004.

———. *Utah's Audacious Stockman: Charlie Redd.* Logan, Utah: Utah State University Press, 1995.

———. "The Mormon Cotton Mission in Southern Utah." *Pacific Historical Review* 25, no. 3 (August 1956): 221–38.

Arrington, Leonard, Feramorz Y. Fox, and Dean L. May. *Building the City of God: Community and Cooperation among the Mormons.* Salt Lake City, Utah: Deseret Book Company, 1976.

Backman, Milton V. Jr. *The Heavens Resound: A Story of the Latter-day Saints in Ohio 1830–1838.* Salt Lake City, Utah: Deseret Book Company, 1983.

Bagley, Will. *Blood of the Prophets: Brigham Young and the Mountain Meadows Massacre.* Norman, Oklahoma: University of Oklahoma Press, 2002.

Baird, Robert. "Welcome, Welcome Sabbath Morning." *Hymns of the Church of the Latter-day Saints.* Salt Lake City, Utah: Church of the Latter-day Saints, 1985.

Barkun, Michael. *Religion and the Racist Right: The Origins of the Christian Identity Movement.* Chapel Hill, North Carolina: University of North Carolina Press, 1996.

Beam, Alex. *American Crucifixion: The Murder of Joseph Smith and the Fate of the Mormon Church.* New York, New York: Public Affairs, 2014.

Bennett, Richard Edmond, Susan Easton Black, and Donald K. Cannon. *The Nauvoo Legion in Illinois: A History of the Mormon Militia, 1841–1846.* Norman, Oklahoma: Arthur H. Clark Company, 2010.

Benson, Ezra Taft. "Our Immediate Responsibility." Speech transcript. Brigham Young University Devotional, October 25, 1966. *Latter-day Conservative.* http://www.latterdayconservative.com/ezra -taft-benson/our-immediate-responsibility/.

Bibles, D. Dean. "The Transforming Effect of the Natural Resources Defense Council Consent Decree." US Department of the Interior Bureau of Land Management. http://www.blm.gov/wo /st/en/info/history/sidebars/natural_resources/the_transforming _effect.html.

Bigler, David. "The Aiken Party Executions and the Utah War." *Western Historical Quarterly* 38, no. 4 (Winter 2007): 457–76.

Bitton, David, and Maureen Ursenbach. "Riding Herd: A Conversation with Juanita Brooks." *Dialogue: A Journal of Mormon Thought* 9, no. 1 (1974): 11–33. https://www .dialoguejournal.com/wp- content/uploads/sbi/articles /Dialogue_V09N01_13.pdf.

Black, Susan Easton. "How Large Was the Population of Nauvoo?" *BYU Studies* 35, no. 2, art. 7 (1995): https://scholarsarchive.byu .edu/byusq/vol35/iss2/7.

Black, Susan Easton, and Charles D. Tate Jr. *Joseph Smith: The Prophet, the Man.* Provo, Utah: Religious Studies Center, Brigham Young University, 1993.

Bloom, Harold. *The American Religion.* New York, New York: Simon and Schuster, 1992.

The Book of Mormon. Trans. Joseph Smith, Jr. Salt Lake City, Utah: The Church of Jesus Christ of Latter-day Saints, 1981.

Bounsall, Eddie. *Crazy Ed's Saga's and Secrets of Desert Gold,* Mesquite, Nevada: self-published, 1992.

Bower, G. Lynn. *Zion on the Muddy.* Springhill, Utah: Art City Publishing, 2004.

Bowman, Dan. *The Battle of Jefferson and Other Skirmishes in the War on the West.* N.p., self-published, 1996.

Bowman, Matthew. "A Mormon Bigfoot: David Patten's Cain and the Conception of Evil in LDS Folklore." *Between Pulpit and Pew: The Supernatural World in Mormon History and Folklore,* edited by Paul W. Reeve and Michael Scott Van Wagenen. 17–39. Logan, Utah: Utah State University Press, 2011.

———. *The Mormon People: The Making of an American Faith.* New York, New York: Random House, 2012.

Bradley, Martha Sontag. *A History of Kane County.* Salt Lake City, Utah: Utah State Historical Society, 1999.

Bradshaw, Hazel. *Under a Dixie Sun: A History of Washington County by Those Who Loved Their Forebears.* Panguitch, Utah: Daughters of Utah Pioneers Washington County Chapter, 1950.

Brodie, Fawn M. *No Man Knows My History: The Life of Joseph Smith.* New York, New York: Vintage Books, 1995.

Brooks, Juanita. "Indian Relations of the Mormon Frontier." *Utah Historical Quarterly* 12, nos. 1–2 (January–April 1944): 1–48.

———. "The Land that God Forgot." *Utah Historical Quarterly* 29, no. 3 (July 1961): 207–19.

———. *The Mountain Meadows Massacre.* 3rd ed. Norman, Oklahoma: University of Oklahoma Press, 1991.

———. *Quicksand and Cactus: A Memoir of the Southern Mormon Frontier.* Logan, Utah: Utah State University Press, 1982.

Brosnahan, Cori. "Ruby Ridge, Part One: Suspicion." *American Experience*, PBS, n.d. https://www.pbs.org/wgbh /americanexperience/features/ruby-ridge-part-one-suspicion/.

———. "Ruby Ridge, Part Two: Confirmation." *American Experience*, PBS, n.d. http://www.pbs.org/wgbh/americanexperience /features/ruby-ridge-part-two-confirmation/

———. "Ruby Ridge, Part Three: Fear and Faith." *American Experience*, PBS, n.d. http://www.pbs.org/wgbh /americanexperience/features/ruby-ridge-part-three-fear-faith/

"Bundy Ranch: Margaret Houston Assaulted by BLM Coward." Youtube video, April 7, 2014. https://www.youtube.com /watch?v=iT97SRyaJA8.

Bunker, Edward. Unpublished autobiography, transcribed by Michael Bunker. N.p., 2006. http://www.bunker.org/ebauto.html.

Burns, Joe, and Tom Schick. "Controversial Federal Grazing Fees Not a Great Deal for Anyone." Transcript. Oregon Public Broadcasting, January 6, 2016. http://www.opb.org/news/series /burns-oregon-standoff-bundy-militia-news-updates/federal -grazing-fees/.

Burroughs, John. "The Grand Canyon of the Colorado." *Century Magazine* (January 1911): 425–38.

Burt, Olive Wooley. "A Kid Named Jones Had a Dream." *Utah Magazine* 8, no. 6 (June 1946): 26–29.

Burton, Richard. *The City of Saints.* New York, New York: Harper and Brothers Publishers, 1862.

Bushman, Richard Lyman. *Joseph Smith: Rough Stone Rolling.* New York, New York: Vintage Books, 2007.

Butler, Jon. *Awash in a Sea of Faith: Christianizing the American People.* Cambridge, Massachusetts: Harvard University Press, 1990.

Calhoon, Harold P., and Priscilla J. Calhoon. *Utah's Dixie Birthplace.* Washington City, Utah: Washington City Historical Society, 1996.

Cannon, George, ed. *Millennial Star*, 24. London, England: Latter-day Saints Depot, 1862.

Cannon, Brian Q., and Jessie L. Embry, eds. *Utah in the Twentieth Century.* Logan, Utah: Utah State University Press, 2009.

Carmack, Noel A. "Of Prophets and Pale Horses: Joseph Smith, Benjamin West, and the American Millenarian Tradition." *Dialogue: A Journal of Mormon Thought* 29, no. 3 (Fall 1996): 589–94.

Carrier, Scott. "Absolutely, God Told Us to Do This." Podcast audio. *Home of the Brave.* January 13, 2016. http://homebrave.com /home-of-the- brave//absolutely-god-told-us-to-do-this.

Carter, Thomas. *Building Zion: The Material World of Mormon Settlement.* Minneapolis, Minnesota: University of Minnesota Press, 2015.

Cawley, McGregor R. *Federal Land, Western Anger: The Sagebrush Rebellion and Environmental Politics.* Lawrence, Kansas: University Press of Kansas, 1993.

Chaloupka, William. "The County Supremacy and Militia Movements: Federalism as an Issue on the Radical Right." *Publius: The Journal of Federalism* 26, no. 3 (Summer 1996): 161–75.

Chavez, Angelico Fray. *The Dominguez-Escalante Journal: Their Expedition through Colorado, Utah, Arizona, and New Mexico in 1776.* Salt Lake City, Utah: University of Utah Press, 1995.

Chidester, David, and Edward Linenthal. *American Sacred Space: Religion in North America.* Bloomington, Indiana: Indiana University Press, 1995.

Cockin, Paul K. *American Originals: Homemade Varieties of Christianity.* Chapel Hill, North Carolina: University of North Carolina Press, 1997.

Colvin, Gina, and Joanna Brooks, eds. *Decolonizing Mormonism: Approaching a Postcolonial Zion*. Salt Lake City, Utah: University of Utah Press, 2018.

Compton, Tina L., Kirsten Jansen, and Jerold N. Willmore. "The US Constitution and Wilderness Designation." *Contested Landscape: The Politics of Wilderness in Utah in the West*, edited by Doug Goodman and Daniel McCool. Salt Lake City, Utah: University of Utah Press, 1999. 17–34.

Compton, Todd M. *A Frontier Life: Joseph Hamblin, Explorer and Indian Missionary*. Salt Lake City, Utah: University of Utah Press, 2013.

Cook, Rob. "Cattle Inventory: Ranking of All 50 States." *Drovers*. https://www.drovers.com/article/cattle-inventory-ranking-all-50-states.

Cox, Shawna. *Last Rancher Standing: The Cliven Bundy Story, a Close-up View*. New York, New York: Legends Library, 2016.

Crawford, JL. *Zion Album: A Nostalgic History of Zion Canyon*. Springdale, Utah: Zion Natural History Association, 1986.

Cronon, William. "The Trouble with Wilderness or Getting Back to the Wrong Nature." *Uncommon Ground: Rethinking the Human Place in Nature*, edited by William Cronon. New York, New York: W. W. Norton, 1996. 69–90.

Cullimore, James. "Devotional, Brigham Young University," Brigham Young University, January 4, 1977.

Dant, Sara. "The 'Lion of the Lord' and the Land: Brigham Young's Environmental Ethic." *The Earth Will Appear as the Garden of Eden: Essays on Mormon Environmental History*, edited by Jedediah S. Rogers and Matthew C. Godfrey. Salt Lake City, Utah: University of Utah Press, 2019. 29–46.

Dees, Morris, and James Corcoran. *Gathering Storm: America's Militia Threat*. New York, New York: Harper Perennial, 1996.

Dellenbaugh, Fredrick S. *A Canyon Voyage: The Narrative of the Second Powell Expedition Down the Green-Colorado River from Wyoming, and the Explorations on Land, in the Years 1871 and 1872*. Tucson, Arizona: University of Arizona Press, 1984

———. "A New Valley of Wonders." *Scribner's Magazine* 35, no. 1 (January 1904): 1–18.

DeLoughrey, Elizabeth, and George B. Handley. *Post-Colonial Ecologies: Literatures of the Environment*. Oxford, England: Oxford University Press, 2011.

Doctrine and Covenants of the Church of the Latter-day Saints: Carefully Selected from the Revelations of God, and Compiled by Joseph Smith Jr., Oliver Cowdery, Sidney Rigdon, Fredrick G. Williams (Presiding Elders of Said Church). Kirkland, Ohio: F. G. Williams and Co. for the Proprietors, 1835.

Durham, Michael S. *Desert between the Mountains: Mormons, Miners, Padres, Mountain Men, and the Opening of the Great Basin*. New York, New York: Holt and Company, 1997.

Durrant, Jeffery O. *Struggle over Utah's San Rafael Swell: Wilderness, National Conservation Areas and National Monuments*. Tucson, Arizona: University of Arizona Press, 2007.

Dutton, Clarence. "The Physical Geography of the Grand Canyon District." *Second Annual Report of the United States Geological Survey to the Secretary of the Interior 1880–1881*. Washington, DC: Government Printing Office, 1882.

Emerson, Ralph Waldo. *Nature and Other Essays*. Mineola, New York: Dover Publications, 2009.

———. *Self Reliance*. N.p.: CreateSpace, 2017.

Epps, Garrett. "Constitutional Myth #7: The 10th Amendment Protects States Rights." *The Atlantic,* July 2, 2011. http://www.theatlantic.com/national/archive/2011/07/constitutional-myth-7-the-10th-amendment-protects-states-rights/241671/.

Farmer, Jared. *On Zion's Mount: Mormons, Indians and the American Landscape*. Cambridge, England: Harvard University Press, 2008.

Feld, Steven, and Keith Basso. *Senses of Place*. Santa Fe, New Mexico: School of American Research, 1996.

Finicum, LaVoy. *Only by Blood and Suffering: Regaining Lost Freedom*. Rochester, New York: Legends Publishing, Inc. 2015.

Flake, Kathleen. *The Politics of Religious Identity: The Seating of Senator Reed Smoot, Mormon Apostle*. Chapel Hill, North Carolina: University of North Carolina Press, 2004.

Flores, Dan. "Zion in Eden: Phases of Environmental History in Utah." *Environmental Review* 7, no. 4 (Winter 1983): 325–44.

Fluhman, J. Spencer. *A Peculiar People: Anti-Mormonism and the Making of Religion in Nineteenth-century America.* Chapel Hill, North Carolina: University of North Carolina Press, 2012.

Ford, Matt. "The Irony of Cliven Bundy's Unconstitutional Stand." *The Atlantic*, April 14, 2014. http://www.theatlantic.com/politics /archive/2014/04/the-irony-of-cliven-bundys-unconstitutional -stand/360587/

Francaviglia, Richard V. *Believing in Place: A Spiritual Geography of the Great Basin.* Reno, Nevada: University of Nevada Press, 2003.

———. *Go East, Young Man: Imagining the American West as the Orient.* Logan, Utah: Utah State University Press, 2011.

———. "Mapping Deseret: Vernacular Mormon Mapmaking and the Spiritual Geography of the American West." *The Earth Will Appear as the Garden of Eden: Essays on Mormon Environmental History*, edited by Jedediah S. Rogers and Matthew C. Godfrey. Salt Lake City, Utah: University of Utah Press, 2019. 107–30.

Garr, Arnold K., Donald Q. Cannon, and Richard O. Cowan, eds. *Encyclopedia of Latter-day Saint History.* Salt Lake City, Utah: Deseret Book Company, 2000.

Gaunt, LaRene Porter. "Hole-in-the-Rock." *Ensign Magazine,* October 1995. https://www.lds.org/ensign/1995/10/hole-in-the-rock.

Gentry, Leland. "The Danite Band of 1838." *BYU Studies* 14, no. 4 (1974): https://contentdm.lib.byu.edu/digital/collection /byustudies/id/460.

Givens, Terryl L. *The Book of Mormon, a Very Short Introduction.* Oxford, England: University of Oxford Press, 2009.

———. *People of Paradox: A History of Mormon Culture.* Oxford, England: University of Oxford Press, 2007.

Goodman, Doug, and Daniel McCool, eds. *Contested Landscape: The Politics of Wilderness in Utah in the West.* Salt Lake City, Utah: University of Utah Press, 1999.

Grand Staircase Escalante National Monument. "Manager's Annual Report," 2014. https://www.blm.gov/style/medialib/blm/ut

/grand_staircase-escalante/nlcs_mgrs_report.Par.61629.File.dat
/GSENM_ Manager_Report_FY2014_draft1-25-2015.pdf.

Grandstaff, Mark R., and Milton Vaughn Backman Jr. "The Social Origins of the Kirtland Mormons." *BYU Studies* 30, no. 2 (1990): 47–66.

Grattan-Aiello, Carolyn. "Senator Arthur V. Watkins and the Termination of Utah's Southern Paiute Indians," *Utah Historical Quarterly* 63, no. 3 (1995): 268–83.

Godfrey, Matthew C. "We Believe the Hand of the Lord Is in It: Memories of Divine Intervention in Zion's Camp." *BYU Studies* 56, no. 4 (2017): 99–132.

Gordon, Sarah Barringer. "'Our National Hearthstone': Anti-polygamy Fiction and the Sentiment Campaign against Moral Diversity in Antebellum America." University of Pennsylvania Law School, Faculty Scholarship, Paper 1429, 1996.

Haas, Ryan. "LaVoy Finicum Supporters Threatened to Burn Qurans, Kill Police and Oregon Governor." Transcript. Oregon Public Broadcasting, March 26, 2016. http://www.opb.org/news/series /burns-oregon- standoff-bundy-militia-news-updates/finicum -supporters-threaten-to-kill-cops-because-they-are-cops/.

Handley, George B. *Home Waters: A Year of Recompenses on the Provo River*. Salt Lake City, Utah: University of Utah Press, 2010.

Hafen, Lyman. *Far from Cactus Flat: The 20th Century Story of a Harsh Land, a Proud Family and a Lost Son*. St. George, Utah: Arizona Strip Interpretative Associate, 2006.

———. *Roping the Wind: A Personal History of Cowboys and the Land*. Logan, Utah: Utah State University Press, 1995.

Hebner, William Logan. *Southern Paiute: A Portrait*. Logan, Utah: Utah State University Press, 2010.

Herring, Hal, "Can We Make Sense of the Malheur Mess?" *High Country News*, February 12, 2016. https://www.hcn.org/articles /malheur-occupation-oregon-ammon-bundy-public-lands-essay

Hinton, Wayne K. *The Dixie National Forest: Managing an Alpine Forest in an Arid Setting*, Cedar City, Utah: US Forest Service, Dixie National Forest, 1987.

————. "Getting Along: The Significance of Cooperation in the Development of Zion National Park." *Utah Historical Quarterly* 68, no. 4 (Fall 2000): 313–31.

Hirschi, Frank W. "Law of Consecration." *Encyclopedia of Mormonism*, edited by Daniel H. Ludlow. New York, New York: Macmillan, 1992. 312–14.

Hofstadter, Richard. *The Paranoid Style of American Politics and Other Essays.* New York, New York: Vintage Books, 2008.

Horowitz, Mitch. *Occult America: The Secret History of How Mysticism Shaped Our Nation.* New York, New York: Bantam Books, 2009.

Hurlburt, Virgil. "The Taylor Grazing Act." *Journal of Land and Public Utility Economics* 11, no. 2 (May 1935): 203–06.

InfoWars. "Historic! Feds Forced to Surrender to American Citizens." YouTube video. Posted by Alex Jones Channel, April 13, 2014. https://www.youtube.com/watch?v=bD61YFxUga4.

Jacoby, Karl. *Crimes against Nature: Squatters, Poachers, Thieves and the Hidden History of American Conservation.* Berkeley, California: University of California Press, 2003.

Jenson, Andrew. *The Historical Record.* Salt Lake City, Utah: privately published, 1886–1890. https://archive.org/details /historicalrecord01jens/page/n4

Jenson, Mari N. "Can Cows and Conservation Mix?" *BioScience* 51, no. 2 (February 2001): 85–90.

Johnson, Nephi. "Nephi Johnson Autobiographical Sketch, Circa 1863." MS 18420. N.p.: Church History Library, ca. 1863. 1–5.

————. "Nephi Johnson Autobiographical Sketch, Circa 1900." MS 23835. N.p.: Church History Library, ca. 1900. 1–13.

————. "Nephi Johnson Autobiography, Undated." MS 11807, microfilm, 18 frames. N.p.: Church History Library, n.d.

Johnson, Paul E. *A Shopkeepers Millennium: Society and Revivals in Rochester, New York 1815–1837.* New York, New York: Hill and Wang, 2004.

Katz, Brigit. "Shrinking of Utah National Monument May Threaten Bee Biodiversity." *Smithsonian Magazine*, December 17, 2018.

https://www.smithsonianmag.com/smart-news/shrinking-utah
-national-monument-may-threaten-bees-180971052/.

Keeler, Jacqueline. "'It's So Disgusting' Malheur Militia Dug Latrine Trenches among Sacred Artifacts." *Indian Country Today*, February 17, 2016. https://newsmaven.io/indiancountrytoday /archive/it-s-so-disgusting-malheur-militia-dug-latrine-trenches -among-sacred-artifacts-FmyM0FlQ0kalIRhBNbOCyw.

Kelly, Charles. "The Fathers of Capitol Reef National Park." *History Blazer* (September 1995). Utah Government Digital Library. https://historytogo.utah.gov/capitol-reef-national-park/.

Kerr, Andy, and Mark Salvo. "Livestock Grazing in the National Park and Wilderness Preservation Systems." *Wild Earth* 10, no. 2 (2000): 53–56.

Klein, Kerwin Lee. *Frontiers of Historical Imagination: Narrating the European Conquest of Native America, 1890–1990*. Los Angeles, California: University of California Press, 1997.

Knack, Martha. *Between the Boundaries: The Southern Paiutes, 1775– 1995*. Lincoln, Nebraska: University of Nebraska Press, 2001.

———. "Church and State in the History of Southern Paiutes in Cedar City, Utah." *Journal of California and Great Basin Anthropology* 19, no. 2 (1997): 159–78.

Krakauer, Jon. *Under the Banner of Heaven: A Story of Violent Faith*. New York, New York: Anchor Books, 2003.

Lambert, Neal E. "Freedom and the American Cowboy." *BYU Studies* 8, no. 1 (January 1, 1968): 61–71. http://scholarsarchive.byu.edu /cgi/viewcontent.cgi?article=1238&context=byusq.

Lambourne, Alfred. "The Mu-kun-tu-weap." *Improvement Era* 14, no. 6 (April 1911): 528–32.

Larson, Andrew Karl. *I Was Called to Dixie: The Virgin River: Unique Experiences in Mormon Pioneering*. 3rd ed. St. George, Utah: Dixie State College, 1992.

———. "Zion National Park with Some Reminiscences Fifty Years Later." *Utah Historical Quarterly* 37, no. 4 (October 1969): 406–25.

Lee, John D. *Mormonism Unveiled or Life and Confession of John D. Lee*. Albuquerque, New Mexico: Fierra Blanco Publications, 2001.

Lee, Martha F. *Earth First: Environmental Apocalypse*. Syracuse, New York: Syracuse University Press, 1995.

Lenz, Ryan, and Mark Potok. "War in the West: The Bundy Ranch Standoff and the American Radical Right." Southern Poverty Law Center, July 2014. https://www.splcenter.org/20140709/war-west -bundy-ranch-standoff-and-american-radical-right.

Leopold, Aldo. *A Sand County Almanac: Outdoor Essays and Reflections*. New York, New York: Ballantine Books, 1986.

Lewis, David Rich. *Neither Wolf nor Dog: American Indians, Environment and Agrarian Change*. New York, New York: Oxford University Press, 1994.

Lewis, James R. *Odd Gods: New Religions and Cult Controversy*. Amherst, Massachusetts: Prometheus Books, 2001.

Limerick, Patricia Nelson. *The Legacy of Conquest: The Unbroken Past of the American*. New York, New York: W. W. Norton, 1987.

Louter, David. *Windshield Wilderness*. Seattle, Washington: University of Washington Press, 2006.

Lythgoe, Dennis L. *Let 'Em Holler: A Political Biography of J. Lee Bracken*. Salt Lake City, Utah: Utah Historical Society, 1982.

Madsen, Truman G. *Joseph Smith: The Prophet*. Salt Lake City, Utah: Bookcraft, 1989.

McCann, Anthony. "Malheur, Part I: Sovereign Feelings." *Los Angeles Review of Books*, September 7, 2016. https://lareviewofbooks.org /article/malheur-part-i-not/.

———. "Malheur, Part II: Ours but Not Ours." *Los Angeles Review of Books*, September 8, 2016. https://lareviewofbooks.org/article /malheur-part-ii-not/.

McConkie, Bruce R. *A Witness for the Articles of Faith*. Salt Lake City, Utah: Bookcraft, 1999.

McDermott, Ted. "The Domestic Terrorist." *Missoula Independent* 25, no. 24 (June 14, 2015). Copy in possession of the author.

McKiernan, F. Mark. "Sidney Rigdon's Missouri Speeches." *BYU Studies* 11, no. 1 (Autumn 1970): 1–3.

McLane, Dennis. *Seldom Was Heard an Encouraging Word: A History of Bureau of Land Management Law Enforcement.* Guthrie, Oklahoma: Shoppe Foreman Publishing, 2011.

McMillan, Tracy. "19 Great Restaurants to Work For." *Food and Wine*, March 14, 2019. https://www.foodandwine.com/travel /restaurants/best-restaurants-work-jobs.

Meinig, D. W. "The Mormon Culture Region: Strategies and Patterns in the Geography of the American West, 1847–1964." *Annals of the Association of American Geographers* 55, no. 2 (June 1965): 191–220.

Miller, Jay. "Basin Religion and Theology: A Comparative Study of Power (Puha)." *Journal of California and Great Basin Anthropology* 5, nos. 1–2 (Summer–Winter 1983): 66–83.

Miller, Perry. *Errand into the Wilderness.* Cambridge, Massachusetts: Belknap Press, 1964.

Mozingo, Joe. "A Sting in the Desert." *Los Angeles Times*, September 21, 2014. https://graphics.latimes.com/utah-sting/.

Muir, John. *My First Summer in the Sierra.* Mineola, New York, New York: Dover Press, 2004.

———. *Our National Parks.* Layton, Utah: Gibbs Smith, 2018.

Musgrave, Curly. "The Ol' Fifty Mile." *The Heritage.* Recorded 2003. http://tidido.com/a35184374391338 /al55f185bba5f3907573943ca8/t55f185bca5f3907573943d1b.

Nash, Roderick. *Wilderness and the American Mind.* 3rd ed. New Haven, Connecticut: Yale University Press, 1982.

National Park Service. "The Establishment of Capitol Reef National Monument: Wayne Wonderland to Capitol Reef, 1933–1936." *Capitol Reef Administrative History.* National Park Service, n.d. http://www.nps.gov/parkhistory/online_books/care/adhi/adhi8a .htm.

———. "Land Use History." Bryce Canyon National Park. http://www .nps.gov/brca/learn/historyculture/land_use_ history.htm.

———. "Livestock Trailing and Grazing Management Plan—EIS Scoping Newsletter." Capitol Reef National Park. http://www.nps .gov/care/learn/management/upload/2015-03-03-CARE-LGTMP -Public-Scoping-Newsletter.pdf.

Nelson, Paul T. *Wrecks of Human Ambition: A History of Utah's Canyon Country to 1936.* Salt Lake City, Utah: University of Utah Press, 2014.

Nelson, Robert H. "Why the Sagebrush Rebellion Burned Out." *AEI Journal on Government and Society (*May/June 1984): 27–35. https://object.cato.org/sites/cato.org/files/serials/files /regulation/1984/5/v8n3-5.pdf.

Neumann, Roderick. *Imposing Wilderness: Struggles over Livelihood and Nature Preservation in Africa.* Berkeley, California: University of California Press, 2002.

Novak, Shannon A. *House of Mourning: A Biocultural History of the Mountain Meadows Massacre.* Salt Lake City, Utah: University of Utah Press, 2008.

Oakes, Len. *Prophetic Charisma: The Psychology of Revolutionary Religious Personalities.* Syracuse, New York: Syracuse University Press, 1997.

Obenzinger, Hilton. *American Palestine: Melville, Twain and Holy Land Mania.* Princeton, New Jersey: Princeton University Press, 1990.

Orsi, Robert. *Between Heaven and Earth: The Religious Worlds People Make and the Scholars Who Study Them.* Princeton, New Jersey: Princeton University Press, 2005.

Oswald, David. *A Journey Through Mukuntuweap: The History of Zion National Park.* Scotts Valley, California: CreateSpace, 2009.

Our American Public Lands. "Public Opinion Research." Our American Public Lands, n.d. http://www.americanpubliclands .com/public-opinion-research/.

Palmer, William R. "Indian Names in Utah Geography." *Utah Historical Quarterly* 1, no. 1 (1928): 5–26.

Parks, Bradley W. "41 Days and Eight Months Later: Dissecting the Oregon Standoff Trial." Transcript. *Oregon Public Broadcasting,*

October 30, 2016. http://www.opb.org/news/series/burns
-oregon-standoff-bundy-militia-news-updates/trial-not-guilty
-verdict-reaction-bundy/.

Parry, Zachariah. "Cliven Bundy's Battle of Bunkerville: An Attorney's Analysis." Matt Pfau Law Group, June 23, 2014. https://www
.mattpfaulaw.com/2016-1-31-cliven-bundys-battle-of
-bunkerville-an-attorneys-analysis/.

Paulos, Michael Harold. "Under the Gun at the Smoot Hearings: Joseph F. Smith's Testimony." *Journal of Mormon History* 34, no. 4 (Fall 2008): 181–225.

Peacher, Amanda. "Meet the Women of the Occupied Refuge." Transcript. *Oregon Public Broadcasting*, January 22, 2016. http://
www.opb.org/news/series/burns-oregon-standoff-bundy-militia
-news-updates/oregon-militia-meet-the-women-of-the
-occupied-refuge/.

———. "Supporters of Harney County Judge Grasty Rally against Recall." Transcript. *Oregon Public Broadcasting*, August 23, 2016. https://www.opb.org/news/series/burns-oregon-standoff-bundy
-militia-news-updates/steve-grasty-harney-county-judge
-supporters-rally-against-recall-/

Pearl of Great Price. Liverpool, England: F. D. Richards, 1851.

Pendley, William Perry. *Sagebrush Rebel: Reagan's Battle with Environmental Extremists and Why It Matters Today.* Washington, DC: Regency Publishing, 2013.

Petersen, Anne Helen, Ken Bensinger, and Salvador Hernandez. "Planting the Seed: Meet the Man—and the Propaganda Machine—Behind the Hammond Pardon." Buzzfeed News, July 11, 2018. https://www.buzzfeednews.com/article
/annehelenpetersen/forrest-lucas-hammond-pardon-bundy
-trump-pence

Peterson, Levi S. *Juanita Brooks: The Life Story of a Courageous Historian of the Mountain Meadows Massacre.* Salt Lake City, Utah: University of Utah Press, 1988.

Platt, Lyman D., and Karen L. Platt. *Grafton: Ghost Town on the Rio Virgin.* St. George, Utah: Tonaquint Press, 1998.

Plewe, Brandon S., S. Kent Brown, Donald Q. Cannon, and Richard H. Jackson. *Mapping Mormonism: An Atlas of the Latter-day Saint History.* Provo, Utah: Brigham Young University Press, 2012.

Poll, Richard R., Thomas G. Alexander, Eugene E. Campbell, and David E. Miller. *Utah's History.* Logan, Utah: Utah State University Press, 1989.

Powell, John Wesley. *The Exploration of the Colorado River and Its Canyons.* N.p.: Simon and Brown, 2003.

Pratt, Orson. "The Kingdom of God," *A Series of Pamphlets,* Liverpool, England: R. James, 1851.

Pratt, Parley P. "Report to the Legislative Council of Deseret, 5 Feb. 1850." *Over the Rim: The Parley P. Pratt Exploring Expedition to Southern Utah, 1849–50,* edited by William B. Smart and Donna T. Smart. Logan, Utah: Utah State University Press, 1999. 171–86.

Prusha, Francis Paul. *The Indians in American Society.* Berkeley, California: University of California Press, 1985.

Quinn, Michael D. *Early Mormons and Their Magic World View.* Salt Lake City, Utah: Signature Books, 1987.

———. *The Mormon Hierarchy: Origins of Power.* Salt Lake City, Utah: Signature Books, 1994.

———. "National Culture, Personality and Theocracy in the Early Mormon Culture of Violence." *The John Whitmer Historical Journal,* Nauvoo Conference Special Edition (2002). 159–86.

Reeve, Paul W. "'As Ugly as Evil' and 'As Wicked as Hell': Gadianton and the Legend Process among the Mormons." *Between Pulpit and Pew: The Supernatural World in Mormon History and Folklore,* edited by Paul W. Reeve and Michael Scott Van Wagenen. Logan, Utah: Utah State University Press, 2011. 40–65.

———. *Making Space on the Western Frontier: Mormons, Miners and Southern Paiutes.* Urbana, Illinois: University of Illinois Press, 2006.

Reeve, Paul W., and Michael Scott Van Wagenen. "Between the Pew and the Pulpit: Where History and Lore Intersect." *Between Pulpit and Pew: The Supernatural World in Mormon History and Folklore*, edited by Paul W. Reeve and Michael Scott Van Wagenen. Logan, Utah: Utah State University Press, 2011. 1–16.

"The Reformation in Utah." *Harper's New Monthly Magazine* 43 (September 1871): 602–10.

Reid, H. Lorenzo. *Brigham Young's Dixie of the Desert: Exploration and Settlement.* Salt Lake City, Utah: Zion Historical Association, 1964.

Rhodes, Stewart. "Recommended Honorable Exit Strategy for Ammon Bundy." Oath Keepers, January 6, 2016. https://www.oathkeepers.org/a-recommended-honorable-exit-strategy-for-ammon-bundy/.

Rich, Alice C. *Memories of New Harmony.* Unpublished memoir, 1957. Platt Family Center, Washington County Historical Society.

Richardson, Elmo E. "Federal Park Policy in Utah: The Escalante National Monument Controversy of 1935–1940." *Utah Historical Quarterly* 33, no. 2 (Spring 1965): 109–33.

Roberts, B. H. *A Comprehensive History of the Church of Jesus Christ of Latter-day Saints.* Vol. 1–6. Salt Lake City, Utah: Deseret News, 1930.

Roberts, Pat. *The New World Order.* Dallas, Texas: Word Publishing, 1991.

Rogers, Jedediah S. *Roads in the Wilderness: Conflict in Canyon Country.* Salt Lake City, Utah: University of Utah Press, 2013.

———. "The Volatile Sagebrush Rebellion." *Utah in the Twentieth Century*, edited by Brian Q. Cannon and Jessie L. Embry. Louisville, Colorado: University Press of Colorado, 2009. 367–84.

Rogers, Jedediah S., and Matthew C. Godfrey, eds. *The Earth Will Appear as the Garden of Eden: Essays on Mormon Environmental History.* Salt Lake City, Utah: University of Utah Press, 2019.

Rothman, Hal. "Shaping the Nature of Controversy: The Park Service, the Forest Service and the Cedar Breaks Proposal." *Utah Historical Quarterly* 55, no. 3 (Summer 1987): 213–33.

RT. "Armed Militia Occupy Forest Reserve HQ in Oregon, Call 'US patriots' to Arms, Bundy Bros Join Protest." Signs of the Times,

January 3, 2016. https://www.sott.net/article/309698-Armed
-militia-occupy-forest-reserve-HQ-in-Oregon-call-US-patriots
-to-arms-Bundy-bros-join-protest.

Runte, Alfred. *National Parks: The American Experience*. Lincoln,
Nebraska: University of Nebraska Press, 1979.

Schindler, Harold. *Orrin Porter Rockwell: Man of God, Son of
Thunder*. Salt Lake City, Utah: University of Utah Press, 1983.

Schultz, Kathryn. "Letter from Utah, Why Two Chefs in Small-Town
Utah Are Battling President Trump." *The New Yorker*, October 1,
2018. https://www.newyorker.com/magazine/2018/10/01/why
-two-chefs-in-small-town-utah-decided-to-sue-president-trump.

Sepulvado, John. "Explainer: The Bundy Militias' Particular Brand of
Mormonism." Transcript. *Oregon Public Broadcasting*, January 3,
2016. http://www.opb.org/news/article/explainer-the-bundy
-militias-particular- brand-of-mormonism/.

———. "Why the Bundy Militia Mixes Mormon Symbolism with
Anti-government Sentiment." *PBS Newshour*, January 4, 2016.
http://www.pbs.org/newshour/updates/why-the-bundy-militia
-mixes-mormon-symbolism-with-anti-government-sentiment/.

Shipps, Jan. *Mormonism: The Story of a New Religious Tradition*.
Urbana, Illinois: University of Illinois Press, 1985.

———. *Sojourner in the Promised Land: Forty Years among the
Mormons*. Urbana, Illinois: University of Illinois Press, 2000.

Short, John Rennie. *Imagined Country: Society, Culture and
Environment*. New York, New York: Routledge, 1991.

"The Silver Mountains of Utah." *Harper's New Monthly Magazine* 52,
no. 317 (October 1876): 641–51.

Skousen, Cleon W. "One Hundred Things Destroying America."
Latter-day Conservative, 1982. http://www.latterdayconservative
.com/articles/100-things-destroying-america/.

———. *Prophecy and Modern Times: Finding Hope and
Encouragement in the Last Days*. Salt Lake City, Utah: Izzard Ink
Publishing, 2017.

———. *The Making of America: The Substance and Meaning of*

the Constitution. Washington, DC: The National Center for Constitutional Studies, 1985.

Skousen, Joel. *The Secure Home: Architectural Design, Construction, and Remodeling of Self-Sufficient Residences and High Security Retreats.* N.p.: self-published, 2013.

Smaby, Beverly P. "The Mormons and the Indians: Conflicting Ecological Systems in the Great Basin." *American Studies* 16, no. 1 (Spring 1975): 35–48.

Smith, Craig S. "James E. Talmage and the 1895 Deseret Museum Expedition to Southern Utah." *Utah Historical Quarterly* 84, no. 2 (Spring 2016): 137–50.

Smith, Jedediah. "The Volatile Sagebrush Rebellion." *Utah in the Twentieth Century*, edited by Brian Q. Cannon and Jessie L. Embry. Logan, Utah: Utah State University Press, 2009. 367–84.

Smith, Joseph. *History of the Church of Jesus Christ of Latter-day Saints.* 7 vols., introduction and notes by B. H. Roberts. Salt Lake City, Utah: The Church of Jesus Christ of Latter-day Saints, 1932–1951.

Smith, Lucy Mack. *History of Joseph Smith by His Mother.* Provo, Utah: Strafford Books, 2005.

Smith-Cavros, Eileen. *Pioneer Voices of Zion Canyon.* Springdale, Utah: Zion Natural History Association, 2006.

Snow, Wilbert. *Codleine's Child: The Autobiography of Wilbert Snow.* Middleton, Connecticut: Wesleyan University Press, 1968.

Soja, Edward. *Postmodern Geographies: The Reassertion of Space in Critical Theory.* London, England: Verso Publishing, 1989.

Spence, Mark David. *Dispossessing Wilderness: Indian Removal and the Making of National Parks.* Oxford, England: Oxford University Press, 1999.

Spendlove, *Etta H. Memories and Experiences of James Jepson, Jr.* MS no. A-31. Salt Lake City, Utah: Utah State Historical Society, 1934. 9–10.

Spivak, Randi, and Ryan Beam. "Public Land Enemies: 15 Federal Lawmakers Plotting to Seize, Destroy and Privatize America's

Public Lands." Center for Biological Diversity, March 2017. https://www.biologicaldiversity.org/campaigns/public_lands _enemies/pdfs/PublicLandsEnemies.pdf

Stegner, Wallace. *The Gathering of Zion: The Story of the Mormon Trail.* New York, New York: McGraw Hill Book Company, 1964.

———. *Mormon Country.* Lincoln, Nebraska: University of Nebraska Press, 1942.

Stoffel, Richard W., and Michael J. Evans. *Kaibab Paiute History: The Early Years.* Freedonia, Arizona: Kaibab Paiute Tribe, 1978.

Sutter, Paul S. *Driven Wild: How the Fight Against Automobiles Launched the Modern Wilderness Movement.* Seattle, Washington: University of Washington Press, 2002.

Swaine, Jon, Douglas MacMillian, and Michelle Boorstein. "Mormon Church Has Misled Members on $100 Billion Tax-Exempt Investment Fund Whistleblower Alleges." *The Washington Post,* December 17, 2019. https://www.washingtonpost.com /investigations/mormon-church-has-misled-members-on -100-billion-tax-exempt-investment-fund-whistleblower -alleges/2019/12/16/e3619bd2-2004-11ea-86f3-3b5019d451db _story.html.

Taylor, John. "The Object of the Gathering of the Saints— Conflict Between the Powers of God and Evil—The World Growing Worse—Work of God Progressing—Exhortation to Righteousness and the Spirit of Union." Speech, August 31, 1879. *Journal of Discourses* 21: 1–8.

Taysom, Stephen C. *Shakers, Mormons, and Religious Worlds: Conflicting Visions, Contested Boundaries.* Bloomington, Indiana: University of Indiana Press, 2011.

Templeton, Amelia, and Conrad Wilson. "Deceased Militant LaVoy Finicum: Rancher, Patriarch, Bundy Believer." Transcript. *Oregon Public Broadcasting,* January 27, 2016. http://www.opb.org /news/article/robert-lavoy-finicum-dead-rancher-bundy-burns -oregon/.

Thoreau, Henry David. *Walking.* Red Wing, Minnesota: Cricket House Books, 2010.

Topp, Brent. *What's on the Other Side? What the Gospel Teaches*

Us About the Spirit World. Salt Lake City, Utah: Deseret Book Company, 2012.

Turner, Fredrick Jackson. *The Frontier in American History*. New York, New York: Henry Holt and Company, 1921.

Turner, James Morton. "The Specter of Environmentalism: Wilderness, Environmental Politics, and the Evolution of the New Right." *Journal of American History* 96, no. 1 (June 2009): 123–48.

Turner, John. *Brigham Young: Pioneer Prophet*. Cambridge, England: Belknap Press, 2012.

Twain, Mark. *Roughing It*. London, England: Signet Classics, Penguin, 2008.

Underwood, Grant. *The Millenarian World of Early Mormonism*. Urbana, Illinois: University of Illinois Press, 1999.

Utah American Western Center, University of Utah. *Paiute History*. http://www.utahindians.org/archives/paiutes/history.html.

Waite, Nathan. "Remembering, Branding, Claiming: How Mukuntuweap National Monument Became Zion National Park." Utah State History Conference, Salt Lake City, Utah, September 6, 2013.

Walker, Peter. *Sagebrush Collaboration: How Harney County Defeated the Takeover of the Malheur Wildlife Refuge*. Corvallis, Oregon: Oregon State University, 2018.

Walker, Robert W., Richard E. Turley, and Glen M. Leonard. *Massacre at Mountain Meadows*. Oxford, England: Oxford University Press, 2011.

Wariner, Ruth, *The Sound of Gravel*. New York, New York: Flatiron Books, 2017.

Watkins, T. H. "Untrammeled by Man: The Making of the Wilderness Act of 1964." *Audubon* 90, no. 6 (November 1989): 74–90.

Weber, Samuel R. "'Shake Off the Dust of Thy Feet': The Rise and Fall of Mormon Ritual Cursing." *Dialogue: A Journal of Mormon Thought* 46, no. 1 (Spring 2013): 108–39. https://www.dialoguejournal.com/wp-content/uploads/sbi/articles/Dialogue_V46N01_526d.pdf

Wehrle, Christopher, and Robin Clegg. "The Evolution of the Wilderness Concept." *Contested Landscape: The Politics of Wilderness in Utah in the West,* edited by Doug Goodman and Daniel McCool. Salt Lake City, Utah: University of Utah Press, 1999. 3–16.

Westover, Tara. *Educated: A Memoir*. New York, New York: Random House, 2018.

Whipple, Maurine. *This Is the Place, Utah*. New York, New York: Alfred A. Knopf, 1945.

White, Richard. "Are You an Environmentalist or Do You Work for a Living? Work and Nature." *Uncommon Ground: Rethinking the Human Place in Nature*, edited by William Cronon. New York, New York: W. W. Norton, 1996. 171–85.

———. "Toward a Reconstruction of Mormon and Indian Relations, 1847–1877." *BYU Studies* 29, no. 4 (Fall 1989): 23–38.

Williams, Terry Tempest. *The Hour of Land: A Personal Topography of America's National Parks*. New York, New York: Farrar, Strauss and Giroux, 2016.

Wilson, Conrad. "Bundy's Attorney Pleads Not Guilty in Courthouse Scuffle Case." Transcript. *Oregon Public Broadcasting*, January 6, 2017. http://www.opb.org/news/series/burns-oregon-standoff-bundy-militia-news-updates/marcus-mumford-plea/

Wilson, E. O. *Creation: An Appeal to Save Life on Earth*. New York, New York: W. W. Norton, 2017.

Wiles, Tay. "Bundy Supporter Gets 68 Years." *High Country News*, July 26, 2017. https://www.hcn.org/articles/public-lands-bunkerville-defendant-sentenced-to-68-years-in-prison.

Winkler, Albert. "The Circleville Massacre: A Brutal Incident in Utah's Black Hawk War." *Utah Historical Quarterly* 55, no. 1 (1987): 4–21.

Wister, Owen. *The Virginian*. New York, New York: Penguin Books, 1988.

Woodbury, Angus. "A History of Southern Utah and Its National Parks." *Utah Historical Quarterly* 12, nos. 3–4 (July–October 1944): 111–209.

Woodruff, Wilford. *Waiting for World's End: The Diaries of Wilford Woodruff*, edited by Susan Staker. Salt Lake City, Utah: Signature Books, 1993.

Wooten, Larry C. Email to Andrew D. Goldsmith. "Disclosure and Complaint Narrative in Regard to Bureau of Land Management Law Enforcement Supervisory Misconduct and Associated Cover-ups as well as Potential Unethical Actions, Malfeasance by the United States Attorney's Office Prosecutors from the district of Nevada, (Las Vegas) in Reference to the Cliven Bundy Investigation." November 27, 2017. http://www.thiswestisourwest.com/index.cfm/draining-the-swamp/whitleblower-larry-wooten-letter/.

Worster, Donald. *Rivers of Empire: Water, Aridity and the Growth of the American West*. New York, New York: Pantheon Books, 1985.

Wynn, Mark. *Faith and Place: An Essay in Embodied Religious Epistemology*. Oxford, England: Oxford University Press, 2009.

Y2 Consultants. *Study on Management of Public Lands in Wyoming*. http://slf-web.state.wy.us/osli/News/FinalStudyFedLand.pdf.

Yard, Robert Sterling. *The New Zion National Park: Rainbow of the Desert*. Washington, D.C.: National Parks Association, 1919.

Yorgan, Ethan R. *Transformation of the Mormon Culture Region*. Urbana, Illinois: University of Illinois Press, 2003.

Young, Brigham. *Journal of Discourses by Brigham Young, His Counselors, Twelve Apostles and Others*. 26 vols. Liverpool, England: F. D. and S. W. Richards, 1854–1886.

Zaitchik, Alexander. *Common Nonsense: Glen Beck and the Triumph of Ignorance*. Hoboken, New Jersey: Wiley and Sons, 2010.

———. "Meet the Man Who Changed Glenn Beck's Life." *Salon*, September 16, 2009. https://www.salon.com/2009/09/16/beck_skousen/.

———. "Fringe Mormon Group Makes Myths with Glenn Beck's Help." *Intelligence Report*, Southern Poverty Law Center, February 23, 2011. https://www.splcenter.org/fighting-hate/intelligence-report/2011/fringe-mormon-group-makes-myths-glenn-beck's-help.

Index

F

Facebook 210, 245, 252, 286. *See also* Bundy Ranch Facebook page
Falling Man 222
Fantasyland 240
Federal Bureau of Investigation (FBI) 152, 153, 154, 155, 156, 171,
    172, 189, 202, 207, 208, 209, 228, 231, 252, 284
Federal Land Policy and Management Act (FLPMA) 139, 140, 141,
    256
Finicum, Robert LaVoy 183, 184, 203, 206, 207, 208, 215, 216, 292
Fish and Wildlife Service 101, 188, 238, 253, 256
Follett, King 55
Food and Wine 277
Forest Service 6, 101, 120, 130, 139, 156, 189, 190, 253, 257, 292
Freeman Institute 171. *See also* National Center for Constitutional
    Studies (NCCS)
Free Speech Areas 229
Fry, David Lee 209, 245

G

Gale, William Potter 161
Galland, Dr. Isaac 50
Garfield County News 139, 165, 189
Garfield County, Utah 144, 146, 162, 274, 275, 276, 280, 281, 282
Garn, Jake 146
Garrett, Bill 251
Genesis 26, 235, 236
George, Judge Lloyd D. 191. *See also* rulings, Las Vegas, Nevada
Gillespie, Doug 191, 197, 228
Gleave, Marty 292
Gleave, Stanton 292, 294, 295
globalism, globalists 150, 151, 153, 177, 178, 182, 269
God 8, 13, 14, 15, 16, 17, 18, 21, 22, 26, 27, 28, 29, 30, 31, 33, 35, 36,
    37, 38, 39, 40, 41, 42, 44, 45, 47, 49, 52, 54, 55, 58, 60, 63, 65,
    66, 67, 68, 70, 71, 77, 79, 93, 97, 101, 102, 104, 105, 109, 116,
    119, 129, 136, 149, 151, 153, 155, 173, 174, 178, 180, 183, 184,
    185, 188, 194, 197, 198, 199, 200, 201, 202, 203, 205, 206, 209,
    210, 221, 235, 236, 243, 244, 261, 262, 269, 271, 280, 286, 287.
    See also Lord
Godfrey, Matthew C. 39

K

L

N

S

ABOUT THE AUTHOR

Betsy Gaines Quammen is a historian and conservationist. She received a doctorate in Environmental History from Montana State University in 2017, her dissertation focusing on Mormon settlement and public land conflicts. She has studied various religious traditions over the years, with particular attention to how cultures view landscape and wildlife. The rural American west, pastoral communities of northern Mongolia, and the grasslands of East Africa have been her main areas of interest. After college in Colorado, caretaking for a bed and breakfast in Mosier, Oregon, and serving breakfasts at a café in Kanab, Utah, Betsy has settled in Bozeman, Montana, where she now lives with her husband, writer David Quammen, three huge dogs, an overweight cat, and a pretty big python named Boots.

TORREY HOUSE PRESS

Voices for the Land

The economy is a wholly owned subsidiary of the environment, not the other way around.
—Senator Gaylord Nelson, founder of Earth Day

Torrey House Press is an independent nonprofit publisher promoting environmental conservation through literature. We believe that culture is changed through conversation and that lively, contemporary literature is the cutting edge of social change. We strive to identify exceptional writers, nurture their work, and engage the widest possible audience; to publish diverse voices with transformative stories that illuminate important facets of our ever-changing planet; to develop literary resources for the conservation movement, educating and entertaining readers, inspiring action.

Visit www.torreyhouse.org for reading group discussion guides, author interviews, and more.

As a 501(c)(3) nonprofit publisher, our work is made possible by the generous donations of readers like you.

Torrey House Press is supported by Back of Beyond Books, The King's English Bookshop, Jeff and Heather Adams, Jeffrey S. and Helen H. Cardon Foundation, Suzanne Bounous, Grant B. Culley Jr. Foundation, Diana Allison, Jerome Cooney and Laura Storjohann, Robert Aagard and Camille Bailey Aagard, Heidi Dexter and David Gens, Kirtly Parker Jones, Utah Division of Arts & Museums, and Salt Lake County Zoo, Arts & Parks. Our thanks to individual donors, subscribers, and the Torrey House Press board of directors for their valued support.

Join the Torrey House Press family and give today at www.torreyhouse.org/give.